A HISTORY OF
ORANGE COUNTY
VIRGINIA

From its Formation in 1734 (O. S.) to the end
of Reconstruction in 1870; compiled
mainly from Original Records

With a Brief Sketch of the Beginnings of
Virginia, a Summary of Local
Events to 1907, and a Map

By W. W. SCOTT
*State Law Librarian, Member of the State Historical
Society, and for ten years State Librarian
of Virginia*

CLEARFIELD

Originally published
Richmond, Virginia, 1907

Reprinted
Regional Publishing Company
Baltimore, Maryland, 1974

Reprinted from a volume in the
George Peabody Branch, Enoch Pratt Free Library
Baltimore, Maryland, 1974

Library of Congress Cataloging in Publication Data
Scott, William Wallace, 1845-1929.
A history of Orange County, Virginia.
Reprint of the 1907 ed. published by E. Waddey Co., Richmond.
1. Orange Co., Va.--History. I. Title.
F232.06S4 1974   917.55'372'033   73-16490

Reprinted for Clearfield Company by
Genealogical Publishing Company
Baltimore, Maryland, 1990, 1996, 1999, 2007, 2010

ISBN: 978-0-8063-0595-0

Made in the United States of America

To my Father,

GARRETT SCOTT,

Presiding Justice of the County of Orange from the creation of that office until displaced by the proscription that followed the war. He long enjoyed the confidence, esteem and affection of all the people of his native county, and throughout this tract of years.

"Wore the white flower of a blameless life."

Also, in grateful memory of his niece,

ELIZABETH HENSHAW,

of that part of Orange now called Kentucky; to whose generosity, after the war, I owe my education at the University of Virginia.

Historians ought to be precise, faithful, and unprejudiced; and neither interest nor fear, hatred nor affection, should make them swerve from the way of truth, whose mother is history, the rival of time, the depositary of great actions, witness of the past, example to the present, and monitor to the future.—*Cervantes*.

— praecipuum munus annalium reor, ne virtutes sileantur, utque pravis dictis factisque ex posteritate et infamia metus sit.— *Tacitus, Annales III. 65.*

PREFACE.

I have undertaken to write this book because I thought that the history of Orange was notable enough to deserve preservation.

It is much to be regretted that some competent person did not do this work long ago; for in the lapse of time and the neglect of opportunity many things that ought to have been preserved can not now be narrated with confidence as history, hardly as tradition.

Though much has perished, much remains. I have read with diligence the minute books of the county court from its organization in 1734 down to 1870; and can assert with complete candor that no known resource which I thought might afford information as to the past has been neglected.

Name after name of places and people once locally historic has passed into oblivion and beyond the reach of the investigator. Regret is vain, and can not restore what is lost; my effort has been to save what is left, and to perpetuate it for posterity.

Fortunately the county records are in excellent preservation, and the order books of the county court contain the history of the county, in the main, so far as it may now be written.

I have been advised by judicious and well meaning friends to omit some of the more shocking details, such as the burning of Eve at the stake, the beheading of Peter, the cutting off of ears, burning in the hands, etc.

I have not been able to take this view, deeming it but a sorry attempt at writing history to suppress the truth.

Indeed I think these so-called cruel episodes in the state of society then existing redound rather to the credit than to the reproach of our ancestors; when sternness in the administration of the law was an essential, not to say a cardinal, virtue.

The sequence of the chapters, though far from being chronological (which is the ideal sequence) is the best I could devise. Facts, far apart in time but relating to the same general subject, have to be grouped in the chapter treating of that subject. Otherwise there could be no orderly narration of them.

I have gone but little into the deed and will books, fearing that there is already too much detail, which, for the benefit of the antiquarian, has generally been put into appendices of which there are so many that I look for the criticism that "the book has appendicitis:" which, however, is the prevailing fashion.

And genealogy has been altogether eschewed.

Grateful acknowledgements are extended to Mr. Charles E. Kemper, of Staunton, himself a historian of excellent fame; to Mr. W. G. Stanard, the well known antiquarian and editor of the Virginia Historical Magazine; and to our courteous and obliging clerk, Mr. C. W. Woolfolk.

I submit the book to the public with the assurance that it is the truth as far as I have been able to ascertain it after diligent seeking; the simple truth, unwarped by fear, favor, or affection.

It has been written with no sordid motive, but I hope a sufficient number of copies may be sold to reimburse the cost of publication, and, perhaps with too much vanity, I look to the appreciation of my friends and of posterity for my main and enduring reward.

W. W. SCOTT.

EXPLANATIONS.

As sundry archaic terms are unavoidably employed in this work the following definitions are deemed necessary.

"*Style.*" The old style prevailed when the county was formed, and until 1752, when the year began March 25th; January, February, and March, up to the 25th, constituting the last three instead of the first three months of the year. The change of 'style' consisted in dating the year from January 1st instead of March 25th; and the addition of the eleven days was a mere incident.

"*Tithable.*" For many years taxes were levied only on persons, not on property, and a tithable, generally speaking, was such a person as was subject to taxation; usually all male persons sixteen years of age, and servants of that age of both sexes.

"*Pounds, shillings, etc.*" The colonial pound was not the pound sterling. The pound was twenty shillings, the shilling twelve pence, equivalent to \$3.33$\frac{1}{3}$, and 16$\frac{2}{3}$ cents, respectively.

"*Gentleman.*" This term then, as now, was one of great vagueness, but always imparted a certain social or official distinction. The grades appear to have been servants, yeomen, planters, who appear to have been "gentlemen" or not, according to their property and family connections. To become a justice, sheriff, vestryman, etc., was to acquire the entitlement, at least, of "Gentleman."

"*Prison Bounds.*" An area, not exceeding ten acres, about the jail where prisoners not committed for treason or felony had liberty, on giving security, to continue therein until discharged: mostly for the benefit of persons imprisoned for debt, the privilege lasting only one year.

"*Benefit of Clergy.*" This was immunity from capital punishment for a first offense, applying at first only to people who could read, but later greatly extended so as to embrace even slaves. Abolished about 1796.

"*The Test.*" In colonial times this oath was that the affiant doth believe that there is not the "real presence" in the elements of the communion of the Lord's Supper.

The chief authorities relied on are the order books of the county court and other county records, Hening's Statutes at Large, manuscript records in the State Library, the Virginia Magazine of History and Biography, and other publications of the Virginia Historical Society.

CONTENTS.

CHAPTER I.
The Seating of Virginia.................................. Page 13

CHAPTER II.
The Genesis of Orange.................................. 17

CHAPTER III.
Organization of the County............................. 26

CHAPTER IV.
The Courthouses... 33

CHAPTER V.
The Colonial Churches................................... 42

CHAPTER VI.
Other Old Churches—The Dissenters..................... 46

CHAPTER VII.
Indian Antiquities....................................... 52

CHAPTER VIII.
French and Indian Wars................................. 58

CHAPTER IX.
Orange in the Revolution............................... 63

CHAPTER X.
Germanna and the First Settlers........................ 77

CHAPTER XI.
Progress to the Mines................................... 87

CHAPTER XII.
The Knights of the Horseshoe........................... 98

CHAPTER XIII.
Physical Features...................................... 114

CHAPTER XIV.
Social and Economic................................... 121

CHAPTER XV.
Crimes and Punishments............................... 133

CHAPTER XVI.
The Orange Humane Society........................... 138

CHAPTER XVII.
From 1848 to 1861.................................... 144

CHAPTER XVIII.
The War Period....................................... 148

CHAPTER XIX.
Reconstruction, 1865 to 1870.......................... 160

CHAPTER XX.
Fiscal and Statistical, 1870 to 1907.................... 166

CHAPTER XXI.
Miscellaneous... 174

CHAPTER XXII.
Biographical Sketches................................. 181

CHAPTER XXIII.
Historic and Other Homes............................. 202

CHAPTER XXIV.
Being a Personal Retrospect........................... 216

CONTENTS 11

APPENDICES.

	Page
Importations	225
Census, 1782	230
Will of President Madison	239
War of 1812	244
War of The Revolution	247
Commissions, 1734–1783	258
Roster of the Montpelier Guards During John Brown Raid, 1859	263
Roster of Confederate Soldiers, 1861 to 1865	264
Members of the Various Conventions	278
Members of the Colonial House of Burgesses	279
Index	281

LIST OF ILLUSTRATIONS.

Montpelier	Frontispiece
At Burlington	126
Barboursville	36
Cameron Lodge	88
Church of the Blind Preacher	46
Clifton	176
Frascati	18
Hawfield	96
Map of Orange County	13
Mayhurst	160
Montebello	112
Mount Sharon	56
Pleasant View	144
Rocklands	80
Soldier's Rest	72
Somerset	64
Tomb of Madison	206
Woodley	168
Wood Park	136

In the interest of economy, these illustrations appear all together preceding page 13.

MAP OF
ORANGE COUNTY,
VIRGINIA

Scale of Miles

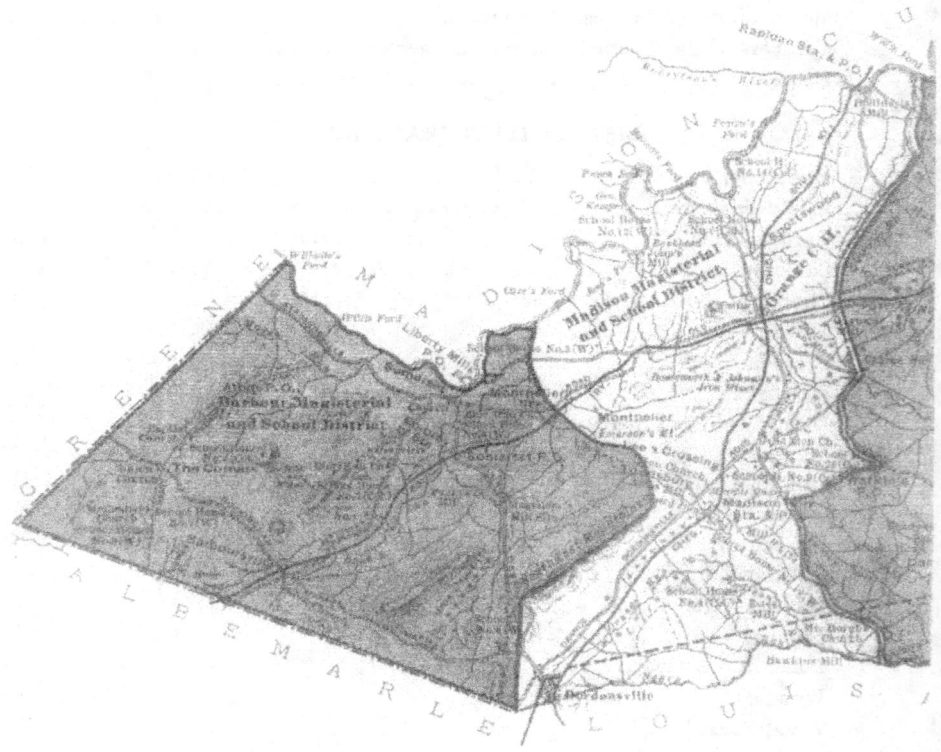

BARBOURSVILLE

AT BURLINGTON

CAMERON LODGE

CHURCH OF THE BLIND PREACHER

CLIFTON

FRASCATI

HAWFIELD

TOMB OF MADISON

MAYHURST

MONTEBELLO

MONTPELIER

MOUNT SHARON

PLEASANT VIEW

ROCKLANDS

SOLDIER'S REST

SOMERSET

WOODLEY

WOOD PARK

History of Orange County

CHAPTER I.

The Seating of Virginia.

A brief sketch of the beginnings of Virginia seems a necessary introduction to a history of Orange. For though this history will be mainly confined to the present narrow limits of the County, it ought to be known to those who may read it that Orange was once a principality in extent, embracing in her limits five prosperous states of the Union, and parts of two others.

All of North America between Florida and Nova Scotia was known as Virginia for a number of years; Queen Elizabeth having been so charmed by Sir Walter Raleigh's sea captains' accounts of the coasts of the Carolinas in 1585 that she named the country Virginia in honor of herself, the "Virgin Queen."

Unfortunately all of Raleigh's attempts to found a colony on these shores failed, and the unknown fate of the one at Roanoke Island, North Carolina, remains a pathetic mystery.

It was not until 1607, in the reign of James I, that a settlement was made in Virginia proper. The charter of 1606 to the "Virginia Company of London" granted the right to found a colony one hundred miles square anywhere between the thirty-fourth and forty-first degrees of north latitude; that is, between the mouths of Cape Fear river in North Carolina and Hudson river in New York; and to the "Virginia Company of Plymouth" a similar right between the thirty-eighth and forty-fifth degrees; that is, between the Potomac river and Nova Scotia. Either company might occupy in the overlapping region, but neither should make a settlement within one hundred miles of the other.

Under this charter Jamestown was founded May 13, 1607, by the Virginia Company of London. A second charter was granted this company in 1609 by the terms of which the boundaries of the colony were extended along the coast two hundred miles, north and south, from Point Comfort, and "up into the land throughout from sea to sea, west and northwest, and also all the islands lying within one hundred miles along the coasts of both seas."

Of course these boundaries were never actually attained. From 'sea to sea' must have meant from the Atlantic to the Pacific ocean, and the line projected "west and northwest" embraced nearly all of the Great Lakes and the states of Ohio, Indiana, Illinois, Michigan, Wisconsin, and a part of Minnesota. To this latter part, known subsequently as the Northwest Territory, Virginia claimed title under the charter. She also acquired title to it later, by conquest of her own soldiers under George Rogers Clark, under orders from Patrick Henry, the then governor, during the Revolutionary War. But to quiet dissension, she ceded it to the federal government in 1784, only reserving land therein sufficient to fulfil her promise of land grants to her soldiers in the Revolutionary and Indian wars.

It was probably all of a hundred years from the settlement at Jamestown before a white man, unless simply as a hunter or Indian trader, set his foot anywhere in Orange. The movement toward the 'frontiers' was very slow, and almost exclusively along the main water courses. In Colonel Byrd's famous "Westover Manuscripts" are published the depositions of Francis Thornton and John Taliaferro. Thornton deposed that in 1703 there were but two settlements above his house on the lower side of Snow Creek, which is about fifteen miles below Fredericksburg, the uppermost of which was about four miles below the Falls, that is Falmouth: Taliaferro, that in 1707 there were but three settlements above his house on Snow Creek, on the south side of the Rappahannock.

Indeed the settlement at Jamestown languished till towards 1620, though soon afterwards the Colony began to grow and prosper. In 1622 the population numbered 4,000 persons, and though from 1609 to 1610, after John Smith's return to England, there had been a period known as the "Starving Time" when many people were famishing or barely subsisting on roots, herbs, acorns, berries, walnuts and even on skins and snakes, in 1622 there was great abundance of grain, fruit, and vegetables; wine and silk were made in considerable quantities, sixty thousand pounds of tobacco was grown, and cattle had increased rapidly.

Women were imported and sold to the colonists, and the price of a wife rose from one hundred and twenty to a hundred and fifty pounds of tobacco.

In that year, 1622, occurred the great massacre, incited by Opechancanough, when hundreds of men, women, and children were treacherously slain, and all the cattle were driven off.

It was long before the colony recovered from this blow, and the extension of the frontiers toward the mountains was greatly delayed by it and by the general hostile attitude of the Indians.

CHAPTER II.

The Genesis of Orange.

In 1634, just one hundred years before the formation of Orange, "the country was divided into eight shires which are to be governed as the shires in England. And lieutenants to be appointed the same as in England, and in a more especial manner to take care of the war against Indians. Sheriffs shall be elected as in England, to have the same powers as there; and sergeants and bailiffs, where need requires." (1 Hen., 224.)

Of these original shires one was named Charles River; so called after the river as named by the colonists in honor of King Charles. The Indian name of the whole river had been Pamaunkee (spelled Pomunkey by Hening) which means, according to Campbell the historian, "where we took a sweat."

It is not known when these political divisions ceased to be called shires and became known as counties, but in 1642-3 the name of the shire Charles River, then called County, was changed to York, and the river below the confluence of the Mattaponi was called York River. The boundaries of these counties were not defined towards the frontiers, and it is assumed that, like Spotsylvania, they extended as far "as might be convenient."

The genesis here becomes somewhat confused. Lancaster County is first mentioned by Hening in 1652, when it had two representatives at a session of the House of Burgesses.

It is included because subsequent formations relate back to it and seem to constitute it a link in the line.

New Kent was formed from York in 1654.

Old Rappahannock from Lancaster in 1656, ceasing to be a county name in 1692, when two counties, Richmond and Essex, were formed from it.

And thus Orange, as will be seen later, furnishes the paradox of being alike the daughter and the mother of a Rappahannock County.

King and Queen was formed from New Kent in 1691.

Essex from old Rappahannock in 1692.

King William from King and Queen in 1701.

Spotsylvania from Essex, King William, and King and Queen in 1720; and

Orange from Spotsylvania in 1734.

This is believed to be the genealogy of Orange, direct and collateral. To complete its geography, its dismemberment and line of descent is here added.

Augusta and Frederick, embracing all the territory of Orange lying north and west of the top of the Blue Ridge, were formed in 1738.

Culpeper, embracing Madison and Rappahannock, was formed from Orange in 1748.

Madison was formed from Culpeper in 1792, and named for James Madison.

Rappahannock was formed from Culpeper in 1833.

Greene, named in honor of Gen. Nathaniel Greene, was formed from Orange in 1838, the last dismemberment.

While it might be interesting, it would be beyond the scope of this book to attempt even an outline history of the many counties named in this genesis. Spotsylvania, as the immediate territory from which Orange was formed, must be briefly considered.

In 1720, the seat of government being at Williamsburg, the following Act "for erecting the counties of Spotsylvania and Brunswick" was passed by the "General Assembly," for so the law-making power was called even at that early date:

"*Preamble*, That the frontiers towards the high mountains are exposed to danger from the Indians, and the late settlements of the French to the westward of the said mountains.

Enacted, Spotsylvania County bounds upon Snow Creek up to the Mill, thence by a southwest line to the river North Anna, thence up the said river as far as convenient, and thence by a line to be run over the high mountains to the river on the northwest side thereof, so as to include the northern passage through the said mountains, thence down the said river until it comes against the head of Rappahannock, thence by a line to the head of Rappahannock river, and down that river to the mouth of Snow Creek; which tract of land from the first of May, 1721, shall become a county, by the name of Spotsylvania County." 4 Hening, 77.

The County was named for Lieutenant-Governor Spotswood, then acting governor of the Colony.

Without the help of boundaries subsequently established and maintained to this time, it would be difficult to define the lines laid down in the statute. Interpreted by these it may be safely affirmed that on the east and south the County was bounded as now; "Snow

Creek," the line with Caroline County, empties into the Rappahannock ten or fifteen miles below Fredericksburg: the North Anna is the southern boundary up to the Orange line: "up the North Anna as far as convenient" is obscure but unimportant, and may be interpreted as meaning all the way to its source. The ultimate source of this river is a spring on the Johnson place, near the top of the Southwest mountains, and but a few feet from the turnpike leading from Gordonsville to Harrisonburg. Taking this spring, which is not far from the Albemarle line, as the starting point for the "line over the high mountains to the river on the northwest side thereof so as to include the northern passage through the said mountains," we have approximately the present lines of Orange and Greene counties with Albemarle to the top of the Blue Ridge. This about forces the conclusion that the "northern passage" means Swift Run Gap, through which this same 'pike crosses the Blue Ridge. At the time the County was formed the only passage across the mountains had been made by Governor Spotswood in 1716, known as the "Expedition of the Knights of the Horseshoe." The "river on the northwest side" of the mountain is our Shenandoah, then called "Sherrando" and "Shenando", and by Spotswood "the Euphrates;" down this river until it comes "against the head of Rappahannock:" this would bring us about Front Royal, the county seat of Warren; thence by a line to the head of Rappahannock River, say about the corner of Fauquier, Warren, and Rappahannock, and then down to the beginning, following the line of the sources of the

Rappahannock, and the Rappahannock itself to Snow Creek. These boundaries can be easily traced on any modern map of Virginia.

By the same Act fifteen hundred pounds was appropriated, to be paid to the Governor, of which five hundred for a church, courthouse, prison, pillory and stocks where the governor shall appoint them in Spotsylvania, he to employ workmen, provide material, etc.: one thousand pounds, of which one-half to Spotsylvania, to be distributed in arms and ammunition among such persons as shall hereafter go to seat the said County; that is, to each Christian titheable one fire lock musket, one socket, bayonet fitted thereto, one cartouch box, eight pounds bullet, two pounds powder, until the whole one thousand pounds be laid out, the account to be laid before the General Assembly. The arms appropriated to the defence of the County, and both the real and personal estate of the persons taking them made liable to their forthcoming in good order; and to be stamped with the name of the County, and liable to seizure of any militia officer if found without the bounds. Inhabitants made free of public levies for ten years, and the whole County made one parish by the name of St. George. Because foreign Protestants may not understand English readily, they and their titheables made free for ten years if any such shall entertain a minister of their own. This last clause was for the benefit of the Germans settled at Germanna.

While Orange was yet a part of Spotsylvania, and, indeed, before Spotsylvania itself was formed, thousands and thousands of acres of land to the westward, even as far as to the Mississippi, had been granted to individuals by the Crown, acting mainly through the Governors of the Colony; and titles to much land in Orange of today are traced back to Spotsylvania, King and Queen, and the land office at Richmond. The "Madison Grant," for example, was made while the grantee was still a resident of King and Queen.

ORANGE COUNTY was formed from Spotsylvania in 1734, and was named not from the "color of its soil" as erroneously stated by Howe and others, for there is no soil of orange color in the County; but for William, Prince of Orange, one of England's most worthy kings. Next to "good Queen Anne" he appears to have been the best beloved by the colonists of all their kings; King William, King and Queen, Williamsburg, and William and Mary College were all named in his honor, two of them in honor of him and his Queen.

In colonial times it was not uncommon for parishes to be formed before the counties which afterwards contained them were established. Such was the case with Orange, and the boundaries of the County can only be stated in connection with those of the parish of St. Mark. The Act defining St. Mark is as follows:

Enacted, Whereas many inconveniences attend the parishioners of St. George parish, in the county of Spotsylvania, by reason of the great length thereof, that from January 1, 1730, the said parish be divided into two distinct parishes: From the mouth of the Rapidan to the mouth of Wilderness Run; thence up the said Run to the bridge; and thence southwest to Pamunkey River: the part below the said bounds to be known as St. George Parish, and all that other part which lies above the said bounds be known as St. Mark.

The freeholders were required to meet at Germanna on that day and there "elect and choose twelve of the most able and discreet persons of their parish to be vestrymen." When Orange was established, just four years later, the dividing line between these parishes was made the boundary line between Orange and Spotsylvania, so it becomes necessary to determine what that line was. It is manifest that Orange never touched the Pamunkey River as we now know that river, and the conclusion is unavoidable that we must understand some point on the North Anna, which probably, at that time, was called the Pamunkey, because it was the main branch of that stream; which point is the present corner of Spotsylvania with Orange on the North Anna.

The Act establishing the County was passed at the August session, 1734. (4 Hen., 450.) Leaving out unnecessary words it reads:

An Act for dividing Spotsylvania County.

Whereas divers inconveniences attend the upper inhabitants of Spotsylvania County, by reason of their great distance from the Courthouse and other places usually appointed for public meetings: Be it therefore enacted, by the Lieutenant-governor, Council and Burgesses, of this present General Assembly, and it is hereby enacted by the authority of the same; That from and immediately after the first day of January now next ensuing, the said County of Spotsylvania be divided by the dividing line between the parish of St. George and the parish of St. Mark; and that that part of the said county which is now the parish of St. George remain and be called and known by the name of Spotsylvania County; and all that territory of land adjoining to and above the said line, bounded southerly by the line of Hanover County, northerly by the grant of the Lord Fairfax, and westerly by the utmost limits of Virginia, be thenceforth erected into one distinct county, to be called and known by the name of the county of Orange.

A Court for the County was directed to be constantly held by the justices thereof on the third Tuesday in every month.

For the encouragement of the inhabitants already settled and which shall speedily settle on the westward of the Sherrendo River, it was further enacted that they should be free and exempt from the payment of public, county and parish levies for three years next following, and that all who might settle there in the next three years should be so exempt for the remainder of that time.

The terms of the statute need explanation in this, "southerly by the line of Hanover." Louisa was then part of Hanover. "The grant of the Lord Fairfax" on the north. As then understood, Lord Fairfax's southern limit was the Rappahannock River, as it is known to-day. There was much and long continued contention and litigation about this line, however, between Fairfax and the colonial authorities, but it was finally settled that the Fairfax grant embraced all the land lying between the Potomac and Rappahannock rivers up to the head springs of each river, and that the head spring of the Rappahannock was the source of what is now known as Conway or Middle River, which source is near the corner of Greene and Madison counties, near the crest of the Blue Ridge. As this contention was not settled till long afterwards, the northerly boundary of Orange continued to be the present Rappahannock River until Culpeper was cut off in 1748, and it remains the boundary of Culpeper to this day.

The Genesis of Orange

A map showing a "survey according to order in the years 1736 and 1737 of the Northern Neck of Virginia, being the lands belonging to Lord Fairfax," is published in the report of the commissioners appointed to settle the boundaries between Maryland and Virginia in 1873. On it South River is called "Thornton," the Rapidan above the mouth of South River, is called "Staunton's River," and below the mouth is put down as "Rappahannock River, South Branch, called Rapidan," and the Rappahannock above the mouth of the Rapidan is called "Cannon", and, higher up, "Hedgeman's River."

CHAPTER III.

Organization of the County.

It must be borne in mind that " Old Style " was yet in effect in the Mother Country and her colonies when Orange was established: that is, that the New Year was reckoned from March 25, and not from January 1; and that the New Style did not become effective until 1752. Thus, though the first court was held in January 1734, there were yet two months to elapse before the year 1735 began: that is, that January, February, and March came after December of the same year. This will make plain the otherwise apparently curious date of the appointment of Col. Henry Willis, the first county clerk.

The first minute on the records of the County is in these words:

Orange County.—Be it remembered that on the twenty-first day of January, in the year 1734, a Commission of the Peace directed to Augustine Smith, Goodrich Lightfoot, John Taliaferro, Thomas Chew, Robert Slaughter, Abraham Field, Robert Green, James Barber, John Finlason, Richard Mauldin, Samuel Ball, Francis Slaughter, Zachary Taylor, John Lightfoot, James Pollard, Robert Eastham, Benjamin Cave, Charles Curtis, Joist Hite, Morgan Morgan, Benjamin Borden, John Smith and George Hobson, and a dedimus for administering the oaths etc., to the said Justices being read, the said John Finlason and Samuel Ball pursuant to the said dedimus administered the oaths appointed by Act of Parliament to be taken instead of the oaths of Allegiance and Supremacy the oath appointed to be taken by an act of Parliament made in

ORGANIZATION OF THE COUNTY

the first year of the Reign of his late Majesty King George the First, entituled an Act for the further Security of his Majesties Person and Government and the Sucession of the Crown in the heirs of the late Princess Sophia, being Protestants and for extinguishing the hopes of the pretended Prince of Wales and his open and secret Abettors, unto Augustine Smith and John Taliaferro who severally subscribed the Test and then the said John Finlason and Samuel Ball administered the oaths of a Justice of the Peace and of a Justice of the County Court in Chancery unto the said Augustine Smith and John Taliaferro. And afterwards the said Augustine Smith and John Taliaferro pursuant to the said dedimus administered all and every of the said oaths unto Thomas Chew, Robert Slaughter, Abraham Field, Robert Green, James Barber, John Finlason, Samuel Ball, Francis Slaughter, John Lightfoot, James Pollard and Benjamin Cave who severally subscribed the Test.

At a Court held for the County of Orange on the twenty-first day of January, 1734, Present Augustine Smith, John Taliaferro, and the Justices to whom they had just administered the oaths:

A Commission to Henry Willis, Gent., under the hand and Seal of office of the Honorable John Carter, Esq., Secretary of Virginia, bearing date the thirtieth day of October, 1734, to be clerk of the Court of this County being produced in Court and read, the said Willis having taken the oaths, etc., and subscribed the Test, was sworn Clerk of this County.

This Henry Willis was the same gentleman mentioned by Colonel Byrd as the "top man of Fredericksburg." Note the date of his commission. October was then really the eighth month and January was the eleventh month of the calendar year. He was the ancestor of Col. George Willis of Woodpark; of Mr. Henry Willis and of Mrs. Ambrose Madison, of Woodbury Forest. Why a person not a citizen of the County should have been made clerk does not appear, but he continued to be such until his death, in the summer of 1740. Jonathan Gibson, Gent., was appointed and qualified as clerk at the September term of that year.

Mr. William Robertson's house, on Black Walnut Run, was designated as the place where court should be held, by the Governor's order, till the court could agree upon a place and have the Governor's approbation.

Benjamin Cave qualified as sheriff, with Thomas Chew and James Barbour as his sureties, and William Henderson as under-sheriff.

James Wood, Gent., produced a commission from the president and masters of William and Mary College, dated November, 1734, to be surveyor for the county. Zachary Lewis and Robert Turner were sworn as attorneys to practise in the County. The court unanimously recommended John Mercer to the Governor for appointment to prosecute the King's causes in their court. James Coward and John Snow were named as overseers of the highway.

A number of the justices were desired to view the Rapidan above and below Germanna for a convenient place to keep a ferry, and to wait on Colonel Spotswood to know on what terms he would let such a place. Later he agreed that he would let his land for a ferry there for 630 pounds of tobacco, with sufficient land for two hands to work, but debarred the keeping of tippling houses and hogs running at large, and public notice was ordered of the letting of the ferry and plantation at a subsequent term, and that advertisements be set up at the churches.

The minutes were signed by Augustine Smith and attested by Henry Willis "Cl. Cur.," a Latin abbreviation for *clericus curiae*, clerk of the court, which attestation was continued throughout his and his successor's terms, and then abandoned. Similarly, they always endorsed indictments found, *Vera Billa*, a true bill.

At the next term many constables and surveyors of the highway were appointed, among the latter Christopher Zimmerman, "from the German Road to Potatoe Run;" John Howard, "from the Chapple Road to the Rapidan Cave's Ford;" John Garth, "from the fork of Elk Run to Staunton's River," as the north branch of the Rapidan was then called; Alexander Waugh, "from Germanna Road to Pine Stake;" Benjamin Porter, "from Todd's Branch to mouth of Robinson;" Edward Haley, "from Taliaferro Road to the Tombstone;" William Smith, "from the Tombstone to the Chapple;" and John Snow "from Todd's Path to Chew's Mill." It would be interesting to designate many of these localities to-day, especially the Tombstone, but the names have nearly all passed out of the public memory.

Three justices, who afterwards became famous in Frederick and Augusta, qualified at this term: Joist Hite, Morgan Morgan, and Benjamin Borden; and John Barnett, from whom no doubt comes our Barnett's Ford of to-day, was appointed surveyor of the highway from the Mountain Road along Mr. James Taylor's "rowling" road and thence to the Rapidan. A rowling road was one over which tobacco hogsheads were rolled to market.

At June term, John Mercer, Gent., produced in court a commission from Hon. William Gooch, his Majesty's lieutenant-governor, which was approved by the Court, and the said Mercer admitted accordingly.

The first jury ever impanelled in the County was at the August term following, to try an action for assault and battery between James Porteus and Jonathan Fennell, alias Fenney, as follows: Benjamin Porter, foreman; Francis Browning, Francis Williams, James Stodgill, Leonard Phillips, William Richeson, George Head, John Conner, John Bomer, William Bohannon, William Crosthwait, Isaac Bletsoe. The verdict was for fifteen shillings damages. The first grand jury appeared in November, Robert Cave, foreman; Abraham Bletsoe, Francis Browning, William Bryant, William Pannill, Edward Franklin, Philip Bush, Anthony Head, William Kelly, Henry Downs, John Bransford, David Phillips, John Howard, George Anderson, Mark Finks, William Carpenter and George Woods.

The following minutes seem worthy of notice: in 1738, a petition for division of the county by inhabitants of Sherrando. This was effective the same year, when Augusta and Frederick counties were formed, embracing all of Virginia lying beyond the Blue Ridge. But Augusta, though formed in 1738, did not really organize as a separate county until about 1745.

Petition of John Lewis and others, of Beverley Manor, for a road to the top of the Blue Ridge, and of Joist Hite, who lived in Frederick County, for a road through Ashby's "bent" (gap).

Ordered, that the County Standard be removed from the house of Colonel Lightfoot, deceased, to that of Major Robert Slaughter.

In 1739 the road was laid off from Beverley Manor, beginning at the North mountains, in Augusta, and ending at the top of the Blue Ridge, "to the bounds of Goochland County," now Albemarle, probably Rockfish Gap, where the Chesapeake and Ohio Railway now crosses.

In 1741 a road was ordered to be opened from Evan Watkins's ferry by a course of marked trees to the head of Falling Spring and over the Tuscarora branch, thence to Opequon Creek, thence to Spout Run, by the King's road leading by Joist Hite's to a fall in the same near the Sherrando ford, and that all tithables from the Potomac between Opequon and the mountain this side the little Cape Capon, and many others, proceed to work the same.

Two more roads, to show the dimensions of the County: May, 1745, James Patton and John Buchanon, Gent., having viewed the way from Frederick County line through that part of this County called Augusta, made their report: "Pursuant, etc., we have viewed, laid off and marked the said road as followeth: to begin at Thom's Brook at Frederick County line, thence to Benjamin Allen's ford and Robert Calwell's path, thence across Beard's ford on North River and Alexander Thompson's ford on Middle River, thence to the Tinkling Spring, to Beverley Manor line, to Gilbert Campbell's ford on north branch of James River, thence to Cherry Tree bottom on James River, thence to Adam Harmon's on the New or Wood's River."

In August of the same year: "Ordered, that George Robinson and Simon Akers view the way from the forks of Roan Oak (Roanoke) to the gapp over the mountains to meet the line of Brunswick County, and from the Catawba Creek into the said way."

In 1748 Culpeper, including all of Orange lying between the whole length of the Rapidan and the Rappahannock rivers, was cut off, and our former "principality" is reduced to the dimensions of Orange and Greene of to-day.

And to dispose of Greene once for all, it may be said here that there was angry contention about this dismemberment, with numerous petitions and counter petitions and protests, but the separatists finally prevailed in 1838.

The old County, though shorn of her territory, has never been shorn of her good name; and her illustrious offspring who have made her famous and historic, were born and reared in the limits of the Orange of to-day!

CHAPTER IV.

The Courthouses.

Mr. William Robertson's house, on Black Walnut Run, was designated as the place where court should be held, by the Governor's order, till the Court could agree upon a place, and have the Governor's approbation, and there the first term was held on the 21st of January, 1734, (Old Style.)

At the same term the sheriff, Thomas Chew, was ordered to build a prison at his plantation, "a logg house, seven and a half feet pitch, sixteen long and ten wide, of loggs six by eight at least, close laid at top and bottom, with a sufficient plank door, strong hinges and a good lock, and that two hundred pounds of tobacco and cask be paid him for building the said house."

A debate was had as to the most convenient place to build a courthouse. The Court divided, one party for the centre of the County and the other for the Raccoon Ford, then some distance higher up the river than now, eight for the former and six for the latter. The question was whether the mouth of the Robertson or Raccoon Ford was nearer the centre, Justices Smith, Taliaferro, Chew, Barbour and Taylor favoring a point just below the mouth of the Robertson on the south side of the Rapidan. Mr. Lightfoot agreed that this was nearest the centre, but insisted on the north side of the

Rapidan. Robert Slaughter was in favor of the centre, when the same should be ascertained. Messrs. Field, Green, Finlason, Ball, Pollard, and Francis Slaughter declined to answer the last question, as to the centre, but insisted on Raccoon Ford, or thereabouts, and the north side of the river. All which the Court ordered should be particularly represented to the Governor.

At the March term ensuing there was an order from the Governor that some of the justices attend the general court and have a hearing about placing the courthouse, and they agree to go at their own charges.

At this term also the following letter from Colonel Spotswood was ordered to be recorded:

> Whereas I have been desired to declare upon what terms I will admit the Courthouse of Orange County to be built upon my land in case the Commissioners for placing the same should judge the most convenient situation thereof to be within the bounds of my Patent. And forasmuch as I am not only willing to satisfy such commissioners that no obstruction in that point will arise on my part, but am also disposed to make those terms as easie to the County, as can well be expected; I do therefore hereby declare that I consent to the building of a courthouse, prison, pillory and stocks on any part of my lands not already leased or appropriated; and that I will convey in the form and manner which the Justices of the County can in reason require such a quantity of land as may be sufficient for setting the said buildings on, with a convenient courtyard thereto, for the yearly acknowledgment of one pound of tobacco. And moreover, that I will allow to be taken gratis off my land all the timber or stone which shall be wanted for erecting and repairing the said buildings.
>
> Given under my hand at Germanna the 6th day of January 1734–5
>
> A. SPOTSWOOD.

The date of this letter would indicate that negotiations had been begun with Colonel Spotswood before the formal organization of the County. The records disclose no appointment by the court of commissioners to confer with him.

At the June term, 1735, Charles Carter and William Beverley reported as to the agreement they had been ordered to make with Colonel Spotswood for land to set the courthouse on, but nothing appears to have come of it, for in Ocober, 1736, a proposal being made where to build it, the Court, after debate, agreed that it be built at the place appointed by the commissioners "near the Governor's Ford on the south side of the Rapidan." At the same term application was made to the Governor for orders to alter the place of holding court from Black Walnut to Mr. Bramham's house in December next, "it being near where the courthouse is, with all expedition, going to be built," and notice was given that workmen meet at the November term to undertake the building.

At November, after debate where to build, the Court agreed with John Bramham that he lease twenty acres of land to build it on for 120 pounds of tobacco per annum, and that the plot should" include the convenientest spring to Cedar Island ford."

Thomas Chew and William Russell were appointed to lay off the land and designate the location of the Courthouse.

The next term was accordingly held at Bramham's house, and it was at this location of the courthouse that Peter was decapitated and his head stuck on a pole, and that Eve was burned at the stake, as appears from the orders published in the text.

In July, 1738, notice was given that at the next term the Court would agree with workmen to finish the courthouse, and at the February term following Peter Russell was employed to keep the building clean, and "provide candles and small beer for the Justices;" so it appears that it had taken nearly two years to complete it after work was actually begun. And it seems certain that the first real courthouse owned by the County was located near the present Somerville's Ford, and on land now belonging to the Hume family. Henry Willis was paid 13,100 pounds of tobacco for building the prison, and 3,350 pounds for finishing the courthouse. He took out license to keep an ordinary there November, 1739.

January, 1742-3. Ordered, that the sheriff cause the lock provided for the justices' room to be put to the door; that he provide glass for the windows of the said room, and cause the windows to be glassed; and that he cause the tops of the chimneys to be pulled down and amended to prevent it from smoking.

June 1749. "The Court judging the present situation inconvenient to the inhabitants are of the opinion that the court ought to be held near the dividing line of the lands of Erasmus Taylor and Timothy Crosthwait," appointed Benjamin Cave, Geo. Taylor, Taverner Beale, Wm. Taliaferro, John Willis, Francis Moore and Henry Downs, or any five of them, to meet and agree on the most convenient place for a courthouse, with power to agree on the manner thereof, and with workmen to erect a prison, pillory, and stocks.

The Courthouses

No doubt the occasion of this removal was the fact that Culpeper, then embracing Madison and Rappahannock, had been cut off from Orange the year before, leaving the courthouse absurdly near the very edge of the County.

A proclamation under the hand of Hon. Thomas Lee, president of His Majesty's Council and Commander-in-Chief of the Colony and Dominion of Virginia, dated the 4th inst., adjourning the Court from the courthouse to the house of Timothy Crosthwait was read, and adjournment was immediately had to the said house "till to-morrow morning at 8 o'clock," and on the 24th day of November, 1749, Court began its sessions at our present County seat. And it was ordered, that Thomas Chew, Geo. Taylor, and Joseph Thomas provide deeds for two acres of land from Timothy Crosthwait to build a courthouse on, and that they lay off the "prison bounds."

1751, August. Ordered, that workmen be engaged to build an addition to the courthouse for the justices' room, sixteen feet by twelve. September: Crosthwait agreed to make a deed for the two acres whereon the courthouse and prison are now built, for five shillings.

May 30, 1752. Note that now the year begins on January 1st, and not March 25th as heretofore. Court agreed with Charles Curtis, builder of the courthouse, to receive the same and to allow him £72 as a full reward for the same, he having already received £32, equal in all to about $350. The first term of the court in this building was held July 6th, 1752, and this was the building next preceding the "old courthouse" standing to-day, and remodeled into the storerooms occupied as drug and hardware stores, facing the railroad.

1754. An addition ordered to the courthouse twenty feet long, same pitch and width as the building, "to have a brick chimney," and be according to dimensions to be indicated by Thos. Chew, Wm. Taliaferro, and James Madison.

1764. Prison repaired; iron grating, and iron spancel and chain ordered.

1768. Pillory and stocks ordered, and extensive repairs to the courthouse.

1787. Court received prison on the undertaker's double ceiling the walls with one and a half inch oak plank inside, to be nailed on with a proportion of 20-penny nails.

1799. Ordered that the sheriff make known by advertisement and proclamation that proposals will be received by the Court for building a new courthouse where the present one stands.

1801. Robt. Taylor, Francis Cowherd, Robt. T. Moore, and John Taylor appointed commissioners to let building of an office 16 wide, 20 long, and 10 pitch, of brick.

1802. The three last named, with Dabney Minor and William Quarles, appointed commissioners to have laid off by Pierce Sandford two acres of ground at this place on which to erect the public buildings, and that Robt. Taylor be appointed to let the building of the office formerly ordered, 24 feet long, 16 wide, and 10 feet pitch. This was probably the old clerk's office in rear of the Bank of Orange.

THE COURTHOUSES 39

1802, April. Ordered, that the building of the courthouse and office be let at the same time, and either publicly or privately.

1804, March. Commissioners appointed to view courthouse and office, and receive or condemn same, or make any compromise as to deductions which the undertakers may be willing to agree to. At the April term this item appears in the County levy: "To balance for building new courthouse and office, including additional work and painting, $2,340.47." This is the building now standing and facing the railroad, as above referred to.

July. Commissioners appointed to sell the old courthouse and office and apply proceeds to enclosing the public lot with post and rail fence in a strong and neat manner, and to building pillory, stocks, and whipping post.

1836. Jail ordered built, and probably completed within the year. This jail stood nearly in front of the old courthouse as it now is, and just across the railroad from it.

In 1852 the Legislature authorized the County Court to sell all or a part of the then public lot, and apply the proceeds of sale to the purchase of another lot, on which to erect a new courthouse and any building proper to be attached thereto.

The site on which the present courthouse stands, known as the "Old Tavern lot" was obtained by exchange, and the edifice constructed thereon after the plans of a paid architect, is not a very good one. The clerk's office remained for many years on the old lot, the Board of Supervisors neglecting all appeals for a fireproof building.

Finally, on the motion of the writer, a rule was issued against them by the Court to shew cause for not complying with the statute requiring a fireproof building for the public records, and they proceeded at once to build the little structure now known as the clerk's office, which if fireproof is also convenience proof, and a reproach to the County. It was completed in 1894. The present jail was built, nearly on the site of the first Baptist church in the town, in 1891.

In January, 1832, a petition numerously signed was presented to the Legislature asking for authority to organize a lottery to raise $5,000, "to pave roads in Courthouse Village." Among the signers were Reynolds Chapman, James B. Moore, Joseph Hiden, Lewis B. Williams, Thos. A. Robinson, Mann A. Page, John Woolfolk, Philip S. Fry, Wm. B. Taylor, Geo. P. Brent, Richard M. Chapman, Peyton Grymes, John H. Lee, and many others. The Act authorizing the lottery was duly passed, and Messrs. Woolfolk, Williams, Richard Chapman, Hiden, and James G. Blakey named therein as commissioners to conduct the same. Nothing appears to have come of it, and the streets were first paved, or macadamized, by the Army of Northern Virginia in the winter of 1863-64, as a military necessity.

The village was first incorporated in 1834, as the Town of Orange, with James Shepherd, Richard Rawlings, Richard M. Chapman, Garland Ballard, Albert Nichols, Samuel Dinkle and Mann A. Page as trustees.

The charter was repealed some years later, the petitioners for the repeal asserting that it had remained a dead letter. It was again incorporated in 1855, but seems not to have assumed any special municipal functions until the present charter of 1896 was passed by the Legislature.

CHAPTER V.

The Colonial Churches.

There appear to have been four State Churches in Orange in colonial times, the first at Germanna, built under the direction of Governor Spotswood about 1724 with the fund of five hundred pounds appropriated for that and other purposes when Spotsylvania was formed.

The next oldest was in the Brooking neighborhood near (old) Cave's ford, about three miles northwest of Somerset, and was later removed to the vicinity of Ruckersville. Capt. May Burton, a Revolutionary officer, was long a lay reader there.

In Bishop Meade's "Old Churches and Families of Virginia" is a chapter by Rev. Joseph Earnest, who was for some years rector of the church at Orange, about the early churches in the County. While his information was not exact, this chapter is the most valuable account of them now obtainable. He narrates that he had been told that the second oldest church was frequented as a place of worship as early as 1723, which is manifestly an error. Most probably it was built about 1740 when St. Thomas Parish was cut off from St. Mark.

The "Middle," or "Brick," church, stood on the hill near where the Pamunkey road crosses Church Run.

It was built between 1750 and 1758 of durable materials, and as late as 1806 time had made little impression on it. One of the first effects of the "freedom of worship" and the practical confiscation of the glebes and church properties was, that the people's consciences became very "free" also to do as they pleased with the church belongings.

This church was actually and literally destroyed, the very bricks carried off and the altar pieces torn from the altar and attached to pieces of household furniture. The ancient communion plate, a massive silver cup and paten, with the name of the parish engraved on it, came to be regarded as common property. Fortunately by the exercise of vigilance the plate was rescued, and is now in possession of St. Thomas Church at Orange.

Nor did the despoilers overlook the churchyard when the work of destruction began. Tombstones were broken down and carried off to be appropriated to unhallowed uses. The Rev. Mungo Marshall, of hallowed memory, rector from 1753 to 1758, was buried there, but his grave was left unmarked. Years afterward a connection of his bequeathed a sum of money upon condition that the legatee should not receive it until he had placed a tombstone over Mr. Marshall's grave, which condition was soon fulfilled. That slab was taken away and used first to grind paints upon, and afterwards in a tannery on which to dress hides! What an injury was done to the history of the County in the destruction of the many tombstones there! for not a vestige remains of church or churchyard.

At a meeting of the vestry of the parish Sept. 1, 1769, there were present: Rev. Thomas Martin, Erasmus Taylor, James Madison, Alexander Waugh, Francis Moore, William Bell, Rowland Thomas, Thomas Bell, Richard Barbour, and William Moore.

In 1786 the congregation in Orange, there being no Episcopal clergyman in the County, engaged the services of James Waddel, the blind Presbyterian minister, to preach for them two years. Forty pounds were subscribed, and the subscription was expected to reach sixty pounds. He not only preached for them but also administered the Sacrament of the Lord's Supper.

The Pine Stake Church, supposed to have been built about the same time as the last, was several miles below "Hawfield," and about a mile and a half east of Everona, near the road to old Verdiersville. It was standing in 1813. During the Revolution "Parson" Leland, as he was called, a Baptist preacher who is referred to at length elsewhere, asked to preach there, which the vestry declined to permit, James Madison, the elder, writing the letter for them.

The principal families connected with the Church in colonial times were the Barbours, Bells, Burtons, Campbells, Caves, Chews, Conways, Daniels, Madisons, Moores, Ruckers, Shepherds, Scotts, Taylors, Taliaferros, Thomases, Waughs, Whites, and Willises.

The glebe farm was near the courthouse, and is now owned by Mr. Wambersie.

In 1739 John Becket, clerk, a synonym for clergyman, was presented for not giving his attendance according to law, and for not administering the Sacrament of the Lord's Supper at his chapel in St. Mark Parish. The presentment was dismissed.

In 1741 Rev. Richard Hartswell of the Parish of St. Thomas, lately cut off from St. Mark, was presented for being drunk on the information of one Tully Joice who had been presented the same day for swearing an oath, thus indicating spite work, as the presentment was promptly dismissed.

As early as 1763, on motion of James Madison, the loss of two duplicate bills of exchange was ordered recorded. These bills represented a subscription of twenty-five pounds sterling to the "Society for the Propagation of the Gospel in Foreign Parts," and show how soon missionary work was begun in Orange.

CHAPTER VI.

Other Old Churches—The Dissenters.

In a County where so many denominations exist, prudence impels strict adherence to the records in narrating their history.

When the County was formed and until the end of the Revolution, the Church of England was the Established or State Church, and church matters were regulated by laws passed by the "General Assembly" or law-making power. Thus it was the civil authorities, mostly composed of State Churchmen, however, not the church authorities, which enforced the law; and if this fact had always been borne in mind it is likely that much polemical asperity and recrimination might have been avoided.

The ecclesiastical regulations of those days would be deemed tyrannical and oppressive in these, but they applied alike to all citizens. The laws compelled everybody to attend religious worship, and numerous were the fines imposed with great impartiality on persons for absenting themselves from the parish church; Churchmen as well as dissenters. At one period, 1690 to 1720, the law was that if the fine was not paid, the offender should be imprisoned and even receive corporal punishment; so it seems that it was not dissenters only who were "persecuted." And, as early as 1714, the German Protestants at Germanna were exempted by statute from paying parish levies, and authorized to employ a minister of their own faith.

A special chapter has been devoted to the colonial churches of the establishment: only four others appear to have existed in colonial times; "Hebron," the Lutheran Church in Madison, built in 1740; "the church of the blind preacher," James Waddel (for so he spelled his own name); old "Blue Run" and "Pamunkey." In those days these were always spoken of as "Meeting Houses," even in the records.

Of these in Orange County, old "Blue Run," situated about midway between Liberty Mills and Barboursville, is probably the oldest. It was constituted in 1769, by the "Separate Baptists," Elijah Craig being the first pastor. As early as 1774 there is record of a motion by Zachary Burnley "to turn the road that leads from the 'Meeting House' down to Blue Run bridge;" and there is still standing near the church what appears to be an indestructible stone vault of the Webb family, erected in 1783. Since the war, the old wooden edifice, still in excellent preservation, has been turned over to the negroes, the Baptist congregation having erected a new building near Somerset.

It is not known when the Presbyterian Church of the blind preacher, rendered memorable by William Wirt, in the "British Spy," was built, but it was certainly one of the earlier churches of the county. It stood on the north side of the Orange highway, about a half mile northeast of Gordonsville: proper appreciation of its historical associations would insure a permanant marking of the site while it is yet remembered.

In the heyday of the "Sons of Temperance," 1850–56, the historic old building was taken down and the lumber used to build a temperance hall at Gordonsville, which after the war was used for some years as a schoolhouse. Finally it was condemned that a street might be opened, and the material was bought by a negro preacher, who reconverted in into another structure, a fate as pathetic as that of old Blue Run; for so we treat our historic treasures, having so many!

And it may as well be recorded here that an old Baptist church known as "Zion Meeting House," which stood about two miles south of Orange courthouse, on the Gordonsville road, was abandoned for a new church at Toddsberth shortly before the war, the lumber of which was sold and put into new buildings at the courthouse, one of which was for years used as a barroom!

North Pamunkey is another Baptist church edifice of historic association. It was organized in 1774 by Aaron Bledsoe and E. Craig with twenty members. Aaron Bledsoe was its first pastor and its original name was North Fork of Pamunkey, from the stream nearby. In 1792 the membership was about three hundred and fifty, and it was used as a place of worship for thirty-seven years before being heated in any way.

The present edifice, practically on the site of the old log structure, the fourth on the same site, was completed in 1849.

Other Old Churches—Dissenters 49

Modern churches abound, almost to the impoverishment of preachers. At Gordonsville the whites have six churches and a chapel, the negroes several; the whites have four at Orange; at and near Somerset there are three, at Barboursville three; at and near Unionville several; and the county is dotted with them from end to end, the whites having thirty-two in all, the negroes seventeen.

Saint Thomas, at the Courthouse, was frequently attended during the war by Generals Lee, Stuart, and other Confederate officers of distinction; and New Zion, at Toddsberth, was occupied as a shoe shop in the winter of 1863-4. General Mahone bought up all the leather that he could, detailed all the shoemakers of his division, and took possession of the church. To his and their credit, no injury was done to the church, and when the campaign opened in the spring, his command was well shod.

The following items are condensed from the order books. In 1737 William Williams, Gent., a Presbyterian minister, took the oaths, subscribed the test, and likewise a declaration of his approval of such of the thirty-nine articles of religion as is required, and certified his intention of holding his meetings at his own plantation and that of Morgan Bryan.

Subsequent records show him to have been very litigious and at odds with very many people for sundry years. He brought suit at one time against nearly one hundred persons, for damages for a certain scandalous paper reflecting on him, but recovered nothing, though some of the signers did retract.

Here is a very curious order of 1768:

"Elijah Morton is discontinued, the Court conceiving him to be an unfit person to act as Justice of the Peace, for that in a plea of debt" he declined, when requested by James Madison to make a quorum to try the cause, because one of the parties told him he did not wish it to be tried at that term; and yet when said Madison and Zachariah Burnley went into court and made a quorum the said Morton ascended the bench and sat in the cause; "and for that," the order concludes, "the said Morton is a promoter of schisms and particularly of the sect called Anabaptists!"

In 1773 Joseph Spencer, being brought before the court by a warrant under the hand of Rowland Thomas, Gent., for a breach of his good behavior in teaching and preaching the gospel as a Baptist not having a license; and it appearing that he did teach and preach as aforesaid, he at the same time insisting that he decented [dissented] from the principles of an Anabaptist; ordered, that he be committed to the custody of the sheriff until he give bond conditioned not to teach or preach without first obtaining a license as the law directs. Bond was required in a penalty of one hundred pounds, and he was allowed the liberty of the prison bounds on giving security.

At the next term leave was given him to live in the courthouse, he indemnifying the County against loss, and on his petition, his bond was reduced to twenty pounds, and William Morton and Jonathan Davis became his sureties for his good behavior.

In 1781 Elijah Craig and Nathaniel Sanders, dissenting Baptist ministers recommended by the elders of their society, were licensed to perform the marriage ceremony.

These are the only items of note in the records as to the treatment of dissenters by the Court.

CHAPTER VII.

Indian Antiquities.

There is a notable Indian Mound near the Greene line. The following description of it is condensed from a special report of the United States Bureau of Ethnology in 1894:

"The country along the upper portion of the Rappahannock and its tributaries was inhabited by tribes known collectively as the Manahoac. They probably migrated westward and united with tribes beyond the Ohio whose names they took. They and the Monacan were allied against the Powhatan.

"It will be proper to describe here a mound, evidently a tribal burial place, situated in the former territory of the Manahoac, and due probably to their labor.

"The mound stands on the right bank of Rapidan river, a mile east of the boundary between Orange and Greene. Originally it was elliptical in form, with the longer axis nearly east and west; but the river in shifting its channel some years ago, undermined and carried away the eastern portion, probably from one-half to two-thirds of the entire structure. For several years, some of the earth fell in at every freshet, thus keeping a vertical section exposed to view. The different strata of bone were plainly visible, and when the water was low fragments of human bones were strewn along the shore beneath. The river shifted again, and the mound soon assumed its natural shape. At present the base measures 42 by 48 feet, with the longer axis nearly north and south. A considerable part of it has been hauled away, leaving a depression at the middle fully 20 feet across and extending almost to the bottom of the mound. As a result, the interior was very muddy, the bones extremely soft and fragmentary, and excavation difficult.

"The highest point left by these destructive agencies was six feet; the river had probably left it fully ten feet high. If the statements concerning its original form and extent be correct, the apex was at least twelve feet above the base, the latter being not less than 50 by 75 feet.

"The earth was removed from an area 28 by 40 feet. At seven feet was found the outer edge of a bone deposit measuring 6 by 15 feet. There were indications in several places that skeletons had been compactly bundled, but most of the bones were scattered promiscuously, as if they had been collected from some place of previous interment and carelessly thrown in, there being no evidence of an attempt to place them in proper order. In the mass were two small deposits of calcined human bones, and beneath it were graves or burial pits.

"This bone bed, which was at the level of the natural surface, was the largest found. Two feet above it, and four feet within its outer margin, was another, much smaller; and numerous others were found in all the portion removed. There was no attempt at regularity in position or extent; in some places only such a trace as may have resulted from the decomposition of a few bones; in others, as many as fifteen or twenty skeletons may have been deposited. They occurred at all levels below a foot from the upper surface of the mound, but no section showed more than four layers above the original surface of the ground, though it was reported that six strata had been found near the central portion, which would indicate that the burials were carried nearly to the top of the mound.

"In the skeletons all ages were represented, for among the bones were those of very young children, while of others many of the teeth were worn to the neck.

"Numerous small deposits of human bones, almost destroyed by fire, were scattered through the mound. The bones in some of the graves appeared to have been placed in their proper position, but it was impossible to ascertain this with certainty. One of the deeper pits had its bottom lined with charcoal; none of the others had even this slight evidence of care or respect.

"No relics of any kind were deposited with the bones; a rough mortar, two arrowheads, and some fragments of pottery were found loose in the debris.

"It is plain that this spot was for a long period the burial place of a small tribe or clan, among whom prevailed the habit of stripping the flesh from the corpse before interment, or of depositing the body elsewhere for a time and afterwards removing the bones to this ossuary. That no stated intervals elapsed between consecutive deposits is shown by the varying position and size among the different bone beds, and by the overlapping of many of the graves beneath.

"It is impossible accurately to estimate the number of skeletons found; certainly not fewer than 200, possibly 250, which figures represent approximately one-fourth of the number deposited, if the statements as to the original size of the mound be correct.

"In its construction this mound corresponds closely with one opened by Jefferson on the Rivanna, a few miles above Charlottesville. 'The contents were such as on the whole to give the idea of bones emptied promiscuously from a bag or basket and covered with earth, without any attention to their order.' That the bones near the top were in a better state of preservation than those towards the bottom is due probably less to their being of much later deposit than to the dryness of the earth near the top. A party of Indians passing about 1751 where this barrow is, near Charlottesville, went through the woods directly to it, without any instructions or inquiry, and having staid about it some time, with expressions construed to be those of sorrow, returned to the high road, which they had left about six miles to pay this visit, and pursued their journey."

For a fuller account the reader is referred to a pamphlet of the Smithsonian Institution, entitled, "Archæologic Investigations in the James and Potomac Valleys."

As so little is known about the Indians who once inhabitated this section, it has been thought worth while to transcribe the few orders relating to them made by the county court.

In 1730, "William Bohannon came into court and made oath that about twenty-six of the Sapony Indians that inhabit Colonel Spotswood's land in Fox's neck go about and do a great deal of mischief by firing the woods; more especially on the 17th day of April last whereby several farrows of pigs were burnt in their beds, and that he verily believes that one of the Indians shot at him the same day, the bullet entering a tree within four feet of him; that he saw the Indian about one hundred yards from him, and no game of any sort between them; that the Indian after firing his gun stood in a stooping manner very studdy [steady] so that he could hardly discern him from a stump, that he has lost more of his pigs than usual since the coming of the said Indians; which is ordered to be certified to the General Assembly."

1742. Sundry Indians, among them Manincassa, Captain Tom, Blind Tom, Foolish Zack, and Little Zack, were before Court for "terrifying" one Lawrence Strother, who testified that one of them shot at him, that they tried to surround him, that he turned his horse and rid off, but they gained on him till he crossed the run. Ordered, that the Indians be taken into custody by the sheriff until they give peace bonds with security, and that their guns be taken from them until they are ready to depart out of this Colony, they having declared their intention to depart within a week. They gave bond.

There is no record extant of any Indian massacre, large or small, in the original limits of the County east of the Blue Ridge.

Indian Antiquities.

The Tomahawk branch, which crosses the Gordonsville road about a mile and a half south of the courthouse, is a preserved Indian name, one of the very few in the County. It was here that the organization known as the "Culpeper Minute Men" camped when first on their way to join the army of the Revolution. (Slaughter's "St. Mark's.")

CHAPTER VIII.

French and Indian Wars.

If Orange as a County ever sent an organized command to any of the French and Indian Wars no record of it has been found. The records do disclose that sundry of her citizens participated in these wars, but in every instance in a company or regiment from some other county; the names of but few appear in the record—among them that of Ambrose Powell, ancestor of Gen. A. P. Hill—who rose to the dignity of a commission during all the years that these wars were waged.

Therefore, any detailed account of these wars would be out of place here, and only such facts will be narrated as may throw some light on the services of citizens who did participate in them.

In 1758 an expedition, the second one, was set on foot for the capture of Fort Duquesne, (the modern Pittsburg, then believed to be in the limits of Augusta County), under General Forbes, a British officer. Washington was commander of the Virginia troops which consisted of two regiments, his own and Col. William Byrd's, about two thousand men in all. A Colonel Bouquet, of Pennsylvania, commanded the advanced division of the army, and Captain Hogg, of Augusta, had a company in Washington's regiment.

FRENCH AND INDIAN WARS. 59

The fort was finally captured, but the loss in Washington's regiment alone was 6 officers and 62 privates. Colonel Byrd was of the "Westover" family, an ancestor of the Willises of Orange. The Captain Overton referred to in the extracts following, was from Hanover, but he was in an earlier expedition in 1755. His company was the first organized in Virginia after Braddock's defeat, and the great Presbyterian preacher, Rev. Samuel Davies, addressed it by request on the eve of its departure for the frontiers. The history of these wars is narrated at large in Waddell's "Annals of Augusta County," second edition, and in Withers's "Chronicles of Border Warfare." The order books show as follows:

August, 1779. David Thompson, soldier in Captain Hogg's Rangers, 1758; sergeant in Colonel Bouquet's regiment in 1764.

Jacob Williams and Jacob Crosthwait, in Colonel Byrd's regiment, 1758.

September Term. Benjamin Powell, sergeant, Thomas Fitzgerald and John Williams, soldiers, in Colonel Byrd's regiment, 1758.

Isaac Crosthwait, Thomas Walker, Charles Walker, in Hogg's rangers.

October. Daniel McClayland, Colonel Byrd's regiment, 1759. William Vawter, sergeant, John Furnes, (Furnace), Hogg's rangers.

James Cowherd, ensign, Colonel Bouquet's regiment; William Bullock and William Rogers, in Colonel Washington's regiment, 1758; Francis Hackley, John Lucas, Thomas Powell, Richard Lamb, John Lamb, James

Gaines, Thomas Morris, Charles Pearcey, William Cave, soldiers, and Michael Rice, sergeant, in Colonel Byrd's regiment.

Henry Shackleford, Henry Hervey, John Warner, Simon Powell, soldiers, and James Riddle, non-commissioned, Hogg's rangers.

1780. William Brock, in Colonel Stephen's regiment, 1762. Colonel Adam Stephen was probably from Frederick County, where Stephensburg is named for him.

Patrick Fisher, Littleberry Low, William Lamb, David Watts, Charles Watts, James Lamb, soldiers, William Cave, non-commissioned, in Colonel Byrd's regiment; William Watson, in "Captain Overton's company of regulars for defence of this State," in 1755.

William Sims and Francis Gibbs, in Hogg's rangers; James Roberts, in "Captain Wagoner's company of regulars for defense of this State," 1757; Ambrose Powell, Gent., staff officer in Virginia forces, 1755.

William Smith, Captain Hogg's rangers.

In Thwaites's edition of Withers it is said that Col. William Russell, at one time high sheriff of Orange, did some frontier service in the early part of these wars, and in 1753 was sent as a commissioner to the Indians in the region where Pittsburg now stands. His son, of the same name, was at the battle of Point Pleasant; was second in command at King's Mountain, and retired at the end of the Revolution as brevet brigadier-general.

The records in the Land Office at Richmond show that the following Orange people received bounty land for service in these wars. Their names are also listed in Crozier's "Virginia Colonial Militia:" Jacob Crosthwait, Francis Gibbs, William Smith, William Brock, William Rogers, Richard Bullard, James Gaines, Michael Rice, John Lamb, Richard Lamb, William Cave, James Riddle, Thomas Morris, John Furnace, David Thompson, Isaac Crosthwait, William Vaughan, Ambrose Powell, Littleberry Lane, Henry Shackleford, Patrick Fisher, Charles Watts, Simon Powell, David Watts.

Francis Cowherd, long known as Major Cowherd, who was a justice of the peace and high sheriff of Orange after the Revolution and who attained the rank of captain in the Revolutionary army, was a soldier in Colonel Field's regiment at the battle of Point Pleasant. His home, "Oak Hill," is about two miles northeast of Gordonsville, and is still owned by his descendants. Just before the battle he and a comrade named Clay were out hunting, a little distance apart, and came near to where two Indians were concealed. Seeing Clay only, and supposing him to be alone, one of them fired at him; and running up to scalp him as he fell, was himself shot by Cowherd, who was about a hundred yards off. The other Indian ran off. (Withers's Chronicles.)

Another anecdote related by his cotemporaries is, that in the battle of Point Pleasant Cowherd was behind a tree, fighting in Indian warfare fashion, when Colonel Field ran up to the same tree. He offered to seek another, but the Colonel commanded him to remain where he was, saying it was his tree, and that he would go to another. In making his way to it he was killed by the Indians, greatly lamented by the army. He was of the Culpeper family of Field, was a lieutenant of a company from that county at Braddock's defeat, and was greatly distinguished as an Indian fighter. (See again Withers's Chronicles.)

Mention is made of the Chew brothers, distinguished in these wars, in the Biographical Sketches.

Hancock Taylor, a brother of Colonel Richard, father of the President, was killed by the Indians in Kentucky in 1774.

There is a so-called "patriotic" association, known as the "Society of Colonial Wars," and descendants of those who participated in the French and Indian wars are eligible to membership therein.

CHAPTER IX.

Orange in the Revolution.

The part the County took in the Revolution must be exhibited rather in details than by a connected narrative.

The royalist Governor, Lord Dunmore, often prorogued—that is, dissolved—the Burgesses from 1773 to 1776, for what he considered their contumacious attitude towards the Crown. The Burgesses, instead of going to their several homes, as he expected, began in 1774 to assemble at the Raleigh Tavern, at Williamsburg, then the capital, and form themselves into revolutionary conventions—one or more in 1774, two in 1775, in all of which Orange was represented by Thomas Barbour and James Taylor; and finally into the world-famous Convention of 1776, in which James Madison, Jr., and William Moore were the delegates from the County. So odious did the name of Dunmore become that a county named for him, once in the domain of Orange, lost its identity under that name, and was re-christened Shenandoah.

While these conventions were being held the people at home became greatly aroused and began to organize for a conflict that seemed inevitable, by choosing committees of safety, putting the militia on a war footing and selecting from them, for regular training and discipline, the more active and resolute, called "Minute Men."

By an ordinance of the Convention of 1775, the colony was divided into eighteen districts, one of which consisted of the counties of Orange, Culpeper, and Fauquier; each district was required to enlist a battalion of 500 men in 10 companies of 50 each, with the requisite officers, a colonel, lieutenant-colonel, and major, 10 captains and lieutenants, a chaplain, surgeon, etc.

The first organization from this district appears to have been designated "The Culpeper Minute Men," supposedly because Culpeper was the middle county; for it is certain that Lawrence Taliaferro of Orange, was its first colonel.

It participated in the battle of Great Bridge, the first battle of the Revolution fought on Virginia soil, in December, 1775, and was then commanded by Stevens, afterwards General Stevens, of Culpeper.

The committees of safety were very great factors in the war, and really constituted a sort of military executive in each county.

It is not to be doubted that each committee kept a formal record of its proceedings, which would furnish invaluable historical data; but very few complete records have been found in any of the counties, and practically all that are preserved are in the fourth series of Peter Force's American Archives, published by order of Congress, and now become quite rare.

The following extracts, copied from these Archives, are believed to be the whole record of the Orange committee that has been preserved:

ORANGE COMMITTEE OF SAFETY.

*At a meeting of the Freeholders of the County of Orange, Virginia, on Thursday the 22nd day of December, 1774, the following gentlemen were elected a Committee for the said County, viz:

James Madison, James Taylor, William Bell, Thomas Barbour, Zachariah Burnley, Rowland Thomas, William Moore, Johnny Scott, James Walker, William Pannill, Francis Moore, James Madison, Jun., Lawrence Taliaferro, Thomas Bell, and Vivian Daniel.

And at a meeting of the said Committee at the Court House, on Monday, the 2nd day of January, 1775, James Madison, Esquire, was elected Chairman, and Francis Taylor, Clerk of said Committee.

Published by order of the Committee.

FRANCIS TAYLOR, *Clerk*.

March 11, 1775.

†An accusation being lodged with the Committee of Orange County against Francis Moore, Jun., of his having violated the Eighth Article of the Continental Association by gaming: the said Moore was cited, and appeared before the Committee convened Feby. 23, 1775. The testimony of a witness, as well as the confession of the accused, convinced the Committee that the charge was well founded; but Mr. Moore gave such evidence of his penitence, and intention to observe the Association strictly for the future, and alleging, moreover, that he was not thoroughly aware of the extent of the prohibition contained in that Article, that the Committee think it proper to readmit him into the number of friends to the public cause, till a second transgression.

---

*Peter Force's American Archives, Fourth Series, Vol. I., p. 1056.
†Ibid: Vol. II. p. 126.

It need scarcely be added, that this mitigation of the punishment prescribed in the Eleventh Article, proceeds from a desire to distinguish penitent and submissive, from refractory and obstinate offenders.

FRANCIS TAYLOR, *Clerk*.

March 27, 1775.

*The Committee of Orange County being informed that the Reverend Mr. John Wingate had in his possession several pamphlets containing very obnoxious reflections on the Continental Congress and their proceedings, and calculated to impose on the unwary; and being desirous to manifest their contempt and resentment of such writings and their authors, assembled on Saturday, the 25th of March, 1775, at the Court House of the said County. The Committee were the rather induced to meet for this purpose, as it had also been reported that there were a considerable number of these performances in the Country, introduced amongst us in all probability to promote the infamous ends for which they were written; that they were to be sold indiscriminately at Purdie's office in Williamsburgh, and that unfavorable impressions had been made on some people's minds by the confident assertions of falsehoods and insidious misrepresentations of facts contained in them. The intentions of this Committee were made known to Mr. Wingate, and a delivery of the pamphlets requested in the most respectful manner, without the least suspicion that Mr. Wingate had procured them with a design to make an ill use of them, or that he would hesitate a moment as to a compliance; but to their great surprise, he absolutely refused, urging that they belonged to Mr. Henry Mitchell of Fredericksburgh, and he could do nothing without his express permission. The Com-

---

*Peter Force's American Archives, Fourth Series, Vol I. p. 234-5.

mittee then proceeded to expostulate with him on the subject, and to insist upon him that as he regarded his association engagements, the favour of the Committee or the good of the publick, he would not deny so reasonable a request. They told him they would engage to make ample satisfaction to Mr. Mitchell for any damage he might sustain and that there would not be the least reason to fear that Mr. Mitchell would be displeased, who was well known to be an associator, and acknowledged by himself to be a hearty friend to the cause which these pamphlets were intended to disparage and counteract; and that if Mr. Mitchell was not this hearty friend we hoped him to be, it must be an additional argument for the Committee to press their request, and for him to comply with it. Mr. Wingate still persisted in his refusal to deliver them up, but added that he would let the Committee have a sight of them, if they would promise to return them unhurt. This could by no means be agreed to, as they were justly apprehensive that it would be their duty to dispose of the pamphlets in a manner inconsistent with such a promise. At length the Committee, finding there was no prospect of working on Mr. Wingate by arguments or entreaties, peremptorily demanded the pamphlets, with a determination not to be defeated in their intentions. In consequence of which they were produced to the Committee who deferred the full examination and final disposal of them till the Monday following.

On Monday, the 27th instant, they again met at the same place, according to adjournment, and after a sufficient inquiry into the contents of five pamphlets under the following titles, viz: 1st, "The Congress Canvassed, etc.," by A. W. Farmer; 2nd, "A View of the Controversey between Great Britain and her Colonies," by the same; 3d, "Free Thoughts on the Proceedings of the Continental Congress, etc.," by

A. Farmer; 4th, "Short Advice to the Counties of New York," by a Country Gentleman; 5th, "An Alarm to the Legislature of the Province of New York, etc.;" most of them printed by Rivington of New York;

Resolved, That as a collection of the most audacious insults on that august body (the Grand Continental Congress) and their proceedings, and also on the several Colonies from which they were deputed, particularly New England and Virginia, of the most slavish doctrines of Provincial Government, the most impudent falsehoods and malicious artifices to excite divisions among the friends of America, they deserved to be publicly burnt, as a testimony of the Committee's detestation and abhorrence of the writers and their principles.

Which sentence was speedily executed in the presence of the Independent Company and other respectable inhabitants of the said County, all of whom joined in expressing a noble indignation against such execrable publications, and their ardent wishes for an opportunity of inflicting on the authors, publishers, and their abbettors, the punishment due to their insufferable arrogance and atrocious crimes.

Published by order of the Committee,

FRANCIS TAYLOR, *Clerk*.

May 9, 1775.

*The Committee for Orange County met on Tuesday, the 9th of May. Taking into their consideration the removal of the powder from the public magazine, and the compensation obtained by the Independent Company of Hanover; and observing also that the receipt given by Captain Patrick Henry to his Majesty's Receiver General refers the final disposal of the money to the next Colony Convention, came to the following Resolutions:

---

*Peter Force's American Archives, Fourth Series, Vol. I, p. 339–40.

1. That the Governour's removal of the Powder lodged in the Magazine, and set apart for the defence of the Country, was fraudulent, unnecessary, and extremely provoking to the people of this Colony.

2. That the resentment shown by the Hanover Volunteers, and the reprisal they have made on the King's property, highly merit the approbation of the publick, and the thanks of this Committee.

3. That if any attempt should be made, at the ensuing Convention, to have the Money returned to His Majesty's Receiver General, our Delegates be, and they are hereby instructed, to exert all their influence in opposing such attempt, and in having the Money laid out in Gunpowder for the use of the Colony.

4. That the following Address be presented to Captain Patrick Henry, and the gentlemen Independents of Hanover:

*GENTLEMEN: We, the Committee for the County of Orange, having been fully informed of your seasonable and spirited proceedings in procuring a compensation for the Powder fraudulently taken from the County Magazine by command of Lord Dunmore, and which it evidently appears his Lordship, notwithstanding his assurances had no intention to restore, entreat you to accept their cordial thanks for this testimony of your zeal for the honour and interest of your Country. We take this occasion also to give it as our opinion, that the blow struck in the Massachusetts Government is a hostile attack on this and every other Colony, and a sufficient warrant to use violence and reprisal, in all cases where it may be expedient for our security and welfare.

This address is signed by all the members of the committee except Messrs. Wm. Bell, Pannill, Francis Moore and V. Daniel, and was prepared by James Madison, Jr., according to Mr. Wm. C. Rives's "Life of Madison." As he was then only about twenty-three and at no time much of a warrior, the statement seems improbable; nor does his fame need bolstering by mere conjecture.

---
*Peter Force's American Archives, Fourth Series. Vol. I, p. 339-40.

It will be observed that this record ends on May 9, only a few days after the "Embattled farmers" of Massachusetts had "fired the shot heard round the world," the opening gun of the Revolution at Concord, April 19, 1775.

Membership of the Committee was quite a badge of distinction, and descent from a Committeeman constitutes a clear title to membership in the societies known as "The Sons" and "The Daughters of the Revolution."

Recurring to the order books, the first record of impending disorder is in 1775, when nine patrolmen are paid 1,679 pounds of tobacco for patrolling the county the preceding year.

In March, 1776, Thomas Barbour is appointed sheriff "agreeable to an order of the Convention," the first official recognition by the Court of existing Revolution. In July of that year the justices take the oath prescribed by the Convention, "to be faithful and true to the Commonwealth of Virginia, and to the utmost of their power support, maintain and defend the constitution thereof as settled by the General Convention, and do equal right and justice to all men." A noble oath! It was first administered to Francis Moore who then administered it to the other justices, to James Taylor, clerk, and to John Walker, "King's Attorney."

Virginia had declared her independence of the Crown on the 29th of June, 1776, five days before the general Declaration in July. The public officers appear to have simply held over by taking the Convention oath. But in May, 1777, commissions from Patrick Henry, the first governor of the new "Commonwealth," directed to James Madison, Francis Moore, William Bell, Rowland Thomas, Reuben Daniel, Zachary Burnley, Thomas Bell, William Moore, Andrew Shepherd, Thomas Barbour, Johnny Scott, Benjamin Grymes, James Madison, Jr., Uriel Mallory, Catlett Conway, and Jeremiah White, were received: and they constituted the first bench of justices under the new regime. It does not appear that James Madison, Jr., ever qualified.

Richard Adams was ordered to deliver to Johnny Scott 60 bushels of salt belonging to the County, agreeable to an order of his Excellency, the Governor.

These companies are named in current orders: Johnny Scott's, Captain Bruce's, Captain Craig's, Captain Conway's, Francis Moore's, Captain Smith's, Captain Mills', and Captain Conney's. Captain seems to have distinguished sufficiently without the Christian name.

William Bell was appointed to administer the prescribed oath, "to oblige all the inhabitants to give assurance of allegiance to the State," and certain dissenting ministers, John Price, Elijah Craig, Nathaniel Sanders, Bartlett Bennett, and Richard Cave, took the oaths of allegiance and fidelity.

In 1778 allowances of money were ordered to Peter Mountague, Jere Chandler, and Joseph Edmondson, soldiers in service; to Sarah Staves, a poor woman having two sons in service; to Usley McClarney, widow of Francis who had died in service; to Margaret Douglas, a poor woman, son in Continental army; and to Solomon Garrett's family, he being in Continental service.

Thirty-six pounds were allowed Mountague's family. Zachary Burnley becomes county lieutenant in place of James Madison, resigned. He resigns in 1781, and is succeeded by James Madison, Jr. Jane Hensley, having son in Continental Army, is allowed 25 pounds.

In 1781, Ordered, agreeably to Act of Assembly for supplying army with clothes, provisions, and wagons, that each tithable person pay the sheriff seven pounds, current money, to purchase a wagon and team and hire a driver. This tax realized about $50,000, and the purchase was made and the outfit delivered to Benjamin Winslow, deputy commissioner.

The sheriff was ordered to pay James Madison $6,500 for repairing public wagons, Benjamin Head $36,000 to purchase a wagon and team for the public, and Edmund Singleton $800 for collars for the team. John Coleman is named as an ensign in Continental service.

In 1782 the companies in the County were commanded by Captains Miller, Burton, Buckner, Herndon, Hawkins, Lindsay, Waugh, Graves, Stubblefield, and Webb.

A special term of the court was held for several days in April, 1782, to adjust claims for property impressed or furnished for the public service. These claims cover nearly forty full pages of the order book, and only a few of the more notable ones can be inserted here. They were mostly for provisions, horses, brandy, guns, etc.; a great many supplies having been furnished when the "Convention Troops," as the prisoners taken at Saratoga were called, subsequently confined in barracks near Charlottesville, were marched through the County.

A guard was constantly kept at Brock's Bridge, quite a detachment to judge from the quantity of supplies furnished it.

James Madison's name often appears. He owned quite a blacksmith's shop, and appears to have got good prices for all his supplies, which generally are rated as something extra. He furnished supplies to Halifax and Pittsylvania militia returning from Noland's Ferry where they had escorted prisoners taken at York; Indian meal to Convention troops marching from the barracks to Winchester in 1781; was paid $35 "for a gun, one of the best, imported," impressed for the Orange militia, and for "a well fixed wagon, the naves (hubs) of the wheels boxed with iron," impressed at Richmond by Stephen Southall, assistant quartermaster general.

Robert Thomas's gun was impressed for the Orange militia guarding the Convention prisoners in 1778. Moses Hase was paid for two bushels of "country-made salt," impressed by George Morton, commissary, Orange militia.

There is incontestible evidence that the Orange militia were several times in actual service in the field, a fact that no history of the Revolution discloses, certainly not so as to identify them. How long and on what occasions they served can not now be ascertained, but these selected entries prove the fact:

William Hawkins furnishes supplies to Prettyman Merry, lieutenant Orange militia for 18-months men marching from Orange to Fredericksburg; allowances to William Webb, for beef for Orange militia on march to camp; to James Coleman, for supplies impressed by William Thomas, commanding officer of guard at Brock's Bridge; to William Morton, for wagon impressed for Orange militia from August 17 to October 31, 1781, and for a wagon impressed at Guilford courthouse, North Carolina, October, 1781, by order of General Stevens; to Zachary Herndon, for wagon with Orange militia 27 days, October and November, 1781, and to same in May, June, and July, 1781, 75 days; to George Morton, for wagons impressed for Orange militia 135 days, John Taylor, colonel commanding.

In a cotemporaneous official manuscript volume labeled, "Virginia Militia" in the State library, published in full in the "Virginia Magazine of History and Biography," see volume 14, page 80, are to be found these entries:

"*1777, Sept. 29.* Scott, Captain John, for pay of his company of Orange Militia to 28 inst, and 9 days to return, £211. 5s. 3d.

September 30. Ditto for ditto. For one day detained, per account, £8. 7s. 5d."

These examples must suffice. They seem to indicate that certainly part of the service was at the seige of York, as Yorktown was then called. Other items of general interest are these: Benjamin Johnson, supplies for prisoners and militia marching from Fredericksburg to Charlottesville or Staunton, and for oats for wagon horses with the "Flying Hospital."

Charles Porter, for use of his house taken for quarters for Marquis de Lafayette by C. Jones, assistant quartermaster general, June, 1781, 3 days. Daniel Thornton, for guarding the Marquis on his march through Orange.

It has been impossible to locate with exactness Charles Porter's house, thus rendered historic, but it is believed to have been near the old Raccoon Ford, some distance above the present ford, it being known that the Marquis was delayed some days there awaiting reënforcements. In an order of March, 1786, laying off the County into districts for overseers of the Poor, Middle District begins "at Charles Porter's and runs along the Marquis's road to Brockman's Bridge," which almost identifies the house as being on the river where this road crossed it.

Mary Bell, for entertaining William Clark, express rider and his horse, stationed at her house by H. Young, quartermaster general, State volunteers.

This Mary Bell was afterwards County jailer for several years.

Andrew Shepherd, for a mare rode express, by order of the County Lieutenant, to give notice to captains of militia to assemble their companies, May, 1781, by order of the Executive.

Other items pertaining to the Revolution, and giving names of Orange people who participated in it will be found in condensed form in an appendix. The curious reader is referred to the order book for 1782, April Special Terms, for further information.

In order to verify the statement heretofore made as to the Orange soldiers being designated at first as "Culpeper Minute Men," the following petition, from the original, now on file in the State library, is published at length. It is endorsed, "The Petition of

Philip Ballard praying for a pension, December 28th, 1829, referred to Revolutionary claims, and is in the words following:

THE PETITION OF PHILIP BALLARD, AN OLD SOLDIER:

To the Senate and House of Representatives of Virginia— Your petitioner begs leave to represent that he enlisted in the service of the State of Virginia as early as 1775 in what was then called the Minute Service in Captain Joseph Spencer's Company from Orange County, Va., who was attached to Col. Tolerver's (Taliaferro), of said County, Regiment, and was from thence marched to Culpeper C. H. and thence to what was called the Great Bridge, at which place your petitioner was engaged in the Battle that took place between the British and General Wolford, after which your petitioner was discharged. Your petitioner then enlisted in the service for two years in Captain Burley's (Burnley) Company who was commanded by Major Robert and Col. Francis Taylor. After the expiration of that time your petitioner enlisted two years more and was attached to Captain Chapman's Company who was commanded by Major Wails (?) and Colonel Crocket. etc.

The affidavit of G. Stallings was filed in verification of this petition.

CHAPTER X.

Germanna and the First Settlers.

Who were the first English settlers may be best ascertained from the family names mentioned in the earlier court proceedings as narrated in other chapters. In most instances these were the people who resided in the County before and at the time of its formation, though some that are oftenest named, and appear to have been of the most conspicuous of the landed gentry, never became actual residents. The great Baylor and Beverley grants, and other very large ones, appear to have been speculative only, for the grantees never lived in the County. Their lands were under the management of bailiffs, as they were then called, who had large numbers of servants under their control. Thus the census of 1782 (Appendix) shows that on the Baylor estate there were 84 blacks and not one white person. The real owners of the land attended court regularly, to acknowledge their many deeds of bargain and sale, and then returned to their homes in Tidewater.

Yet a good many people did actually take up their abode in this frontier county while it was still a part of Spotsylvania, and some of their names are household words to-day; Spotswood, Chew, Cave, Madison, Moore, Willis, Taliaferro, Thomas, Barbour, Scott, Smith, Taylor, Waugh, Porter, Head, Fry, Lightfoot, and many more; the general narrative must be looked to to learn who they were, and what they did. They all appear covetous of great landed possessions, but they appear also to have been resolute and public-spirited citizens, an ancestry of which their descendants may well be proud.

Far and away the most ancient and most historic settlement was Germanna, "in the peninsula formed by the Rapidan." Indeed there are few places in all Virginia, which is to say in all America, that surpass Germanna in historic interest during the colonial period; Jamestown, Williamsburg, York, and a few more; yet to-day Germanna constitutes not much more than a name and a memory, rich as are its associations with the past, with the beginnings that foreshadowed Orange at its zenith.

It is first mentioned in a statute, that somehow escaped the vigilance of Hening when compiling that vast treasure house of Virginia history, the "Statutes at Large." In the State library is an old volume entitled "Acts of Assembly passed in the Colony of Virginia from 1662 to 1715," printed at London in 1727.

About the last Act in it is one to exempt certain German Protestants from the payment of levies for seven years, and for erecting the parish of St. George, passed in 1714: "Whereas certain German protestants, to the number of forty-two persons or thereabouts, have been settled above the falls of the River Rappahannock, on the southern branch of the said river, called Rapidan, at a place named Germanna, in the County of Essex, and have there begun to build and make improvements for their cohabitation, to the great advantage of this colony and the security of the frontiers in those parts from the intrusions of the Indians," it is enacted that they shall be free from the payment of all public and county levies for seven years, as should be any other German Protestants who might settle there, always providing, however, that they did not leave Germanna and settle elsewhere.

The next section creates the parish of St. George, extending for five miles on each side of the town, exempts it from all parish levies from the Parish of St. Mary, in Essex, and from the cure of the minister thereof, and "from all dependencies, offices, charges and contributions" of the same, and of "all levies, oblations, obventions and all other parochial duties whatsoever" relating to the same.

Here are disclosed some interesting historical facts: that Germanna was in Essex County at that time; that a special parish was established of which the ecclesiastical historians have taken no note whatever, the St. George parish of subsequent years being a wholly distinct one, though embracing the original parish of that name; and, most of all, that these "Strangers in a strange land" were placed there as a sort of buffer against the Indians, a rather cool and somewhat cruel thing to have done.

These German Protestants who came in 1714 were in fact the "First Settlers" of Orange, then a part of Essex, afterwards of Spotsylvania, and not called Orange until 20 years later; and as such their names ought to be chronicled, and something of their history narrated. In brief it is as follows:

GERMANNA, FIRST GERMAN COLONY.

Three German colonies came to Virginia during the administration of Governor Spotswood and settled at or near Germanna. The first consisted of 12 families numbering 42 persons, as shown by an Order of the Virginia Council passed April 28, 1714. This Order provided that a fort should be built for them, that two cannon and some ammunition should be furnished, and a road cleared to the settlement. The Order also shows that the colony had only recently arrived in Virginia. They were the first actual settlers in what is now Orange County, and this was the beginning of Germanna. Mr. Charles E. Kemper, of Staunton, Va., a lineal descendant of one of the families, in an article contributed to the April number, 1906, of the Virginia Magazine of History and Biography (Vol. XIII., pp. 367-70) gives their names as follows:

Jacob Holtzclaw, wife Margaret, sons John and Henry; John Kemper, wife Alice Kathrina; John Joseph Martin, wife Maria Kathrina; John Spillman, wife Mary; Herman Fishback, wife Kathrina; John Henry Hoffman, wife Kathrina; Joseph Coons, wife Kathrina, son John Annalis, daughter Kathrina; John Fishback, wife Agnes; Jacob Rector, wife Elizabeth, son John; Melchior Brumback, wife Elizabeth; Tillman Weaver, mother Ann Weaver; Peter Hitt, wife Elizabeth.

In 1724 these Germans were proving their importations in the Spotsylvania County Court in order to take up lands under the Head-right Act, and stated that they had arrived in Virginia in April, 1714.

All these first colonists belonged to the German Reformed Church, the great German branch of the Presbyterian family of churches. They were natives of the old principality of Nassau-Siegen, now a part of Westphalia, Germany, and their homes were in and near the city of Siegen and the town of Muesen. They organized, at Germanna, the first congregation of the German Reformed church in the United States, and John Fontaine records in his Journal the first description of a religious service in America conducted by the adherents of this denomination. They removed from Germanna in 1721 and settled on Licking Run, about eight miles south of Warrenton near present Midland station, where they first acquired lands. The locality was then in Stafford, later Prince William, and is now Fauquier. Their new home was known as Germantown.

Rev. Henry Haeger was their pastor. He was a man of much erudition, lived to a great age, and died in 1737. These colonists were induced to leave their homes in Germany by the Baron de Graffenreid, acting for Governor Spotswood who was then making preparations to develop his iron mines in the vicinity of Germanna, and this business enterprise of the Governor was the sole cause of their coming to America and Virginia.

SECOND GERMAN COLONY.

The second colony, which came in 1717, was entirely distinct from the first; in fact, when leaving Germany its destination was Pennsylvania, and not Virginia, and it finally reached Virginia through force of circumstances for which they were not responsible and which they could not control. This colony was composed chiefly of Lutherans. It numbered about eighty persons, comprised in twenty families, coming from Alsace, the Palatinate and adjacent districts in Germany.

In 1719 a third colony, also mostly Lutherans, consisting of forty families, came to Virginia and settled in the vicinity of Germanna. Comparatively nothing is known of the antecedent history of this last group of Germans. The colony of 1717 became involved in litigation with Governor Spotswood, of whose treatment they more than once complained.

The records of Spotsylvania show their names as follows: John Broil, Frederick Cobbler, Christopher Zimmerman, wife Elizabeth, children John and Andrew; Henry Snyder, wife Dorothy; Michael Smith, wife Kathrina; Michael Cook, wife Mary; Andrew Kerker, wife Margarita, daughter Barbara; William Carpenter, wife Elizabeth; Christopher Pavler, (or Parlur) wife Pauera; Jacob Broil; John Broil, wife Ursley, children Conrad and Elizabeth; Nicholas Yeager, wife Mary, children Adam and Mary; Philip Paulitz; Robert Turner, wife Mary, children Christopher, Christianna, Kathrina, Mary and Parva; Conrad Auberge, Balthaser Blankenbaker, Michael Clore, Andrew Ballenger, George Sheible, George Meyer, Michael Kaffer, Matthias Blankenbaker, Michael Holt, Zerechias Fleshman, Hendrick Snyder, George Utz.

Quite a number of them proved their importations at Germanna in 1726 and 1727, and their names are given in the Virginia Magazine of History and Biography, April No., 1906

The colonists of 1717 and 1719 seem to have remained at Germanna, or in that neighborhood, until 1725 or 1726, when they removed to the Robertson river section (in Madison County), where they had acquired lands.

In the same magazine, Vol. XIV. pp. 136-170, Rev. William J. Hinke, of Philadelphia, contributes a number of valuable documents relating to the German element of Madison County, which, with Mr. Hinke's notes, constitute the most valuable sources of history of these two colonies, and tell best the story of their early fortunes in Virginia. Many of these names are familiar in Madison to-day, and the list last given sounds like an echo of the roll-call of the Madison Troop in the Confederate war. Hebron church, near the Robertson River, remains a monument of their devotion and Christian character.

The history of these Germans is very interesting, and has been written at large by several authors, the best and most comprehensive account of them being the "Kemper Genealogy," which treats of the earliest colony, that of 1714. Gen. James L. Kemper, Governor of Virginia soon after the war, was a descendant of one of these colonists; and their descendants are to be found not only in Virginia, but throughout the South and West.

The limitations of this book preclude the following up of their fortunes, but the truth of history impels the statement that the colonists of 1714 were the real first actual settlers of Orange. And if Governor Spotswood were in fact the "Tubal Cain of Virginia," it was these Germans who won that title for him. In the "Kemper

Genealogy" it is stated with emphasis that the colony of 1714 was not a Palatinate Colony. "They did not leave their homes not knowing where they were going, nor because they were compelled to. They were engaged to go, and knew where they were going, and what they were to do. They came from one of the thriftiest and most intelligent provinces of Germany; they were master mechanics, and were an intelligent, progressive set of people."

The Rev. Hugh Jones, in his "Present State of Virginia," published about 1724, thus describes Germanna: "Beyond Governor Spotswood's furnace above the Falls of Rappahannock River, within view of the vast mountains, he has founded a town, called Germanna from the Germans sent over by Queen Anne, who are now removed up further. He has servants and workmen at most handicraft trades, and he is building a church, courthouse, and dwelling house for himself; and with his servants and negroes he has cleared plantations about it, proposing great encouragement for people to come and settle in that uninhabited part of the world, lately divided into a county," that is Spotsylvania.

This would seem to fix the date of the first English settlement there as about 1724; and incidentally to dispose of the rather incredible statement made by Mr. William Kyle Anderson, in his "Taylor Genealogy" that "Bloomsbury," the former home of Col. James Taylor, now owned by the Jerdone family, about three miles below present Orange courthouse and some twenty above Germanna, was built so early as 1722.

A subsequent chapter, "The Progress to the Mines," is the best extant description of this historic old place. That there was a "palace" there, with a terraced garden connected by an underground passage with a fort, there is no reason to doubt. Indeed, the terraces remain to this day. It was certainly the county seat of Spotsylvania, as the statute shows. In May, 1732, a statute was passed, "Whereas, the place for holding courts in the County of Spotsylvania, is appointed and fixed at Germanna, and it is found by experience that great inconveniences attend the justices and inhabitants of the said county and others whose attendance is required or who have business to transact at the said courts, for want of accommodation for themselves and their horses, which by reason of the fewness of the inhabitants for many miles round the said place cannot be had," and enacting that these courts be held only at Fredericksburg from the ensuing first day of August.

Then began, no doubt, the decadence of this historic hamlet, which has continued till now. But "a merry place it was in days of yore," where the gentry were feasted at the palace, and "Miss Theky" dispensed other beverages than coffee that would not give a man the palsy. But it ought never to be forgotten that at Germanna began that great adventure, the tramontane ride of the "Knights of the Horseshoe," the first body of Englishmen to cross the Blue Ridge and discover the Goshen beyond; and hence, it may be truly said, the "star of empire began its westward course," nor stopped until the Mississippi had been passed and the Golden Gate to the Pacific had been reached. In later times, mighty armies crossed and recrossed the Rapidan at Germanna, and the thunders of Chancellorsville and the Wilderness shook its ruins to their foundations. Ichabod! The glory of Israel is departed; let the memory of it remain forever!

CHAPTER XI.

Progress to the Mines.

The following sketch of a visit to Colonel Spotswood and his mines in 1732 by Col. William Byrd is inserted with full knowledge of the proverb that "comparisons are odious."

A just consideration of the rights of the readers of this book impels its insertion, the cost of the Westover Manuscripts, from which it is extracted, rendering them practically inaccessible to the average reader.

Colonel Byrd was one of the commissioners to run the boundary line between Virginia and North Carolina, and also a commissioner on the part of the colony to define the southwestern limit of Lord Fairfax's grant, reporting strenuously and conclusively that the modern Rappahannock River was the true boundary; which report, however, did not finally prevail.

He held many positions of dignity and trust in the colony and, it is said, was the friend of Addison, and an occasional contributor to the "Spectator." He amassed the finest private library which had then been seen in America. Born March 28, 1674. Died August 26, 1744.

I took my leave about ten, and drove over a spacious level road ten miles, to a bridge built over the river Po, which is one of the four branches of Matapony, about forty yards wide. Two miles beyond that we passed by a plantation belonging to the company of about five hundred acres, where they keep a great number of oxen to relieve those that have dragged their loaded carts thus far. Three miles farther we came to Germanna road, where I quitted the chair, and continued my journey on horseback. I rode eight miles together over a stony road, and had on either side continual poisoned fields, with nothing but saplings growing on them. Then I came into the main county road, that leads from Fredericksburg to Germanna, which last place I reached in ten miles more. This famous town consists of Colonel Spotswood's enchanted castle on one side of the street, and a baker's dozen of ruinous tenements on the other, where so many German families had dwelt some years ago; but are now removed ten miles higher in the fork of Rappahannock, to land of their own. There had also been a chapel about a bowshot from the Colonel's house at the end of an avenue of cherry trees, but some pious people had lately burnt it down, with intent to get another built nearer to their own homes. Here I arrived about three o'clock, and found only Mrs. Spotswood at home, who received her old acquaintance with many a gracious smile. I was carried into a room elegantly set off with pier glasses, the largest of which came soon after to an odd misfortune. Amongst other favorite animals that cheered this lady's solitude, a brace of tame deer ran familiarly about the house, and one of them came to stare at me as a stranger. But unluckily spying his own figure in the glass, he made a spring over the tea table that stood under it, and shattered the glass to pieces, and falling back upon the tea table, made a terrible fracas among the china. This exploit was so sudden, and accompanied with such a noise, that it surprised me and perfectly frightened Mrs. Spotswood. But it was worth all the damage to show the moderation

and good humour with which she bore the disaster.
In the evening the noble Colonel came home from his
mines, who saluted me very civilly, and Mrs. Spotswood's sister, Miss Theky, who had been to meet him
en cavalier, was so kind, too, as to bid me welcome.

We talked over a legion of old stories, supped about
nine, and then prattled with the ladies till it was time
for a traveller to retire. In the meantime I observed
my old friend to be very uxorious and exceedingly fond
of his children. This was so opposite to the maxims
he used to preach up before he was married, that I
could not forbear rubbing up the memory of them.
But he gave a very good-natured turn to his change of
sentiments, by alleging that whoever brings a poor
gentlewoman into so solitary a place, from all her
friends and acquaintances, would be ungrateful not to
use her and all that belongs to her with all possible
tenderness.

28th. We all kept snug in our several apartments
till nine, except Miss Theky, who was the housewife of
the family. At that hour we met over a pot of coffee,
which was not quite strong enough to give us the palsy.
After breakfast the Colonel and I left the ladies to their
domestic affairs, and took a turn in the garden, which
has nothing beautiful but three terrace walks that fall
in slopes one below another. I let him understand that
besides the pleasure of paying him a visit, I came to be
instructed by so great a master in the mystery of making of iron, wherein he had led the way, and was the
Tubal Cain of Virginia. He corrected me a little there,
by assuring me he was not only the first in this country,
but the first in North America, who had erected a regular furnace. That they ran altogether upon bloom-
eries in New England and Pennsylvania, till his example had made them attempt greater works. But in this
last colony, they have so few ships to carry their iron to
Great Britain, that they must be content to make it

only for their own use, and must be obliged to manufacture it when they have none. That he hoped he had done the country very great service by setting so good an example. That the four furnaces now at work in Virginia circulated a great sum of money for provisions and all other necessaries in the adjacent counties. That they took off a great many hands from planting tobacco, and employed them in works that produced a large sum of money in England to the persons concerned, whereby the country is so much the richer. That they are, besides, a considerable advantage to Great Britain, because it lessens the quantity of bar iron imported from Spain, Holland, Sweden, Denmark and Muscovy, which used to be no less than 20,000 tons yearly, though at the same time no sow iron is imported thither from any country, but only from the plantations. For most of this bar iron they do not only pay silver, but our friends in the Baltic are so nice, they even expect to be paid all in crown pieces. On the contrary, all the iron they receive from the plantations, they pay for it in their own manufactures, and send for it in their own shipping. Then I inquired after his own mines, and hoped, as he was the first that engaged in this great undertaking, that he had brought them to the most perfection. He told me he had iron in several parts of his great tract of land, consisting of 45,000 acres. But that the mine he was at work upon was 13 miles below Germanna. That his ore (which was very rich) he raised a mile from his furnace, and was obliged to cart the iron, when it was made, fifteen miles to Massaponax, a plantation he had upon Rappahannock River; but that the road was exceeding good, gently declining all the way, and had no more than one hill to go in the whole journey. For this reason his loaded carts went it in a day without difficulty. He said it was true his works were of the oldest standing: but that his long absence in England, and the wretched management of Mr. Greame, whom he had entrusted with his affairs, had put him back very much. That, what with neglect and severity, above eighty of his slaves were lost while he was in England, and most of his cattle starved. That his furnace stood still a great part of the time, and all his plantations ran to ruin. That indeed he was rightly served for committing his affairs to the care of a mathematician, whose thoughts were always among the stars. That nevertheless, since his return, he had applied himself to rectify his steward's mistakes, and bring his business again into order. That now he had contrived to do everything with his own people, except raising the mine and running the iron, by which he had contracted his expense very much. Nay, he believed that by his directions he could bring sensible negroes to perform those parts of the works tolerably well. But at the same time he gave me to understand, that his furnace had done no great feats lately, because he had been taken up in building an air furnace at Massaponax, which he had now brought to perfection, and should be thereby able to furnish the whole country with all sorts of cast iron, as cheap and as good as ever came from England. I told him he must do one thing more to have a full vent for those commodities—he must keep a shallop running into all the rivers, to carry his wares home to people's own doors. And if he would do that, I would set a good example, and take off a whole ton of them. Our conversation on this subject continued till dinner, which was both elegant and plentiful. The afternoon was devoted to the ladies, who showed me one of their most beautiful walks. They conducted me through a shady lane to the landing, and by the way made me drink some very fine water that issued from a marble fountain, and ran incessantly. Just behind it was a covered bench, where Miss Theky often sat and bewailed her virginity. Then we proceeded to the river which is the south branch of Rappahannock, about fifty yards wide, and so rapid that the ferry boat is drawn over by a chain, and therefore called the Rapidan. At night we drank prosperity to all the Colonel's projects in a bowl of rack punch, and then retired to our devotions.

29th. Having employed about two hours in retirement, I sallied out at the first summons to breakfast, where our conversation with the ladies, like whip sillabub, was very pretty, but had nothing in it. This it seems was Miss Theky's birthday, upon which I made her my compliments, and wished she might live twice as long a married woman as she had lived a maid. I did not presume to pry into the secret of her age, nor was she forward to disclose it, for this humble reason, lest I thould think her wisdom fell short of her years. She contrived to make this day of her birth a day of mourning for having nothing better at present to set her affections upon, she had a dog that was a great favorite. It happened that very morning the poor cur had done something very uncleanly upon the Colonel's bed, for which he was condemned to die. However, upon her entreaty, she got him a reprieve; but was so concerned that so much severity should be intended on her birthday, that she was not to be comforted; and lest such another accident might oust the poor cur of his clergy, she protested she would board out her dog at a neighbour's house, where she hoped he would be more kindly treated.

We had a Michaelmas goose for dinner, of Miss Theky's own raising, who was now good natured enough to forget the jeopardy of her dog. In the afternoon we walked in a meadow by the riverside, which winds in the form of a horse-shoe about Germanna, making it a peninsula, containing about four hundred acres. Rappahannock forks about fourteen miles below this place, the northern branch being the larger, and consequently must be the river that bounds my Lord Fairfax's grant of the Northern Neck.

30th. The sun rose clear this morning, and so did I, and finished all my little affairs by breakfast. It was then resolved to wait on the ladies on horseback, since the bright sun, the fine air, and the wholesome exercise, all invited us to it. We forded the river a little above the ferry, and rode six miles up the neck to a fine level piece of rich land, where we found about twenty plants of ginseng, with the scarlet berries growing on the top of the middle stalk. The root of this is of wonderful virtue in many cases, particularly to raise the spirits and promote perspiration, which makes it a specific in colds and coughs. The Colonel complimented me with all we found in return for my telling him the virtues of it. We were all pleased to find so much of this king of plants so near the Colonel's habitation, and growing too upon his own land; but were surprised, however, to find it upon level ground, after we had been told it grew only upon the north side of stony mountains. I carried home this treasure with as much joy as if every root had been a graft of the tree of life, and washed and dried it carefully. This airing made us as hungry as so many hawks, so that between appetite and a very good dinner, it was difficult to eat like a philosopher. In the afternoon the ladies walked me about amongst all their little animals, with which they amuse themselves and furnish the table; the worst of it is they are so tender-hearted, they shed a silent tear every time any of them are killed.

October 1st. Our ladies overslept themselves this morning, so that we did not break our fast till ten. We drank tea made of the leaves of ginseng, which has the virtues of the root in a weaker degree, and is not disagreeable.

2d. This being the day appointed for my departure from hence, I packed up my effects in good time; but the ladies, whose dear companies we were to have to the mines, were a little tedious in their equipment. However we made a shift to get into the coach by ten o'clock; but little master, who is under no government, would by all means go on horseback. Before we set out I gave Mr. Russel the trouble of distributing a pistole among the servants, of which I fancy the nurse had a pretty good share, being no small favourite. We drove over a fine road to the mines, which lie thirteen measured miles from the Germanna, each mile being marked distinctly upon the trees. The Colonel has a great deal of land in his mine tract exceedingly barren, and the growth of trees upon it is hardly big enough for coaling. However, the treasure under ground makes amends, and renders it worthy to be his lady's jointure. We lighted at the mines, which are a mile nearer Germanna than the furnace. They raise abundance of ore there, great part of which is very rich. We saw his engineer blow it up after the following manner. He drilled a hole about eighteen inches deep, humouring the situation of the mine. When he had dried it with a rag fastened to a worm, he charged it with a cartridge containing four ounces of powder, including the priming. Then he rammed the hole up with soft stone to the very mouth; after that he pierced through all with an iron called a primer, which is taper and ends in a short point. Into the hole which the primer makes, the priming is put, which is fired by a paper moistened with a solution of saltpetre. And this burns leisurely enough, it seems, to give time to the persons concerned to retreat out of harm's way. All the land hereabouts seems paved with iron ore; so that there seems to be enough to feed a furnace for many ages. From hence we proceeded to the furnace, which is built of rough stone, having been the first of that kind erected in the country. It had not blown for several moons, the Colonel having taken off great part of his people to carry on his air furnace at Massaponax. Here the wheel that carried the bellows was no more than twenty feet diameter; but was an overshot wheel that went with little water. This was necessary here, because water is something scarce, notwithstanding it is supplied by two streams, one of which is conveyed 1900 feet through wooden pipes, and the other 60. The name of the founder employed at present is one Godfrey, of the kingdom of Ireland, whose wages is three shillings and six-pence per ton for all the iron he runs, and his provisions. This man told me that the best wood for coaling is red oak. He complained that the Colonel starves his works out of whimsicalness and frugality, endeavouring to do everything with his own people, and at the same time taking them off upon every vagary that comes into his head. Here the coal carts discharge their loads at folding doors, made at the bottom, which is sooner done, and shatters the coal less. They carry no more than one hundred and ten bushels. The Colonel advised me by all means to have the coal made on the same side the river with the furnace, not only to avoid the charge of boating and bags, but likewise to avoid breaking of the coals, and making them less fit for use. Having picked the bones of a sirloin of beef, we took leave of the ladies, and rode together about five miles, where the roads parted. The Colonel took that to Massaponax, which is fifteen miles from his furnace, and very level, and I that to Fredericksburg, which cannot be less than twenty. I was a little benighted, and should not have seen my way, if the lightning, which flashed continually in my face, had not befriended me. I got about seven o'clock to Col. Harry Willis's, a little moistened with the rain; but a glass of good wine kept my pores open, and prevented all rheums and defluxions for that time.

3d. I was obliged to rise early here that I might not starve my landlord, whose constitution requires him to swallow a beef-steak before the sun blesses the earth with its genial rays. However, he was so complaisant as to bear the gnawing of his stomach, till eight o'clock for my sake. Colonel Waller, after a score of loud hems to clear his throat, broke his fast along with us. When this necessary affair was despatched, Colonel Willis walked me about his town of Fredericksburg. It is pleasantly situated on the south shore of Rappahannock River, about a mile below the falls. Sloops may come up and lie close to the wharf, within 30 yards of the public ware-houses, which are built in the figure of a cross. Just by the wharf is a quarry of white stone that is very soft in the ground, and hardens in the air, appearing to be as fair and fine grained as that of Portland. Besides that there are several other quarries in the river bank, within the limits of the town, sufficient to build a large city. The only edifice of stone yet built is the prison; the walls of which are strong enough to hold Jack Sheppard, if he had been transported thither. Though this be a commodious and beautiful situation for a town, with the advantages of a navigable river and wholesome air, yet the inhabitants are very few. Besides Colonel Willis, who is the top man of the place, there are only one merchant, a tailor, a smith, and an ordinary keeper; though I must not forget Mrs. Levistone, who acts here in the double capacity of a doctress and coffee woman. And were this a populous city, she is qualified to exercise two other callings. It is said that the courthouse and the church are going to be built here, and then both religion and justice will help to enlarge the place. Two miles from this place is a spring strongly impregnated with alum, and so is the earth all about it. This water does wonders for those that are afflicted with a dropsy. And on the other side the river, in King George County, 12 miles from hence, is another spring of strong steel water as good as that at Tunbridge Wells. Not far from this last spring are England's iron mines, called so from the chief manager of them, though the land belongs to Mr. Washington. These mines are two miles from the furnace, and Mr. Washington raises the ore, and carts it thither for 20 shillings the ton of iron that it yields. The furnace is built on a run, which discharges its waters into Potomac. And when the iron is cast, they cart it about six miles to a landing on that river. Besides Mr. Washington and Mr. England, there are several other persons, in England, concerned in these works. Matters are very well managed there, and no expense is spared to make them profitable, which is not the case in the works I have already mentioned.

CHAPTER XII.

The Knights of the Horseshoe.

It has been stated that Governor Spotswood's tramontane expedition started from Germanna. The Governor, and John Fontaine, who had been an ensign in the British army and had lately come to Virginia, came thither from Williamsburg, and Fontaine's quaint Journal constitutes the historical warp and woof of any account that can be given of the expedition.

The gentlemen of the party appear to have been Spotswood, Fontaine, Beverley, the historian of Virginia in 1703, Colonel Robertson, Austin Smith, who abandoned the expedition the second day because of sickness, Todd, Dr. Robinson, Taylor, Brooke, Mason, and Captains Clouder and Smith; the whole number of the party was about fifty, and as Campbell remarks and the Journal shows, they had "an abundant supply of provisions and an extraordinary variety of liquors." Probably but for the frequent manifestations of loyalty by the party in drinking the healths of the royal family and themselves, a better idea could be formed of the route followed. Suffice it to say here that it appears to have been wholly within the confines of what was then Spotsylvania, and afterwards became Orange County.

Rev. Dr. Philip Slaughter, in his "History of St. Mark's Parish" undertook to outline the route, and even to attempt a diagram of it. Manifestly there is so much conjecture in both the outline and diagram that it cannot be accepted as serious history. It confutes itself by its own ingenuity.

Names of places, as given in the Journal, have come down to the present time, as Mine Run, and Mountain Run. The forks of the Rappahannock above Germanna can only mean the confluence of the Robertson and Rapidan rivers; after that all is confusion and pure guesswork until Swift Run is reached.

Fontaine calls the Rapidan the Rappahannock, its true name at that period, throughout the westward journey; returning he calls it the Rapidan, a name it never had until so called by Spotswood about the date of this expedition.

Beverley says, in the preface to the second edition of his "History of Virginia" (1722), contradicting a more absurd statement of Oldmixon; "I was with the present Governor at the head spring of both these rivers (Rappahannock and York) and their fountains are in the highest ridge of mountains;" Dr. Slaughter, that, "as Swift Run Gap is the only 'pass' which the head waters of York, James and Rappahannock approximate, etc." The well ascertained fact is that the ultimate head springs of the York are within a few miles of Gordonsville, and the head spring of the Rappahannock some miles to the east of Swift Run Gap; so both these contentions fall.

Fontaine's statement is simply that they "came to the very head spring of James River where it runs no bigger than a man's arm from under a big stone," where they drank many healths at the very top of the Appalachian Mountains; and that about a musket shot from this spring there is another which runs down on the other side. This statement can be confirmed by any traveller through the gap, and his general description of the near approach to the gap is very realistic as one follows the turnpike, Journal in hand. Of course this head spring of the James is its eastern head spring, and the spring distant from it about a musket shot flows into the Shenandoah and thence into the Potomac.

There is no reason to doubt, and every reason to believe, that this crossing of the Blue Ridge was made in 1716, and was almost certainly the first that had ever been made by any body of white men. So when Spotsylvania was formed four years later, and its southwestern line was run from a "convenient" point on the North Anna to the river on the west side of the great mountains "so as to include the northern passage through the said mountains," and that line has subsisted substantially from that day to this, the conclusion seems unavoidable that Swift Run Gap is the place where Spotswood crossed. The line runs but a few miles southwest of the gap, with no intervening good pass.

The footnote to the Journal sufficiently indicates the bestowal of miniature horseshoes upon these gentlemen adventurers, and any further attempted elaboration of it would be mere conjecture. It is very remarkable, however, that all of these jeweled tokens of the expedition have disappeared. In the Romance, "The Knights of the Horseshoe," by Dr. Caruthers, is published a letter from Judge Brooke of Fredericksburg to the author in which he testifies that he had seen one of them. Campbell, the careful historian, relates that the one which had belonged to Spotswood was small enough to be worn on a watch chain. Some of them, if not all, were set with jewels.

Curious and careless as it may seem, several Virginia historians have published the legend as "*Sic Jurat,*" instead of "*Juvat;*" and even John Esten Cooke in his "Stories from the Old Dominion," forfeiting all doubt as to a typographical error, so writes it and then translates his bad Latin, "So *they swore* to cross the mountains;" an error which is corrected in his graver work, the History of Virginia in the "American Commonwealths" series.

It has been impossible to ascertain where the fiction of "knighthood" originated, a dignity which only royalty or quasi royalty could confer: it seems improbable that the ever loyal Spotswood would have presumed to establish an "Order" of his own.

In a former paragraph it has been stated with confidence that this crossing of the Blue Ridge was almost certainly the first by any body of white men; which statement was not made in ignorance of other claims to that distinction. In an "Abridgement of the Public Laws of Virginia in force and use, June 10, 1720, London, 1728," in the Library of Congress, at page 163-165, there appears an address of the Burgesses to the King, in which it is distinctly stated that there are only two known "passes" through the Blue Ridge: the Northern pass and the one on Roanoke leading to the south. Three white men, an Indian and a "former servant" appear to have passed through Wood's Gap, near the North Carolina line, as early as 1671, but nothing was accomplished by them towards opening up the great Valley of Virginia,

"The Discoveries of John Lederer in Three Several Marches from Virginia," published in London in 1672, so discredits itself by travellers' tales, as to forfeit all claim to be called history. From the top of the Blue Ridge he "saw the Atlantic Ocean washing the Virginia shore" and sundry other impossible things; and it seems to be agreed that if, perchance, he did ascend the Blue Ridge he certainly did not descend the western slope. (See Amer. Anthropologist, IX, 45.)

THE VIRGINIANS OF THE VALLEY.
Sic Juvat.

The knightliest of the knightly race,
  Who, since the days of old,
Have kept the lamps of chivalry
  Alight in hearts of gold.
The kindliest of the kindly band
  Who rarely hated ease,
Yet rode with Spotswood 'round the land
  And Raleigh 'round the seas!

Who climbed the blue Virginia hills
  Amid embattled foes,
And planted there, in Valleys fair,
  The lily and the rose;
Whose fragrance lives in many lands,
  Whose beauty stars the earth,
And lights the hearts of many homes
  With loveliness and worth.

We thought they slept! these sons who kept
  The names of noble sires,
And slumbered while the darkness crept
  Around their Virgin fires!
But still the Golden Horseshoe Knights
  Their Old Dominion keep,
Their foes have found enchanted ground
  But not a Knight asleep.

The above poem, written by Ticknor, of Georgia, about 1861, seems an appropriate introduction to the Journal, as copied from the "Memoirs of a Huguenot Family."

JOHN FONTAINE'S JOURNAL.

Williamsburg, 20th August, 1716. In the morning got my horses ready, and what baggage was necessary, and I waited on the Governor, who was in readiness for an expedition over the Appalachian mountains. We breakfasted, and about ten got on horseback, and at four came to the Brick-house, upon York River, where we crossed the ferry, and at six we came to Mr. Austin Moor's house, upon Mattapony River, in King William County; here we lay all night and were well entertained.

21st. Fair weather. At ten we set out from Mr. Moor's, and crossed the river of Mattapony, and continued on the road, and were on horseback till nine of the clock at night, before we came to Mr. Robert Beverley's house, where we were well entertained, and remained this night.

22d. At nine in the morning, we set out from Mr. Beverley's. The Governor left his chaise here, and mounted his horse. The weather fair, we continued on our journey until we came to Mr. Woodford's where we lay, and were well entertained. This house lies on Rappahannock River, ten miles below the falls.

23d. Here we remained all this day, and diverted ourselves and rested our horses.

24th. In the morning at seven, we mounted our horses, and came to Austin Smith's house about ten, where we dined, and remained till about one of the clock, then we set out, and about nine of the clock, we came to the German-town, where we rested that night —bad beds and indifferent entertainment.

German-town, 25th. After dinner we went to see the mines, but I could not observe that there was any good mine. The Germans pretend that it is a silver mine; we took some of the ore and endeavoured to run it, but could get nothing out of it, and I am of opinion it will not come to anything, no, not as much as lead. Many of the gentlemen of the county are concerned in this work. We returned to our hard beds.

25th. At seven we got up, and several gentlemen of the country that were to meet the Governor at this place for the expedition arrived here, as also two companies of rangers, consisting each of six men and an officer. Four Meherrin Indians also came.

In the morning I diverted myself with other gentlemen shooting at a mark. At twelve we dined, and after dinner we mounted our horses and crossed the Rappahannock River, that runs by this place, and went to find out some convenient place for our horses to feed in, and to view the land hereabouts. Our guide left us, and we went so far in the woods, that we did not know the way back again; so we hallooed and fired our guns. Half an hour after sunset, the guide came to us, and we went to cross the river by another ford higher up. The descent to the river being steep, and the night dark, we were obliged to dismount, and lead our horses down to the river side, which was very troublesome. The bank being very steep, the greatest part of our company went into the water to mount their horses, where they were up to the crotch in water. After we had forded the river and come to the other side, where the bank was steep also, in going up the horse of one of our company slipped and fell back into the river on the top of his rider, but he received no other damage than being heartily wet, which made sport for the rest. A hornet stung one of the gentlemen in the face, which swelled tremendously. About ten we came to the town, where we supped, and to bed.

27th. Got our tents in order, and our horses shod. About twelve, I was taken with a violent headache and pains in all my bones, so that I was obliged to lie down, and was very bad that day.

28th. About one in the morning, I was taken with a violent fever, which abated about six at night, and I began to take the bark, and had one ounce divided into eight doses, and took two of them by ten of the clock that night. The fever abated, but I had great pains in my head and bones.

29th. In the morning we got all things in readiness, and about one we left the German-town to set out on our intended journey. At five in the afternoon, the Governor gave orders to encamp near a small river, three miles from Germanna, which we called Expedition Run, and here we lay all night. This first encampment was called Beverley Camp in honor of one of the gentlemen of our party. We made great fires, and supped, and drank good punch. By ten of the clock I had taken all of my ounce of Jesuit's Bark, but my head was much out of order.

30th. In the morning about seven of the clock, the trumpet sounded to awake all the company, and we got up. One Austin Smith, one of the gentlemen with us, having a fever, returned home. We had lain upon the ground under cover of our tents, and we found by the pains in our bones that we had not had good beds to lie upon. At nine in the morning, we sent our servants and baggage forward, and we remained because two of the Governor's horses had strayed. At half past two we got the horses, at three we mounted, and at half an hour after four we came up with our baggage at a small river, three miles on the way, which we called Mine River, because there was an appearance of a silver mine by it. We made about three miles more, and came to another small river, which is at the foot of a small mountain, so we encamped here and called it Mountain Run, and our camp we called Todd's Camp. We had good pasturage for our horses, and venison in abundance for ourselves, which we roasted before the fire upon wooden forks, and so we went to bed in our tents. Made six miles this day.

31st. At eight in the morning, we set out from Mountain Run, and after going five miles we came upon the upper part of Rappahannoc River. One of the gentlemen and I, we kept out on one side of the company about a mile, to have the better hunting. I saw a deer, and shot him from my horse, but the horse threw me a terrible fall and ran away; we ran after, and with a great deal of difficulty got him again; but we could not find the deer I had shot, and we lost ourselves, and it was two hours before we could come upon the track of our company. About five miles further we crossed the same river again, and two miles further we met with a large bear, which one of our company shot, and I got the skin. We killed several deer, and about two miles from the place where we killed the bear, we encamped upon Rappahannoc River. From our encampment we could see the Appalachian Hills very plain. We made large fires, pitched our tents, and cut boughs to lie upon, had good liquor, and at ten we went to sleep. We always kept a sentry at the Governor's door. We called this Smith's Camp. Made this day 14 miles.

1st, September. At eight we mounted our horses, and made the first five miles of our way through a very pleasant plain, which lies where Rappahannoc River forks. I saw there the largest timber, the finest and deepest mould, and the best grass that I ever did see. We had some of our baggage put out of order, and our company dismounted, by hornets stinging the horses. This was some hindrance, and did a little damage, but afforded a great deal of diversion. We killed three bears this day, which exercised the horses as well as the men. We saw two foxes but did not pursue them; we killed several deer. About five of the clock, we came to a run of water at the foot of a hill, where we pitched our tents. We called the encampment Dr. Robinson's

Camp, and the river Blind Run. We had good pasturage for our horses, and everyone was cook for himself. We made our beds with bushes as before. On this day we made 13 miles.

2d. At nine we were all on horseback, and after riding about five miles we crossed the Rappahannoc River, almost at the head, where it is very small. We had a rugged way; we passed over a great many small runs of water, some of which were very deep, and others very miry. Several of our company were dismounted, some were down with their horses, and some thrown off. We saw a bear running down a tree, but it being Sunday, we did not endeavour to kill anything. We encamped at five by a small river we called White Oak River, and called our camp Taylor's Camp.

3d. About eight we were on horseback, and about ten we came to a thicket so tightly laced together, that we had a great deal of trouble to get through; our baggage was injured, our clothes torn all to rags, and the saddles and holsters also torn. About five of the clock we encamped almost at the head of James River, just below the great mountains. We called this camp Colonel Robertson's Camp. We made all this day but eight miles.

4th. We had two of our men sick with the measles, and one of our horses poisoned with a rattlesnake. We took the heaviest of our baggage, our tired horses, and the sick men, and made as convenient a lodge for them as we could, and left people to guard them, and hunt for them. We had finished this work by twelve, and so we set out. The sides of the mountains were so full of vines and briers, that we were forced to clear most of the way before us. We crossed one of the small mountains this side the Appalachian, and from the top of it we had a fine view of the plains below. We were obliged to walk up the most of the way, there being abundance of loose stones on the side of the hill. I killed a large rattlesnake here, and the other people killed three more. We made about four miles, and so came to the side of James River, where a man may jump over it, and there we pitched our tents. As the people were lighting the fire, there came out of a large log of wood a prodigious snake, which they killed; so this camp was called Rattlesnake Camp, but it was otherwise called Brooke's Camp.

5th. A fair day. At nine we were mounted; we were obliged to have axemen to clear the way in some places. We followed the windings of James River, observing that it came from the very top of the mountains. We killed two rattlesnakes during our ascent. In some places it was very steep, in others it was so that we could ride up. About one of the clock we got to the top of the mountain; about four miles and a half and we came to the very head spring of James River, where it runs no bigger than a man's arm, from under a large stone. We drank King George's health, and all the Royal Family's, at the very top of the Appalachian Mountains. About a musket shot from the spring, there is another which rises and runs down on the other side; it goes westward, and we thought we could go down that way, but we met with such prodigious precipices, that we were obliged to return to the top again. We found some trees which had been formerly marked, I suppose, by the northern Indians, and following these trees, we found a good, safe descent. Several of the company were for returning; but the Governor persuaded them to continue on. About five, we were down on the other side, and continued our way for about seven miles further, until we came to a large river, by the side of which we encamped. We made this day 14 miles. I, being somewhat more curious than the rest, went on a high rock on the top of the mountain, to see fine prospects, and I lost my gun. We saw when we were over the mountains the footing of elks and buffaloes, and their beds. We saw a vine which bore a sort of wild cucumber, and a shrub with a fruit like unto a currant. We eat very good wild grapes. We called this place Spotswood Camp, after our Governor.

6th. We crossed the river which we called Euphrates. It is very deep; the main course of the water is north; it is four score yards wide in the narrowest part. We drank some healths on the other side, and returned; after which I went a swimming in it. We could not find any fordable place, except the one by which we crossed, and it was deep in several places. I got some grasshoppers and fished; and another and I, we catched a dish of fish, some perch, and a fish they call chub. The others went a hunting, and killed deer and turkeys. The Governor had graving irons but could not grave anything, the stones were so hard. I graved my name on a tree by the river side; and the Governor buried a bottle with a paper inclosed, on which he writ that he took possession of this place in the name and for King George the First of England.*

We had a good dinner, and after it we got the men together, and loaded all their arms, and we drank the King's health in champagne, and fired a volley, the Princess's health in Burgundy, and fired a volley, and all the rest of the Royal Family in claret, and a volley. We drank the Governor's health and fired another volley. We had several sorts of liquors, viz.; Virginia red

---

*Governor Spotswood, when he undertook the great discovery of the Passage over the mountains, attended with a sufficient guard, and pioneers and gentlemen, with a sufficient stock of provision, with abundant fatigue passed these mountains, and cut his Majesty's name in a rock upon the highest of them, naming it Mount George; and in complaisance the gentlemen, from the Governor's name, called the mountain next in height, Mount Alexander. For this expedition they were obliged to provide a great quantity of horse shoes, (things seldom used in the lower parts of the country, where there are few stones;) upon which account the Governor, upon their return, presented each of his companions with a golden horse shoe, (some of which I have seen studded with valuable stones, resembling the heads of nails,) with this inscription on the one side: *Sic juvat transcendere montes;* and on the other is written the tramontane order. This he instituted to encourage gentlemen to venture backwards, and make discoveries and new settlements; any gentleman being entitled to wear this Golden Shoe that can prove his having drunk his Majesty's health upon Mount George.   HUGH JONES, 1724.

wine and white wine, Irish usquebaugh, brandy shrub, two sorts of rum, champagne, canary, cherry punch, water, cider, etc.

I sent two of the rangers to look for my gun, which I dropped in the mountains; they found it, and brought it to me, and I gave them a pistole for their trouble. We called the highest mountain Mount George, and the one we crossed over Mount Spotswood.

7th. At seven in the morning we mounted our horses, and parted with the rangers, who were to go farther on, and we returned homewards; we repassed the mountains, and at five in the afternoon we came to Hospital Camp, where we left our sick men, and heavy baggage, and we found all things well and safe. We encamped here, and called it Captain Clouder's Camp.

8th. At nine we were all on horseback. We saw several bears and deer, and killed some wild turkeys. We encamped at the side of a run and called the place Mason's Camp. We had good forage for our horses, and we lay as usual. Made 20 miles this day.

9th. We set out at nine of the clock, and before twelve we saw several bears, and killed three. One of them attacked one of our men that was riding after him, and narrowly missed him; he tore his things that he had behind him from the horse, and would have destroyed him, had he not had immediate help from the other men and our dogs. Some of the dogs suffered severely in this engagement. At two we crossed one of the branches of the Rappahannoc River, and at five we encamped on the side of the Rapid Ann, on a tract of land that Mr. Beverley hath design to take up. We made, this day, 23 miles, and called this camp Captain Smith's Camp. We eat part of one of the bears, which tasted very well, and would be good, and might pass for veal, if one did not know what it was. We were very merry, and diverted ourselves with our adventures.

10th. At eight we were on horseback, and about ten, as we were going up a small hill, Mr. Beverley and his horse fell down, and they both rolled to the bottom; but there were no bones broken on either side. At twelve, as we were crossing a run of water, Mr. Clouder fell in, so we called this place Clouder's Run. At one we arrived at a large spring, where we dined and drank a bowl of punch. We called this Fontaine's Spring. About two we got on horseback, and at four we reached Germanna. The Governor thanked the gentlemen for their assistance in the expedition. Mr. Mason left us here. I went at five to swim in the Rappahannoc River, and returned to the town.

11th. After breakfast all our company left us except Dr. Robinson and Mr. Clouder. We walked all about the town, and the Governor settled his business with the Germans here, and accommodated the minister and the people, and then to bed.

12th. After breakfast went a fishing in the Rappahannoc and took seven fish, which we had for dinner; after which Mr. Robinson and I, we endeavoured to melt some ore in the smith's forge, but could get nothing out of it. Dr. Robinson's and Mr. Clouder's boys were taken violently ill with fever. Mr. Robinson and Mr. Clouder left us, and the boys remained behind.

13th. About eight of the clock we mounted our horses, and went to the mine, where we took several pieces of ore; and at nine we set out from the mine, our servants having gone before; and about three we overtook them in the woods, and there the Governor and I dined. We mounted afterwards, and continued on our road. I killed a black snake about five feet long. We arrived at Mr. Woodford's, on Rappahannoc River, about six, and remained there all night.

14th. At seven we sent our baggage and horses before us; and at ten we mounted our horses; we killed another snake, four feet nine inches long. At twelve we came to the church; where we met with Mr. Buckner, and remained till two, to settle some county business; then we mounted our horses, and saw several wild turkeys on the road; and at seven we reached Mr. Beverley's house, which is upon the head of Mattapony River, where we were well entertained. My boy was taken with a violent fever, and very sick.

15th. At seven my servant was somewhat better, and I sent him away with my horses, and about ten the Governor took his chaise, and I with him, and at twelve we came to a mill-dam, which we had great difficulty to get the chaise over. We got into it again, and continued on our way, and about five we arrived at Mr. Baylor's, where we remained all night.

16th. My servant was so sick, that I was obliged to leave him, and the Governor's servants took care of my horses. At ten we sent the chaise over Mattapony River, and it being Sunday, we went to the church in King William County, where we heard a sermon from Mr. Monroe.

After sermon we continued our journey until we came to Mr. West's plantation, where Colonel Bassett waited for the Governor with his pinnace, and other boats for his servants. We arrived at his house by five of the clock, and were nobly entertained.

17th. At ten we left Colonel Bassett's, and at three we arrived at Williamsburg, where we dined together, and I went to my lodgings, and to bed, being well tired, as well as my horses.

I reckon that from Williamsburg to the Euphrates River is in all 219 miles, so that our journey, going and coming, has been in all 438 miles.

[NOTE. The distance from Germanna to Elkton, the supposed point on the Sheanadoah reached by the expedition, is about sixty miles, following the roads of to-day.]

CHAPTER XIII.

Physical Features.

Orange is in the Piedmont belt, about twenty-five to thirty miles from the foot of the Blue Ridge. The mean distance from Washington and Richmond is 85 miles, from tidewater at Fredericksburg, 40 miles.

The County is almost bisected by the South West Mountains, so called because their trend is northeast and southwest. They constitute the main water shed, though by reason of their many convolutions there are variations. Generally speaking, the waters northward of the mountains flow to the Rapidan, those southward to the North Anna; yet towards Gordonsville, north of the mountains, some streams flow into the South Anna. At Gordonsville, Main street is a watershed, the waters on one side flowing into the North Anna, on the other into the South Anna.

A few small streams northwest of Barboursville fall into the Rivanna, and thence into the James. With this exception the waters ultimately reach the Rappahannock and the York. The very head spring of the York is on the Johnson farm, near the crest of the mountains where the Barboursville pike crosses.

The principal streams are the Rapidan (formerly Rapid Anne, and so named by Governor Spotswood), the North Anna, the Pamunkey, the local name for the north fork of the North Anna, Blue Run, Mountain Run, Negro Run, and Wilderness Run. Black Walnut Run is a name identified with the earliest history of the County.

The chief elevations are Clarke's Mountain, about eight miles east of the courthouse, where a signal station was maintained during the war, elevation above tide (according to United States Geological survey, from which all following elevations are taken), 1,100 feet; Quarles's Mountain, two miles east of courthouse, 700 feet; Scott's Mountain, near Madison Run, 1,100 feet; Merry's Mountain, named for Prettyman Merry, prominent citizen during the Revolution, 1,200 feet; Watts's Mountain, in front of Frascati, 1,200 feet; Newman's Mountain, near Montpelier, 800 feet; and Hardwicke's Mountain, a few miles northeast of Barboursville, 900 feet.

The elevation of Gordonsville, according to the profile of the Cheseapeake and Ohio Railroad, is 500 feet, which is 51 feet higher than Charlottesville.

A vein of limestone, so narrow that it is called "the string," runs through the County from Gordonsville to the Rapidan, following the Southern Railroad to Madison Run where it diverges to the right, crossing Church Run at the Taylor farm, thence down through "Hawfield," and on to the river. In former years much lime was burned, both for domestic and agricultural uses, but it was found to be of little value in agriculture.

Professor William B. Rogers, in his "Geology of Virginia," gives the following analyses, the names of present owners being substituted:

Limestone from Col. W. H. Chapman's farm (formerly Colby Cowherd's), one and one-half miles from Gordonsville.
Carbonate of lime.............................79.20
Carbonate of magnesia—trace
Silica..19.60

Limestone from Gibson's quarry (present owner unknown) south side of Rapidan River.
Carbonate of lime.............................90.40
Carbonate of magnesia......................... 6.44
Silica.. 2.00

Limestone from Rawlings quarry—near old Zion Meeting house, two miles from Courthouse (present owner Bowers).
Carbonate of lime.............................73.68
Carbonate of magnesia......................... 9.28
Silica..15.60

Limestone from Todd's quarry—near Madison Run (known as the marble quarry).
Carbonate of lime.............................51.72
Carbonate of magnesia.........................42.72
Silica.. 3.28

In each of these analyses small quantities of alumina and oxide of iron, and water, are noted; too inconsiderable to be enumerated here.

Payne Todd, stepson of President Madison, wasted much money in an effort to develop a marble quarry, which still remains an object of interest, but has long been full of water and become a local "fishing hole."* Beautiful marble was obtained from it, but veined with a very hard quartz so destructive to tools that it was found to be impracticable to work it. Some handsome mantels, still extant, have been made from it.

---

*In 1840 the Legislature incorporated "The Montpelier Marble Company" to quary 'marble, porphyry agate, flagstones for paving and slate for roofing houses in the County of Orange." Todd was the only incorporator. Capital stock not less than $20,000, nor more than $200.000.

Physical Features

In the Marsh Run neighborhood, and extending from a point near the Rapidan to the Greene corner on the Barboursville turnpike, is a range of hills known as the Blue Hills. Underneath these, at varying depths, is a stratum of plumbago or graphite. So far no merchantable quality has been obtained, but a company has been lately formed with a view of exploiting the mineral resources of these hills.

On the divide between the mountain section and the grey land are to be found many fine quarries of a composite stone, mainly sandstone, finely adapted for building purposes.

There are several mineral springs and wells in the County, and great medicinal virtues are locally attributed to some of them.

A noble spring on the old "Willis Grove" farm, the part owned by the late Philip B. Jones, Jr., now the property of Mr. Egbert Leigh, is perhaps the most notable. There is a tradition, which the writer knows to be approximately true, that two old ladies lived near this spring to the ages of 110 and 120 years, respectively, and that both enjoyed extraordinary health during all that time.

There is a mineral well at Mugler's station; a well-known chalybeate spring near the old turnpike near the Spotsylvania line; and several driven wells at Gordonsville are alleged to be strongly impregnated with lithia. "Mineral Hill" near Barboursville, long owned by Mr. James Barbour Newman, though not his residence, has long been celebrated for the virtues of a spring from which the place takes its name; and there are "sulphur pumps" both at Gordonsville and the Courthouse.

The general character of the water, however, outside of the narrow limestone belt, is pure freestone, and with rare exceptions of most excellent quality, though in the red land district many of the springs become tinged with the color of the soil in long wet spells. The number of springs is something wonderful, and no county in the State is better watered, so that having to drive stock any distance to water is unheard of.

There are large deposits of iron ore, which have been worked from time to time, and which were considered so valuable once that several miles of railroad were built to convey the ores to market. It was found out that they contained too much phosphorus to compete with the better classes of ore, and the industry has been abandoned. These deposits lie mainly along the verge of the limestone belt.

Also there are gold mines in the lower part of the County, the "Vaucluse" mine being, perhaps, the best known.

Professor Rogers says: "In Spotsylvania and the adjacent counties, Orange, Louisa, Fluvanna and Buckingham, numerous veins of auriferous rocks have been wrought for some time, from many of which rich returns have been procured, and under improved modes of operation a still larger profit may be expected."

He is the highest authority on the geology of Virginia, but as the improved methods of operating the mines have not yet been tried his forecast remains only a forecast.

Mr. James Barbour Newman, who lived one mile east of Barboursville, and died, universally regretted at the great age of ninety-seven years, kept a very careful record of the rainfall for many years. He published, in the Southern Planter and Farmer, November, 1879, the record from 1851 to 1878, both inclusive, a period of twenty-eight years. Estimating snow at nine for one of water the average yearly precipitation was 39 4–7 inches. The maximum was 52 inches in 1861, the minimum 23 7–8 inches in 1872. It was 28 inches in 1856, and only in these years and 1851 did it fall below 30 inches; only twice in the whole period did it exceed 50 inches, and in one of these by but an eighth of an inch.

Captain William G. Crenshaw began a record of the rainfall at "Hawfield" in 1880, and it has been diligently and carefully continued since his death to this time. His son, Mr. S. Dabney Crenshaw has kindly furnished the following data.

ANNUAL RAIN FALL AT HAWFIELD, ORANGE COUNTY VIRGINIA.
1880 to September 10, 1907 (inclusive).

1880 inches 26.40	1894 inches 33.55
1881 inches 30.77	1895 inches 38.86
1882 inches 42.60	1896 inches 40.44
1883 inches 38.72	1897 inches 47.56
1884 inches 38.43	1898 inches 45.06
1885 inches 33.00	1899 inches 37.37
1886 inches 45.55	1900 inches 41.68
1887 inches 33.20	1901 inches 56.50
1888 inches 49.06	1902 inches 60.99
1889 inches 57.83	1903 inches 48.07
1890 inches 37.84	1904 inches 37.47
1891 inches 48.46	1905 inches 51.43
1892 inches 36.95	1906 inches 57.30
1893 inches 40.82	†1907 inches 33.81

Average for 27 7–10 years 42.93 inches.

---
†To September 10th, 1907.

Mr. Jefferson, in his "Notes on Virginia," gives 47.038 inches as the average of the five years from 1772 to 1777, in Albemarle. Grouping the five years in Mr. Newman's record between 1859 and 1863, very nearly the same average is found.

According to a "Gazetteer of Virginia," prepared by the United States Geological Survey in 1904, the mean magnetic declination in 1900 was 3° 35', and the mean temperature 55° to 60° Fahrenheit.

The elevation above the sea is from 300 to 1,200 feet; area 349 square miles.

CHAPTER XIV.

Social and Economic.

In the early days, almost as a matter of necessity, the "simple life" was the rule for the rich and poor alike.

There was little comfort in the modern sense, and no luxury. The houses were small and rude, few having glazed windows. All the lumber was sawn by hand, usually with a "pit saw": such nails as were used were wrought in the blacksmiths' shops, and almost every article of domestic use was made at home.

There are several houses yet standing in the County built of pit-sawn lumber and with wrought nails. On nearly every plantation there were negro carpenters, smiths, shoemakers, brick masons, etc., and, generally speaking, all the implements of agriculture, which were few and rude, and all house furnishings, were homemade. There were few books and little light at night to read by; the local roads were mostly bridle paths, and, except on rare occasions, horseback was the only mode of travel. A "bridal tour" consisted in the bride's going to the groom's home on the same horse, "riding behind him."

Visiting neighbors spent the day at least, and "calls" were unknown. The well-to-do got their clothes and wines and some furnishings from England, the poorer people wore homespun. Indeed almost down to the war, homespun and homemade garments were not uncommon, whether woolen, hempen or cotton. The negro women were taught to card, spin and weave, and to cut and make the clothes of the children and servants. The ladies had their imported silks and linens, not many of a kind, which lasted a long time and were handed down to their daughters. The planters wore broadcloth on public occasions, with short breeches, silk stockings and knee buckles. Pewter was far commoner than silver or china ware. The return on an execution in 1737 shows "a gun and sword, an old chafing dish, a servant woman, a pewter salt, a pewter dram cup, and a piece of a looking glass."

When the tobacco was hauled to Fredericksburg to market, the return load was usually family supplies, and often oysters in the shell, which, piled in the cellar and sprinkled occasionally with salt water, appear to have "kept" a long time.

Ordinaries, where "entertainment for man and beast" was provided, were very common, and the gentry were usually the proprietors.

The scale of prices was rigorously regulated by the county court every year. Thus, in 1735, this order is entered:

"The Court doth set and rate liquors; Rum, the gallon, eight shillings; Virginia brandy, six shillings; Punch, or Flipp, the quart, with white sugar, one and three pence, with brown sugar, one shilling; French brandy, sixteen shillings; Punch of same, two and six pence; Frill or Madeira wine, quart, two shillings; a hot dyet (diet) one shilling; a cold dyet, six pence; a lodging with clean sheets (always thus in the ratings) six pence;" and so on for oats, pasturages, etc. "Ordered that the several ordinary keepers in this county sell and retail liquors at the above rates, and that they presume not to sell at any other rates, and that if any person do not pay immediately that he pay for the same at the Fall in tobacco at ten shillings the hundred weight."

These ratings during the Revolution constitute a fine historical setting for later experience in Confederate times, as a gill of brandy or rum, two pounds two shillings; of whiskey one pound four shillings; a hot dinner, three pounds, six; a cold dinner, or second table, three pounds. The cost of a small drink of whiskey was thus about $3.50, a price it never attained in the Confederacy.

So in October, 1778, Joseph Woolfolk's executors were bonded in £10,000; in 1779 Reuben Daniel's executors in £30,000; and a negro, condemned to be hung, was valued at $3,333.

They looked after the morals of the people more closely then than now. The church wardens kept an eye on sinners, bound out orphans and the children of parents who did not take care of them, kept down immoral conduct as well as they could, and appear to have been an excellent sort of local inquisitors. In 1742 the court orders the church wardens to bind out Dodson's children, "he taking no care of their education, nor to bring them up in Christian principles," one of many like instances. In 1743 Pat Leonard is ordered to the stocks "for calling the sheriff a liar." Next year three men were presented by the grand jury for Sabbath breaking and riotously entering the German chapel and disturbing the congregation assembled for the worship of God, and putting the people in fear of life and limb. They were fined 200 pounds of tobacco and imprisoned one hour.

For being a vagabond and cheating at cards Jacob Saunders was ordered to receive 25 lashes at the common whipping post, and John O'Neill was committed to jail and required to give security for good behavior for speaking traitorously of King George and Governor Gooch.

Presentments for swearing oaths and for not attending church were very common, and there were also presentments for not "raising corn according to law," and for "setting stops in the rivers," In 1741 Jonathan Gibson, clerk of the Court, and others were fined ten shillings each for not attending church for two months.

As late as 1803 sundry people, including some of the most conspicuous of the gentry, were before court for unlawful gaming. They were Zachary Herndon, Paul Verdier, Thomas Bell, James Madison, John Burnley, Willis White, Edmund Terrell, William Hamilton, John Pollock, William Terrell, Reuben Hamilton, George Hughes, Charles Bell, Thomas Barbour, Jr., William Madison, Jr., Thomas Davison, and Abner Newman. All were presented, and the presentments appear to have been dismissed.

Yet it is well in the memory of many people now living when gaming was more usual than otherwise at Orange, and that it was a regular habit for a "faro" outfit to be brought over from Culpeper every court-day, to remain as long as there was inducement.

So it is related, in the palmy days of the Orange Springs, known at first as the "Healing Springs," where James Coleman was licensed to keep a tavern as early as 1794, while it was yet a place of public resort, that gentlemen used to indulge in a quiet game there, as was also the case at several private residences in the County; and no great harm done. Happily times have changed greatly in this respect, and gaming for stakes appears to be a thing of the past.

Militia musters, both company and regimental, constituted a distinctly social feature down to the war. The companies had their convenient places of assembly for drill, and the contrast between the flamboyant and gorgeous uniforms of the officers and the homespun drab of the privates was very striking. The officers would be assembled for "training" for several days at a time prior to each annual "General Muster," and when that great occasion came the people flocked to see it as they now do to a circus. The appearance of the field and staff mounted on prancing steeds was a triumphal pageant, and when Allan Long and Peter Gilbert struck up "The Girl I left behind me" on fife and drum, the martial spirit became intense, and the maneuvres much involved. The new element in our citizenship, as one of the results of the war, has eliminated "musters" for all time, but they were great while they lasted.

It was a good old fashion, too, long continued and much enjoyed, to give neighborhood dances to the young people. There were simple music, ample refreshments, pretty but inexpensive apparel, and happy people, young and old. It was part of the celebration of Christmas week to have these "parties," though by no means confined to that week. The young people attended them not to display gowns, or the lack of them, but to enjoy themselves in honest, simple, and innocent pleasures, which they did to the full. The poorer people, too, had their pleasant social amusements "during the consulship of Plancus."

Those were the years when the men who afterwards composed the Army of Northern Virginia were reared, and when their mothers and sisters were the women of Orange, such years and such pleasures as their posterity can never enjoy—Arcadian days when people met for pleasure not for display. *Hæc olim meminisse juvabit!*

They were continued for some years after the war, but that violent shock to social and domestic conditions put an end to them, and they remain only as pleasing and pathetic memories.

Educational facilities were few and simple, but such education as there was appears to have been practical and thorough as far as it went. It was the day of "Old-Field Schools," when a neighborhood, or the leading men of it, would employ a teacher for their children, build a log schoolhouse at some convenient point, and throw the doors open to all comers; to boys and girls, the rich and poor alike. The overseers' sons would be at the same desk, when desks were to be had, and in the same classes with the planters' sons; and ordinarily "the three R's" would constitute the curriculum, though Latin was taught to all who wished to learn it. The birch and the ferule were generously administered, and the pedagogue of "The Deserted Village" appears often in the annals of the schools in colonial days. The rich had private tutors occasionally for their sons and daughters, and French, and music on the spinnet, were taught.

There was certainly a fragmentary spinnet in the County some years after the war, a sort of primitive piano.

James Waddel, the blind preacher, taught school at his home near Gordonsville, and Meriwether Lewis, of the Lewis and Clark expedition, and Gov. James Barbour went to school to him there.

Walker Maury, a very noted teacher of his day, had a school at or near Burlington, the home of Mr. James Barbour Newman, near Barboursville. The famous statesman, John Randolph, of Roanoke, was one of his pupils. The house in which he lodged still stands in the yard. Mr. Maury died in charge of the celebrated grammar school at Norfolk in 1786. His son, Leonard Hill Maury, taught a classical school at "Halla Farm," now owned by Mr. R. L. Coleman, near Somerset, early in the last century.

One of Randolph's eccentricities was developed there. His delicate sensibilities were disturbed by noises from contiguous rooms, and he daubed his own with mud mortar to exclude the sound as much as possible. Mr. Newman long preserved a fragment of this as a memento of Randolph.

The girls were not highly educated, in the modern sense, in those days, and the boys, with rare exceptions, finished their education at the neighborhood schools. But they developed into splendid women and fine men whose superiors have not appeared under the modern system. Sessions lasted ten months, and the school hours were from eight to four or later. There were not many text-books, no "hygiene," no athletics nor peripatetic "teams," but there was honest and thorough teaching, and a splendid citizenship, and illustrious citizens, as a result. But aspirations were different then, and it ought never to be lost to memory that "frugality" was a household word among the statesmen of the earlier generations, and considered so fundamental a principle of free government as to be inscribed in the organic law of every state of the Union.

The first mention of a local newspaper is in an order dated in 1830 directing an order of publication in "The Reporter" published at the Courthouse.

A single copy of "The Orange Express," Volume I, number 13, has been lent by Mr. A. J. Stofer, a veteran editor in Orange. It is dated at the courthouse, August 19, 1831, "By William R. Robinson," a brother of the respected merchant, Thomas A. Robinson, who so long sold honest goods on the cornor opposite the present bank of Orange. The motto of the paper was *"in civitate libera linguam mentemque liberas esse debere,"* in a free State speech and thought ought to be free. In an advertisement notice is given of a petition to be presented to the next General Assembly for the division of the County "by a line running nearly north and south from some point on the Albemarle line near Barboursville or Cavesville, across the County to the Madison line, between Willis's Mill and Cave's Mill," which came to naught.

When this paper was discontinued is not known, but the next in order was "The Southern Chronicle," established by Payne and Stofer in 1857, which died during the war. In 1867 Mr. Stofer established the "Orange Expositor," which in the fall of that year was changed to "The Native Virginian," and published at Orange till 1869, and then at Gordonsville by Dr. George W. Bagby (Mozis Addums) and Mr. Stofer. This in turn, after a brief career, was bought by Stofer and carried back to Orange, the name being changed to "The Piedmont Virginian" as at this day.

In September, 1873, "The Gordonsville Gazette" was launched by W. W. Scott and George W. Graham, and conducted by them till 1877, when they sold it. After many vicissitudes of fortune and as many proprietors, it has been lately bought by Mr. Bibb, the present editor. Mr. B. Johnson Barbour and Dr. James C. Hiden were frequent contributors to its columns while Mr. Scott was its editor.

A denominational paper, of the "Disciples," was published a short time at Gordonsville shortly before the "boom," and during the boom, Mr. Albert Sidney Johnston established a paper there which died with it.

The "Orange Observer" was founded in 1882 by Mr. Robinson, father of the present owners.

Looking now to economic and industrial features, the records disclose many things which appear strange to this generation.

The first County levy was not quite twenty-five thousand pounds of tobacco for all the public expenses. More than one thousand was paid out in bounties for wolves' heads, one hundred and forty for an old, seventy pounds for a young wolf's head. Eighty odd wolves were killed that year, and killing them continued to be an industry for a long time, though rapidly diminishing. In 1764 the number had decreased to three old and six young heads, and in 1815 there is an entry of $2 paid for one wolf's scalp, probably the last reward paid.

Attention was quickly given to roads and ferries. An early order is that "the sheriff give notice at every church in the County that the ferry at Germanna is to be let to the lowest bidder, he to be bonded for duly keeping the same."

In 1737 a ferry was established at old Raccoon Ford, William Payne, ferryman, to be kept open on court days and the day after, the minister and sheriff to be set over for 400 hundred pounds of tobacco.

In 1742 a committee was appointed to take subscriptions for a bridge at Germanna, and agree with workmen to build it: if subscription insufficient, balance to be levied by the County not to exceed 3,000 pounds of tobacco. In 1765 Orange and Louisa jointly built Brock's Bridge over the North Anna.

The first pretentious "public improvement" of the highway was by "The Swift Run Turnpike Company," and the road is, or was, the "old turnpike" from the courthouse to Fredericksburg, but projected to go to Swift Run. It was incorporated January, 1810, and in 1816 work was begun on it in Orange. In 1834 the Company "failing to realize 8 per cent. on its capital stock," asked permission of the Court to increase its tolls; which was refused.

It seems almost incredible that tolls were ever paid on such a road; incredible, indeed, that such a road was ever built, if portions of it did not remain as a wonderful exhibit of the engineering and macadamizing of that period.

In 1840 condemnations began for the "Louisa Road," now the Chesapeake and Ohio. This road started at Doswell and ended at Louisa. Later it was projected to Gordonsville which was the western terminus for several years. The first survey for its extension was through Swift Run Gap to Harrisonburg, but Albemarle and Augusta legislators got it diverted to Staunton, thereby losing the bulk of the great Valley trade to Richmond and the State. Early in the fifties the Valley clamored for good highways to a railroad, and turnpikes were constructed across the Blue Ridge to Gordonsville, one from Harrisonburg, the other from New Market. These were toll roads, and of great use to the army during the war. Soon after the war they were taken over by the County as "abandoned turnpikes," but are continued as public highways.

Fredericksburg smarted under the diversion of her former trade to Richmond, and the Narrow Gauge railroad, and the plank road were soon projected, and the latter completed about 1856, a splendid highway at first but soon wearing out. The Narrow Gauge was not completed until about 1875, and until carried further into the interior can never become of great commercial importance.

The Orange and Alexandria, now the Southern, having its terminus first at Gordonsville was completed about 1855. Soon after the Charlottesville and Rapidan railroad was built the Chesapeake and Ohio took a ninety-nine year lease of the nine miles between Gordonsville and the courthouse. In the aggregate there are 50 miles of railroad in the County, operated as follows: by the Southern, 19 miles; Chesapeake and Ohio, $10\frac{1}{2}$; by the Potomac, Fredericksburg and Piedmont (Narrow Gauge), 19 miles.

The chief agricultural products are the cereals, hay, and apples. Little tobacco is now raised, but down to the war tobacco houses dotted every plantation, and it was a staple crop.

Fat cattle, lambs for the early market, and fine horses constitute leading industries, and dairy farming is carried on very successfully.

CHAPTER XV.

Crimes and Punishments.

There are some notable instances of crimes, and particularly of punishments, in the earlier records; punishments that in these days would be called barbarous, but which were the identical punishments for the particular crimes prescribed by the laws of England, then the laws of the colony. A crime by a servant against his master, by a wife against her husband, if sufficiently grave, was "petty treason," as in the cases of Peter and Eve hereafter narrated.

Hog stealing seems to have been so persisted in that special penalties were denounced upon it, until finally a second conviction was punishable by death; and hogs, then as now, had a special fascination for the negroes.

It is to be observed, too, that the "unspeakable crime," though of rarer occurrence in those days than now, was by no means unheard of as has been asserted.

The tradition that Negro Run, formerly Negro-head Run, was so called because the head of a negro who had been drawn and quartered for crime had been set up near it, is not sustained by the records of Orange; if true, the incident must have occurred before the County was formed, but there really seems no substantial basis for it.

The cases that follow are taken from the order books where they still may be read at large by the curious. It must be borne in mind that in those days the County Courts were often constituted "Courts of Oyer and Terminer," that is, to hear and make final determination.

At a Court of Oyer and Terminer held June, 1737, present Goodrich Lightfoot, Robert Slaughter, Robert Green, John Finlason, Francis Slaughter and William Russell, gentlemen justices.

Peter, a negro slave of John Riddle, deceased, being indicted for feloniously murthering his said master upon arraignment plead guilty. On consideration whereof the Court are of opinion that the said Peter is guilty of the said felony; therefore it is considered by the Court that the said Peter be hanged by the neck till he be dead. Memorandum. The said Peter was executed accordingly and it is ordered that the sheriff cut off his head and put it on a pole near the courthouse to deter others from doing the like.

At October term following, Zachary Lewis, King's attorney, informed the Court that at the houses of Lewis Stilfy and John Smith several persons, the famous Benjamin Borden, a justice of the peace, being one of them, do keep unlawful and tumultuous meetings tending to rebellion.

In November, 1740, Zacharias Bell being enlisted into his Majesty's service as a soldier to serve against the Spaniards and having deserted, it is ordered that the sheriff, immediately after the adjourning of this court, do sell the said Bell to the highest bidder as a servant for the space of five years, and apply the money according to law.

Thomas Kennerley ordered ten lashes for stealing a handkerchief, and Alexander Sweeney committed to general court for coining, counterfeiting and debasing the Spanish current coin. John Cranch prays to receive corporeal punishment instead of being sent on to the grand jury; which is administered. Frank, a negro slave hanged for breaking open a store and stealing goods of the value $10, and Cuffy, an accessory to the crime, prayed benefit of clergy and was ordered to be burnt in the hand and receive 39 lashes.

The following, however, is the most sensational item in all the records; the burning at the stake of Eve, a negro woman slave of Peter Montague, for poisoning her master, administering the same in milk served on the table. The indictment in this case, spread out in full on the order book, is a literary curiosity.

She was tried Thursday, January 23, 1745, and found guilty; "Therefore it is considered by the Court that the said Eve be drawn upon a hurdle to the place of execution and there to be burnt," which sentence was executed on the following Wednesday.

A hurdle was a sort of sledge used for hauling traitors to execution.

Mr. Charles S. Waugh, a venerable and highly respected citizen of Orange, remembers that his grandfather pointed out to him the little knoll near the old courthouse about Somerville's Ford where Eve was burnt. A hole was drilled in a rock and the stake inserted. Ploughing this knoll some years ago Mr. Waugh's ploughshare slid over a rock and, recalling the narrative, he carefully scraped off the earth with his knife, and found the round hole drilled in it. There can be little doubt that this was the identical rock to which she was chained.

June, 1753, "On the motion of Daniel McClayland who in a fight lately had a piece of his left ear bit off, it is by the Court ordered to be recorded."

This is an unique order. It will be seen later that cropping ears was a punishment for crime, which stigma Daniel probably sought to avoid by this record.

In September, 1767, Tom, a negro belonging to John Baylor, under two indictments for burglary and felony, not guilty of the first, guilty of the second, and having already received the benefit of clergy, the Court do adjudge that he suffer death. His crime was feloniously breaking the house of Erasmus Taylor, Gent., and stealing goods of the value of 25 cents! Stealing and such modern trifles "came high" in those days, and James Madison, Sr., was the president justice.

July, 1768. Cornelius and Ann Cornelia, vagrants, the said Ann "profainly swearing four oaths before the Court and failing to pay the fine: "ten lashes at the whipping post, they promising to leave the County immediately.

In 1776 Hampshire, a slave of Charles Porter, for notoriously running away and lying out so his master could not reclaim him; "ordered that the sheriff take him to the pillory and nail his ears to the same, and there to stand half an hour and then to have his right ear cut off."

In 1782 appears the first record of the unspeakable crime, when Cary, a negro slave of William Vawter, is hanged for rape.

In 1794, Caleb, a slave, found guilty of hog stealing; "Ordered that the sheriff take him to the pillory and nail one ear thereto, and in one hour thereafter to cut it loose from the nail, then to nail the other ear and in another hour's time to cut that loose from the nail, this being the second offense."

In 1799, a negro from Culpeper hanged for ravishing a married white woman of Orange County.

In 1801, "it appearing that George Morris has been and is still guilty of a flagrant contempt in confining the body of his wife Susannah, ordered that he be attached and kept in custody until he permit her to be entirely at liberty; Robert T. Moore and Dabney Minor dissenting."

In 1818, 1821 and 1823 negroes were hanged for rape, and in 1839 a negro "only seventeen years old" condemned to death for ravishing a white woman is unanimously recommended for executive clemency, or else to transportation, "in consideration of his youth." There's a falling away.

But probably the most unique of all the punishments was that prescribed for habitual absence from church; 50 pounds of tobacco or its equivalent in cash, and in default of payment, "ten lashes on the bare back." This was the law for some forty years, 1680-1720. There is no record of the lash for this offense in Orange, but many of the fine.

CHAPTER XVI.

The Orange Humane Society.

In 1749 William Monroe proved his importation into this colony from Great Britain. This was a formal proceeding before court in order to obtain what was called a "head right," that is, the right to take up 50 acres of land, a sort of bounty and inducement to immigrants.

We hear no more of him till his will is proved in 1769, and that will constitutes no inconsiderable item in the history of the County. By its terms his whole estate, after the death of his wife, was devoted to the cause of education. The estate was to be sold by his executors to the highest bidders, and the money invested; "the principal to be kept intact and the interest arising from the same to be disposed of towards schooling such poor children as my executors shall think most in want."

The land was sold accordingly, and the proceeds invested, and the interest re-invested from year to year; but the executors, fearing that the will was void for uncertainty, failed to make any application of the interest to the purposes of education. There is little doubt that the will was void, but as Monroe left no heirs in this country, certainly none that appeared to claim as such, and so the estate would legally have been

The Orange Humane Society

escheated by the Commonwealth, it was determined to invoke the action of the Legislature to the end that the intent of the testator might be carried into effect.

In January, 1811, The Orange Humane Society was incorporated by the Legislature, and the County Court was authorized and required at the ensuing March term, and every four years thereafter, to elect twelve trustees in whom should be vested the proceeds of the sale of the glebe lands of the church and of this fund, known as "the Monroe Fund;" to be by them managed in such manner as they deemed best and most conducive to promote the object of the Act, and be exclusively appropriated to the poor children, inhabitants of Orange, provided that they should only apply the interest arising from the said funds.

At "the ensuing March term" the Court elected the trustees; Isaac Davis, James Burton, Francis Cowherd, James Barbour, Philip Pendleton Barbour, Fortunatus Winslow, Robert Taylor, Catlett Conway, John Gibson, George Grasty, Thomas Coleman, and Thomas Woolfolk. The mere names of these trustees constitute a sufficient indication of the importance of the trust confided to them.

At that time, under the terms of the statute creating the "General Literary Fund of Virginia," of which Governor Barbour of Orange was the protagonist, there was a Board of School Commissioners in each county charged with the disbursement of the proceeds of that fund in the education of poor children. Just ten years after the Humane Society was organized, James Barbour, its president, having made his annual report in conformity with the order of the Court, and having requested their opinion as to consolidating the fund set apart for the education of the poor children and that under the control of the Society, the Court coincided with him as to the propriety of the measure, and recommended the delegates of the County to use their best endeavors to obtain the passage of a law to that effect. Diligent search has failed to find that such a law was enacted, and it was likely found that it was unnecessary, for from that time on when the Court appointed a trustee of the Society it at the same time appointed him a School Commissioner; so that the trustees and commissioners were one and the same. As late as 1838, the Court, "appointing directors or commissioners for the distribution of the public funds for the education of the destitute, decree that the funds of the Humane Society be exclusively appropriated to the education of the destitute children of the County."

It appears that the fund, at one time, amounted to more than $30,000, for when Greene was formed in 1838, her share was agreed to be one-third, or $10,300. It was carefully managed, and many poor children were educated, the interest only being used. Forty-three hundred dollars was in bank stock, the balance represented by bonds of citizens of the County secured on real estate. Thus matters went on until the war, during which the principal of some of the bonds was paid and reinvested in Confederate bonds. When the war ended these bonds and the bank stock were worthless, and the trustees appear to have lost interest in the Society.

THE ORANGE HUMANE SOCIETY 141

A balance of about $4,000 was still due to Greene, with interest accumulations, and litigation over it ended in a consent decree of October, 1873, in favor of Greene for $5,000, with interest from date. The County school board brought suit, in 1874, for the fund still in the control of the Society, claiming under the Act of 1872 establishing the public school system, and failing in this suit, resort was had to special legislation in 1876 whereby the original charter of 1811 was repealed and the school board authorized to take possession of the assets. Litigation now became fast and acrimonious. Suit was brought to compel the paying again of a bond paid off in Confederate money, and was successful in the lower court. The decree was reversed, however, on appeal, and in Wambersie *v.* the Orange Humane Society, 84 Va., it was held that the Society which had been rejuvenated in 1880 by the appointment of new trustees by William R. Taliaferro, then judge of the County Court, had no legal existence by reason of the repeal of the charter in 1876. Meantime the costs had been enormous, and, what with the losses and the expenses of litigation, there was not much left of this noble charity for the school board to administer. How much came into their hands the records do not disclose; indeed it is said that the records of the school board that first came into possession of the fund have been lost!

It is known that the High School building at the courthouse was paid for, in part or in whole, out of the fund. The visible, available assets, in personal bonds of individuals, amount to less than three thousand dollars. It is understood that the school board will soon assume actual and active control of this remnant, and administer it, in their wisdom, in the interest of education.

Information derived from a prominent citizen of Greene is to the effect that her portion of the fund constitutes a real factor in the public school system. Her portion was one-third of the whole.

A letter written by Gov. James Barbour, in February, 1839, to Hon. John S. Pendleton, then a member of the House of Delegates from Culpeper, protesting against the claim of Greene County for a division of the fund, is filed with the Orange petitions in the State Library, and the following extracts are taken from it. As he was so long president of the Society, and took such a warm interest in its management, this letter, written but a few years before his death, has all the force of an official utterance.

> We commenced with a capital of some $13,000; we have educated over a thousand children, and have increased the capital to about $30,000, retaining and converting the interest in part into principal, and thus looking to the probable demand we have the means that will correspond with the progress of the Society. * * * Not a farthing has been lost. At my instance the Court of Orange have, by appointing the same persons directors of the Humane Society also commissioners of the School Fund, united both these benevolent funds. (Proceeds of sale of the glebe lands, etc.)
>
> My hope and purpose have been to create a fund by the aid of the charitable equal to the establishment of a manual labor school, where the indigent might be so instructed as to become useful citizens, and especially where teachers might be reared—a good supply of which to operate through the State in an object of great importance.

In this letter is to be found the first appeal in Virginia, so much heard in recent years, for industrial and normal schools which, at last, are becoming parts of our educational system.

It seems the irony of fate that this fund, earned in the sweat of his face by a man imported here as an indentured servant who could neither read nor write, and by him dedicated to the education of children as indigent as he had been, should have so dwindled that there is hardly a beneficiary of it in the County to-day; and that probably there is not a score of people now living who ever heard of William Monroe, the philanthropist, whose obscure grave in Greene County lies in flagrant neglect.

For the benefit of the Boards of Supervisors of the two counties, the recipients of his bounty, and especially of their county school boards, it is here stated with confidence that his grave is on the Chapman farm, "on a hill overlooking the river;" that Colonel Bradford of Orange can still point it out, if, as in duty bound, they wish to mark the spot, and so commemorate the first philanthropist of this section of the State.

CHAPTER XVII.

From 1848 to 1861.

In preceding chapters there have been no headline dates, because a system of grouping facts has been followed, not a narration of them in regular sequence.

The War of 1812, for instance, and the Mexican War, have not even been mentioned, for the reason that the County records disclose nothing of interest about either. Indeed neither the County nor any of its citizens, with a few exceptions, bore any conspicuous part in either of these wars, and the meagre facts that can be collected about the War of 1812 (for there seem to be none about the War with Mexico) will be narrated in an appendix.

In 1848 the War with Mexico has just been ended in triumph, and one of its chief heroes, Gen. Zachary Taylor, a son of the County, elected President of the United States.

Everything appears to be serene and matter-of-fact at this period. The industrial and public improvement age has begun. In 1850 a vote of the freeholders is ordered on the question of a subscription of $10,000, to the projected Fredericksburg and Valley Plank Road, which was carried by a handsome majority. It was a great road while it lasted, and Gen. William

Mahone, if for no other reason, ought to be remembered with gratitude for his fine engineering work on this highway. Yet as early as 1859 the directorate turned over the roadbed to the County, "on condition that it shall be kept open as a public highway." The court accepted it on those terms, but the condition has not been faithfully fulfilled.

In 1851 a section of the Blue Ridge Turnpike was opened to travel, and a right of way across the public lot was granted to the Orange and Alexandria Railroad Company (now the Southern) on condition that it keep the public buildings insured against fire.

The public buildings were removed higher up the street some years later, but, though still enjoying the right of way, the company does not keep up the insurance.

At this period was held the great "Reform Convention" to revise the State Constitution, framed by the world-famous Convention of 1829–30, which was utterly cast aside, except that George Mason's Bill of Rights was retained almost word for word. White male suffrage became universal, and every office from constable to judge of the supreme court of appeals, was made elective by the people. Dire things were prophesied of it by the traditionally conservative, but so long as it lasted, practically only to the outbreak of the war, it gave great satisfaction, and the judges elected under its provisions conformed to the highest judicial standards of former and subsequent periods.

The whole State became a storm centre of politics about this time, and the "Know Nothing Party" was launched. It received its definite quietus in 1855, when Henry A. Wise, its leading antagonist, was elected governor.

In 1850 a ten-mile section of the Rockingham Turnpike was opened to travel, and since its completion no macadamized or other improved public highway has been built in the County, except the short reaches at the County seat.

In 1857 the present courthouse was ordered, with permission to the Masons to add a third story for use as a lodge, they to pay one third of the insurance on the building. The Masons did not accept. The court held its first session in the new building in July, 1859.

In 1859 occured the invasion of the State, and the attempt to incite the negroes to armed insurrection, known as the "John Brown Raid." It occasioned wild excitement, and a good deal of local apprehension, and was, indeed, the alarum gun of the war that so soon followed.

The "Montpelier Guards," a fine volunteer company at and about Orange Courthouse, commanded by Capt. Lewis B. Williams, Jr., was promptly ordered to repair to Charlestown, where they remained till Brown and such of his accomplices as had been caught were hanged.

A roster of the company, as then constituted, believed to be complete, is printed in an appendix.

One of the immediate results of this raid was the organization and equipment of many volunteer companies throughout the State. Two, the "Gordonsville Greys," Capt. William C. Scott, and the "Barboursville Guard," Capt. W. S. Parran, were organized in Orange, received arms and equipments, were uniformed, and began regular drills in preparation for the direful conflict which everybody felt was coming, indeed was almost come.

And here, it may be said, ends the history of the Orange of the old régime—a régime which all who can recall it will delight to cherish in their memories, and the like of which no one may hope to look upon again.

But relentless time goes on, and with it the history of the people that made noble sacrifice, suffered and endured; and who, like the brave yeomen of their motherland, never lost "the mettle of their pastures!"

CHAPTER XVIII.

The War Period.

It is not within the scope of this book to treat of the war period, except in the most cursory way, narrating briefly what relates particularly to the County, and more shall not be attempted; but a résumé of local happenings ought to be recorded, with such impartiality as a participant in the struggle may command.

In the presidential election of 1860 the vote in Orange was as follows: for Bell and Everett, the pronounced Union ticket, 427; for Breckenridge and Lane, the States Rights ticket, 475; for Douglas and Johnson, also a pronounced Union ticket, 12; for Lincoln and Hamlin, 0. Thus in a total vote of 914, there was only a States Rights majority of 48, and adding the Douglas vote to Bell's, a majority of only 36; so it will be seen that love for the "Union" was still strong in the County.

After the election of Lincoln, which was followed so soon by the secession of South Carolina and other Southern States, the Secessionists of the County grew bolder and more aggressive, and when the State convention was called to determine the course of Virginia, party feeling became very tense. Rosettes of blue ribbon, called "cockades," appeared everywhere, even at the churches. Men, boys, and even girls, wore them. The Unionists were less demonstrative, but no less resolute. Candidates to represent the County in the convention were numerous and eager. Col. John Willis, Major John H. Lee, Hon. Jeremiah Morton, and perhaps others, aspired to represent the Secessionists. The contest finally narrowed to Mr. Morton, on that side, and Mr. Lewis B. Williams, the elder, who had then been the attorney for the commonwealth for thirty years, for the Unionists. The exact figures are unattainable, but Mr. Morton was elected by a good majoirty.

The convention assembled at Richmond in February, 1861. But there was no secession; the Union party was in control. It is likely there would have been none but for the attempted reinforcement of Fort Sumter by the administration, while peace loving people were yet endeavoring to avert disunion and war.

Another shot was "heard 'round the world," when Sumter was fired on, and the echoes of it have hardly yet ceased to reverberate. At once there were no "Unionists" in Orange; certainly none that disclosed themselves until after the war had ended disastrously, and an office was in sight.

All the people seemed of one mind, and on the night of April 17th the three volunteer companies of the County, with many fresh recruits, hastily assembled, and under orders from Governor Letcher, proceeded to Harpers Ferry and took possession of the national arsenal there, which had been partially burned before their arrival; and war was on.

The Monday following was regular court day, and a vast concourse attended. On that day, Col. Robert E. Lee passed through Orange on his way to Richmond, in response to an invitation from the convention. After long and irrepressible calls from the throng at the depot, which even threatened to block the train, he appeared on the rear platform and bowed acknowledgments. Erect, without a strand of grey in his hair or moustache, and he then wore no beard, he appeared every inch a man and a soldier. The people went wild with enthusiasm at his martial appearance: he bowed, but said not a word.

Orange looked upon him many times afterwards; grown grey, indeed, but never bent. No doubt the Daughters of the Confederacy will some day mark with appropriate tablets the several places in the County still remembered as Lee's and Jackson's "Headquarters."

Soon after court was opened, Mr. B. Johnson Barbour, the only surviving son of Gov. James Barbour, arose, and in a rather faltering but incisive voice addressed the Bench, saying in substance that it was known of all men how he had striven to save the Union of the fathers and to avert the dread calamity of war, but now that Mr. Lincoln, like another Appius Claudius, had cast his lustful eyes upon the fair Virginia, and had called for volunteers to invade the South, there was nothing for patriots to do but to prepare to meet the invaders. He suggested that a subscription for defense be made, and himself pledged a liberal sum.*

---

*This is not stated as matter of record. The writer was present and heard the remarks, and he especially remembers the apt classical allusion. Mr. Barbour was noted for such allusions. The immediate order of the court, and the committee as named by it, fully confirm his recollection.

The following order was thereupon entered: "The Court of this County, at the suggestion of some of the citizens, being of the opinion that, for the defense of our County and State, funds should be raised to an amount not exceeding $4,000, and that such action is approved and desired by the people of the whole County, do appoint Benjamin J. Barbour, Ferdinand Jones, and Philip B. Jones a committee to borrow a sum or sums of money not exceeding $4,000 in the aggregate, from time to time as may be required in the opinion of the committee, to be applied by them as necessity may require; and the court pledge themselves to levy on the land and slaves such amount of money as may be necessary from time to time, to pay the said sums of money so borrowed in installments of one and two years, with all interest that may accrue thereon." It also authorized H. T. Holladay to employ four or six discreet persons to guard the railroad bridge at Rapidan.

At the May term three persons in each magisterial district were appointed to visit the families of soldiers in actual service and furnish to each all necessary meat and bread, pledging the court to levy $500, at the next term for that purpose.

July 22, the day after the first battle of Manassas, when many private houses and some hastily provided hospitals at the Courthouse were full of sick and wounded soldiers, the Court "requested Mr. W. M. Graham to supply them such necessaries as the physician might apply for;" and $1,000 was afterwards appropriated to pay the bill.

The former order authorizing a loan of $4,000 was changed, and the clerk was authorized to issue County bonds for $6,000, for the committee to pay debts already contracted by them, and to procure uniforms, clothing, equipments, and necessary relief to the volunteers and portions of the militia of the County.

In May, 1862, John L. Woolfolk was appointed a commissioner to go to the salt works and purchase 6,000 bushels of salt for the citizens.

At a special term, January, 1863, the slaveholders were required to deliver, in the ratio of their holdings, 200 able-bodied negro men to the sheriff, for work on the defences of Richmond.

The apportionment among individual owners appears at large on the order book.

April, 1863, Ferdinand Jones appointed to borrow $10,000 on the faith of the County, and pay the same to the wives of soldiers in service at the rate of eight dollars per month to each wife and four dollars per month for each child under twelve years of age.

Also an order to William Parker to distribute the county salt so that each inhabitant receive fifteen pounds; charging eight cents a pound for the first ten pounds, and ten cents a pound for the remainder.

In November the sheriff was ordered to list all indigent soldiers disabled or honorably discharged, and their families, and the families of those now in service, and the widows and minor children of such as are dead or may die; and to summon all the justices to the next term to make provision for the families of soldiers in service.

At the December term Ferdinand Jones was appointed agent of the County to purchase supplies for indigent families of soldiers; to furnish them with money as per the former order, or to purchase and supply to each member of a family at the rate of one-half pound of beef, or one-eighth pound of bacon, and one and a half pints of meal or its equivalent in flour, per day; and he is authorized to impress 7,000 pounds of bacon, or 20,000 pounds of beef, and 2,200 bushels of corn at prices fixed by the impressing agent of the Confederate States; and also to borrow $50,000.

May, 1864, Ordered, that it be certified to the post quartermaster for the Eighth Congressional District that there are in the County four hundred persons, members of indigent families of soldiers; that there will be necessary for their subsistence for the next six months, 10,000 pounds of bacon and 1,200 bushels of corn; and that it is impossible to procure same by purchase in the County.

The Confederacy is starving!

September, 1864, Ferdinand Jones directed to borrow $25,000 for same purposes.

The Confederate enrolling officer having been ordered to impress one of every four able-bodied negro men to work on the fortifications at Richmond, the court makes its protest to the Secretary of War, alleging many and weighty reasons why the order should not be enforced in this County.

This is the last war item of interest in the order books, and surely these are enough to show the devotion of the people to their cause. Battle and murder and sudden death had become their daily bread.

They had borne all things, endured all things, believed all things, hoped all things; they had seen things in a mirror darkly, and now were to behold them face to face.

And so ensued Appomattox and the end!

A volume might be written, interesting and inspiring, about Orange soldiers and their valiant conduct in the field from 1861 to 1865, but this must be left in the main to military annalists.

There were three companies from the County in the Thirteenth Virginia Infantry, commanded first by A. P. Hill, who was killed at Petersburg in 1865, having attained the rank of lieutenant-general; secondly by James A. Walker, who later commanded the Stonewall Brigade, became a brigadier-general, and after the war, was lieutenant-governor of the State, and for several terms a member of the United States House of Representatives; thirdly by James Barbour Terrell, of Bath County, whose father was a native of Orange, and who was killed at second Cold Harbor in 1864, his commission as brigadier general, having been signed; a noble record for the regiment! It was next commanded by Col. G. A. Goodman, of Louisa, who went out as a lieutenant in the Gordonsville Greys, and survived the war; and lastly by Lieutenant-Colonel Charles T. Crittenden, of Culpeper, who died recently at the Soldiers' Home. A roster of these companies appears elsewhere.

The regiment bore a brave part in all the great battles of the Army of Northern Virginia except Gettysburg, having been left in charge of Winchester at the time of that battle.

The War Period

There were two companies of artillery from the County, one organized and commanded by Capt. Thomas J. Peyton, and subsequently by Capt. C. W. Fry, who was promoted to the rank of major, but whose commission, captured on the retreat to Appomattox, was never actually received.

The other company, which can not be strictly called an Orange company, was raised and commanded by Capt. William G. Crenshaw, of Hawfield.

A cavalry company, "The Orange Rangers," was enlisted by Capt. G. J. Browning.

Many Orange soldiers served in the Seventh Virginia Infantry, in the Wise Artillery, and in sundry other organizations formed without the County.

The County suffered much from the ravages of the war, being practically on the border from its beginning. The Rapidan was General Lee's line of defence for many months, and his army wintered in the County in 1863-64, his headquarters being on the Rogers farm, near Nason's.

Just before and just after the battle of Slaughter's Mountain, Stonewall Jackson's headquarters were on the farm of Col. Garrett Scott; almost exactly where Rev. F. G. Scott's farm buildings now stand, and near a notable spring known locally as the "Hollow Spring."

Gen. A. P. Hill's were in the yard at "Mayhurst," the residence of Mr. William G. Crenshaw Jr., near Orange; then known as "Howard Place," and owned by Col. John Willis.

The important battles fought in the County were Mine Run, in 1863, and the Wilderness battles of 1864.

There were also cavalry engagments, mostly skirmishes, at Rapidan, Locust Grove, Morton's Ford, New Hope Church, Orange, Liberty Mills, Zoar, Germanna and on the turnpike near Col. Alexander Cameron's, two miles northwest of Gordonsville (the nearest approach of the enemy to that town during the war); and the Thirteenth Virginia Infantry had an insignificant skirmish with cavalry at Toddsberth in July, 1862, where they encountered a reconnoitering party which had been up the County road as high as the "Stone Bridge," about four miles northeast of Gordonsville.

The tragic story of the Magruder and the Burrus families in the war must be narrated in some detail.

For some years prior to the war, Col. James Magruder owned and resided at "Frascati," near Somerset. He was an ardent "old line whig," and an enthusiastic lover of the Union of the States. At the outbreak of the war he had five sons of military age, and three daughters, the eldest having lately been married to Col. Edward T. H. Warren, of Harrisonburg, who afterwards became colonel of the Tenth Virginia Infantry. His eldest son, Edward, a graduate of the Virginia Military Institute, who was teaching school in Rome, Georgia, came to Virginia in command of a company, and attained to the rank of colonel. He was seven times wounded during the war.

Colonel Warren, the son-in-law, was killed in battle. The second son, James Watson, lately graduated from the University, joined the Albemarle Light Horse, Second Virginia Cavalry, was chosen first lieutenant, and was killed in battle near Richmond during Sheridan's raid. The next son, known as Hilleary, was a doctor, and received an appointment as assistant surgeon in one of Ashby's regiments. So much beloved was he by the soldiers, that he was prevailed on to accept a captaincy of one of the companies. He was killed, leading a charge near Rochelle in Madison County, almost in sight of his home. The next son, George, and the youngest, David, were members of the Gordonsville Greys. David was the first man to be wounded in the Thirteenth Infantry; so badly wounded at Munson's Hill, in 1861, that he was disabled for active service for the rest of the war, though he continued in the army on light service, and died soon after the war from the effect of his wound. George was killed in battle, in the Valley. Five sons and a son-in-law; four killed in battle, one seven times wounded, and one disabled!

Mr. Lancelot Burrus, who lived near Pamunkey, had been high sheriff of the County, and enjoyed the respect and esteem of all who knew him. Of his six sons, five enlisted in the Montpelier Guards, the sixth later on, being under age, in the Sixth Virginia Cavalry. Their full names are written down here as a memorial of them, and the names of three of them are inscribed on the Confederate monument in the public square at Orange. Five of them, George Martin, Robert Henry, Thomas Joseph, William Tandy and Lancelot went to Harpers Ferry April 17th, 1861. At the battle of Gaines's Mill, known also as first Cold Harbor, the three first named were killed, William Tandy, slightly wounded, Lancelot wounded, his cartridge box belt cut off, and fourteen bullet holes shot through his clothing; all this in one day and one battle!

John Herschel, the youngest brother, joined the army in 1862, and was wounded in the head, near Luray. Lancelot, was seven times wounded, and had thirty-seven bullet holes through his clothes. And Tandy was in every battle with his regiment from the beginning to the end of the war:

When a friend called to condole with the father of these soldiers, after the battle of Gaines's Mill, the brave old man said to him, "Ah, Mr. W——, I wish I had a million sons, even though they all had to go the same way!"

And these are but types, remarkable though they be, of the resolute fathers and sons in Orange, "in the time of the war."

Mr. Larkin Willis, who lived not far from Germanna, had ten sons in the Confederate army at one time.

There is at Orange, though first organized at Gordonsville, a Confederate veterans' camp, known as the "William S. Grymes Camp," and named in honor of a distinguished and much loved surgeon and countyman who served through the war.

There is also a chapter of the "Daughters of the Confederacy," named for the Thirteenth Virginia Infantry.

An appendix gives the names of such of the Confederate soldiers from the County as could be obtained after much effort. It is known to be very defective; and if the names of soldiers not found therein are to be rescued from oblivion, it must be done by these two organizations, and done at once.

The monument on the public square at the County seat will hand down the names of those who were killed. The names of those who served and survived ought also to be preserved.

CHAPTER XIX.

Reconstruction, 1865 to 1870.

The last chapter brought the record down to Appomattox. It is interesting now to recall the memories of the three or four ensuing years.

The soldiers came back home, if home had been left them, and, settling down to peaceful pursuits, began their struggle with poverty. There was not seed in the County sufficient to pitch a crop, nor money wherewith to buy. So great was the rebound from the field of battle to the serenity of domestic life, that even the old veterans, their bodies racked with many wounds, set to work with their own hands and with good heart to make the best of the situation. The Freedmen's Bureau was constituted by the conquerors, and satraps with shoulder straps and brass buttons were sent to every county to look after the late slaves; the "wards of the nation" as they were then called. The negroes were organized into "Union leagues," and depraved white men, some of them citizens, many of them a low type of northern newcomers, "scalawags" and "carpet-baggers," they were called respectively, did what they could to inflame them to tumult and riot. To the credit of the negroes be it said that many of them, notwithstanding the wiles of their charmers, accepting their freedom as a great boon, continued to be orderly, respectful, and industrious. There was no such "labor problem," even in those trying times as has prevailed for the past ten years.

And it ought to be remembered with perpetual gratitude that the city of Baltimore came to Virginia at that time with gifts in her hands—a real Ceres sowing the seeds of hope—and offered to furnish, on the credit of a crop to be planted, matured, and marketed, such seeds as the planters needed. Everybody took fresh heart and went to work. There was life in the land again. The roar of the cannons had ceased; bloody annals were still related by the fireside, but peace brooded over all.

And, as the order books show, the court sat on, the same justices and other officials "pursuing the noiseless tenor of their way" in the administration of County affairs; and it was not until January term, 1869, that attention is rudely arrested. Here is the caption of the order book of that time.

> At a monthly court held for the County of Orange at the Courthouse on Monday, the 25th day of January, one thousand eight hundred and sixty-nine:
> Present, Garrett Scott, Presiding Justice, Ferdinand Jones, William H. Faulconer, Edward Beazley, and James Coleman.

The first entry under that caption is this:

> HEADQUARTERS FIRST MILITARY DISTRICT,
> State of Virginia.
> *Richmond, Virginia December 31, 1868.*
> Mr. Michael D. Higgins is hereby appointed Clerk of the County and Circuit Courts of Orange County, State of Virginia, to fill the vacancy caused by the removal from office of Philip H. Fry, and is empowered to perform all the duties of the said office according to law until his successor shall be duly elected and qualified.

Before entering on the duties of his office, he will qualify as required by the laws of the State and of the United States.

GEORGE STONEMAN,
Brevet Major-General U. S. A. Commanding."

The cormorants had got hungry and had demanded the mess of pottage.

That this Higgins may not be confounded with the family "native here and to the manner born," let it be stated that he had, a few years before his appointment, come to the County from the North and purchased the estate near Orange now owned by Mr. William G. Crenshaw, Jr.

The minutes of this term, and of the February term which began on George Washington's birthday, were signed by Garrett Scott, who had been presiding justice for twenty years—his last appearance on the Bench.

Now came the period of hard swearing known as "taking the iron clad oath," and so denominated in the record when Higgins took the oaths of office.

There was no March term, but on April 26th there appeared a Court with more facile consciences; "Present John M. Chapman, presiding justice, John Terrell, John M. Shipp, and William H. Faulconer."

Daniel Sheffey Lewis, of Rockingham County, acted as attorney for the Commonwealth during this period, vice Lewis B. Williams who had held the office since 1831.

This "Presiding Justice" appears to have held but the one term. William H. Faulconer was next elected and continued to act as such until March 1870, when the county court ceased to be a Bench of justices.

Other justices, whose names appear as constituting the court during this period, besides those named above, were William L. Duval, Robert Allison and Joseph K. Dobbins.

In 1870 the new constitution of the State, framed in 1867-68 by what is known in history as the "Black and Tan" or "Underwood" convention, became effective; and the State was "readmitted into the Union," which she had been chiefly instrumental in forming and establishing. The delegate from Orange to that Convention was a "carpet bagger," whose name, never before nor since heard of in the County, is now known only to the curious; and which, like those of all his class, would be infamous if it had not been forgotten.

The changes wrought by it were many and grave, and chief among them was the abolition of the county courts administered by justices, an institution almost coeval with the colony, and the creation of the office of county judge.

Each county had to be laid off into townships, and the Governor appointed Garrett Scott, R. L. Gordon, Ferdinand Jones, and William F. Brooking to perform that duty in Orange. Their report is recorded in the current deed book for 1870.

The map herewith shows the boundaries of these townships, now known, by Constitutional amendment, as magisterial districts, which have not been changed since they were established.

Great apprehension was felt at the time lest the negroes, who then constituted a majority of the registered voters, might work havoc in the fiscal matters of the County by electing a majority of the newly created board of supervisors. As they had already flocked in numbers to Gordonsville and Orange, the two principal villages in the County, it was deemed essential that these precincts should be in the same township, so that the white people might maintain political ascendancy in the other three; which is the explanation of the rather remarkable boundaries of the townships.

There has, however, never been a negro supervisor in the County, nor any negro elected to office, and rarely has there been a negro jury; once, when such a jury had been impaneled to try a member of their own race for murder, the prisoner plead earnestly for a jury of white men, which was denied him.

The townships were named Barbour, Madison, Taylor, and Gordon, in memory of four eminent citizens of the County. William G. Williams was chosen by the legislature as county judge. He held his first term, April 1870, and appointed Lewis B. Williams, Commonwealth's Attorney and John G. Williams, Clerk of the courts.

There have been three county judges: William G. Williams, who resigned; William R. Taliaferro; and James W. Morton. The last named was the incumbent when the present constitution, which abolished the county courts, went into effect. He was the recipient of a handsome "loving cup," as a testimonial from the Bar, when his court ceased to be an institution.

Since 1870 matters have gone on in the usual and regular routine, with nothing of such notable moment in the order books as need be narrated here. Such items as have been omitted in the regular narrative, because not susceptible of grouping under the chapter headings, and which are deemed worthy of attention, may be found in a subsequent chapter under the head of "Miscellaneous."

CHAPTER XX.

Fiscal and Statistical, 1870 to 1907.

The narrative having been brought down to the end of Reconstruction, little remains to be told.

The recuperation from the waste of the war, has been remarkable; not more so than that of other counties enjoying like advantages of climate, soil, and market facilities, yet so remarkable as to arrest attention. For it must be remembered that Orange was a theatre of the war, almost from the beginning, and though fabulous prices were paid for the timber and fences destroyed by and for the supplies furnished to the army, yet payment was made in fabulous currency, and the final result was total loss.

There were 6,111 slaves in Orange in 1860, constituting an asset of quite a million and a half dollars, nearly double the value of all other personal property, which was wiped out as with a sponge.

The tax rate on slaves twelve years of age, whether decrepit or not, was $1.20 each, and the auditor's report shows 3,309 of that age, the tax on whom amounted to nearly four thousand dollars.

A table is annexed, that readers may compare for themselves values as assessed in the years 1860, 1866, and 1906. The only change of County lines since 1838 was an adjustment of the line with Louisa, whereby

Orange gained some little territory, yet the returns show a few thousand acres less in 1906 than in 1860. In the latter year, the tax rate on lands was forty cents on the hundred dollars of assessed value; in 1866, fourteen cents, the valuation being nearly the same; in 1906 it was thirty-five cents, of which ten cents for free schools; but the assessments for this year are much lower, though not lower than for a good many years past.

No good reason can be given for this apparent depreciation in value, which is certainly only apparent.

There is now much more arable land, the farming has been greatly improved, and the lands are in much better condition than ever before. There has also been a very great increment of value by reason of new buildings and enclosures, yet the assessment has fallen off from more than $2,700,000 in 1860 to less than $2,000,000 in 1906, and of the latter sum nearly a quarter of a million represents town values which in 1860 were only $84,000 in amount. True, labor was abundant and cheap in 1866, gold was at a premium, the currency inflated, and the land market brisk by reason of an influx of immigrants from England and the northern States. The panic of 1873 depressed all values and for some years thereafter land could hardly be sold at any price. But these conditions no longer prevail, and normal prices have been attained for several years; yet the assessments of the panic time continue not only in Orange but throughout the State.

There can be little doubt that "politics" had much to do with it, the controversy over the State debt, now happily ended, having been a material factor in lowering not actual values, but values assessed for taxation.

There are but few manufactures and special industries in the County; among the latter, stock breeding, dairy farming, and poultry raising. Some years since, there was a cheese factory at Somerset, which manufactured excellent cheese, but it has been found to be more remunerative to ship the cream and milk to the city markets than to manufacture them at home.

There was never a bona fide bank in the County till long after the war, and the early adventures in that line proved disastrous to the depositors, there having been three bank failures in a few years. Now, at the County seat there are two national banks, the "Bank of Orange," with a paid-up capital of $25,000; surplus, $30,000; deposits, $330,000; John G. Williams, president, M. G. Field, cashier; the "Citizens' National Bank," capital, $25,000; surplus, $4,000; deposits, $160,000; R. O. Halsey, president, R. C. Slaughter, cashier; and at Gordonsville there is a "Branch of the Virginia Safe Deposit and Trust Corporation," W. S. Rogers, manager. All these institutions possess the confidence of the people, and their stock commands a premium.

There are two hunt clubs, which go to the field in costume and oftener pursue a bag of anise seed than reynard; the "Tomahawk," Mr. H. O. Lyne, president and Mr. Wallace Sanford, master of hounds; and the Blue Run," Mr. William duPont, president, and Dr. James Andrews, master of hounds.

These clubs in addition to their picturesqueness and

the sport they afford their members, teach the "art of Thrace—centaur like to ride," and promote the breeding and training of hunters which command great prices.

The Orange Horseman's Association, Mr. Thomas Atkinson, president, has become an institution that annually draws a great throng to its exhibition. This undoubtedly constitutes the chief spectacular occasion of the year, and also stimulates the breeding of fine horses.

The building of the Charlottesville and Rapidan Railroad cut off Gordonsville from her main back-country trade, which has now fallen to Barboursville and Somerset. These hamlets have become the main depots of Greene and Madison, respectively, and their trade in the minor products of the farms is something phenomenal.

The County seat is the junctional point of three railroads, and its growth in recent years has been quite susbtantial. Here are two banks, a merchant mill and ice factory, a wholesale store, macadamized streets, granolithic pavements, electric lights, and a library.

Gordonsville has a bank, excellent pavements, electric lights and an uncommonly good system of water works. The water, gathered into two reservoirs from a group of pure freestone springs on the mountain side, is very wholesome, and the natural gravity is sufficient to throw a stream over the greatest elevation in the town. There is one manufacturing plant in successful operation. Here the "Gordon Land Company," launched an unfortunate "boom" in 1890, which, like most booms, ended in disaster.

There are six merchant mills in the county, most of them equipped with the roller-process machinery. There is little valuable timber left, but a considerable business continues in lumber and cross ties.

The "Pamunkey" neighborhood, which embraces the Orange Springs, a very fertile section of the County, lying ten miles below the County seat, has long been celebrated for the thrift and hospitality of its people.

The "Somerset" and "Rapidan" neighborhoods embrace the most beautiful and highly cultivated sections of the County. The landscape, beautiful in itself, with "the long, waving line of the Blue Pyranees," the Blue Ridge, for its northward horizon, is embellished with many handsome homes. The soil is very fertile, and nature has dispensed all her bounties with a lavish hand.

Before the war there were a good many citizens in the County of ample fortunes, as fortunes were then reckoned. Colonel George Willis's family, of Wood Park, used to come to Church at Orange in a coach and four, and fine equipages were more the rule than the exception; after the war hardly anybody was left even "well-to-do," though some of the County people have now amassed handsome fortunes. In more recent years gentlemen of great means, attracted by the salubrity of the climate, the ever pleasing landscape, the historic associations and the many other features which render the country so dear to its people, have acquired homes in Orange, whose combined fortunes aggregate millions. In most cases they have adapted themselves to their new environment, and have enlarged and adorned homes that were long cherished even in their former and simpler settings. They have introduced the newest methods in farming, have brought in many varieties of improved stock, and thus have stimulated agricultural activities in their respective neighborhoods; better than all, they have shown themselves, with rarest exception, to be liberal minded and public spirited, and wholly without the offensive arrogance and display of the newly rich,

In 1906 Madison district was authorized by a vote of all the districts to contract a loan of $25,000 for the improvement of its public highways; a beginning of the "Good Roads" system so much talked about of late. The universal hope is that this loan will enure to the general welfare.

In 1907 there are seventy-four public free schools in the County, forty-five white and twenty-nine colored, with fifty white and twenty-four colored teachers; eight graded and one high school; school population, 2,004 white, 2,451 colored; Edmund W. Scott, Somerset, county superintendent.

The net revenue paid into the State treasury in 1905, by the County was $16,125.60.

In 1906 the County levy was at the rate of twenty cents on the $100 for general purposes, and ten cents for schools. The magisterial district levy was from five to ten cents for schools, and twenty to thirty for roads. The receipts of the County for the year were: on real estate, $3,609.47; personal estate, $1,878.96; railroads, $1,034.29; telegraph and telephone lines, $33.65; other sources, $968.00; for schools, $3,279.85. Total $10,804.22.

Total district receipts for schools, $2,933.08; for roads, $7,638.74; all purposes, $10,571.82. Grand total, county and districts, $21,376.04.

There were ninety Confederate pensioners, to whom the State paid $2,110.00.

Population in 1860, whites, 4,407; free negroes, 188; slaves, 6,111; total, 10,700. In 1900, whites, 7,052; negroes, 5,519; total 12,571.

Mr. Woolfolk, the County clerk, furnishes the following figures as to the denomination of the white people's churches: Episcopal, 4; Presbyterian, 3; Methodist, 7; Baptist, 13; Disciples, 4; Roman Catholic, 1; Free, 1.

COMPARATIVE STATEMENT OF TAXABLE VALUES OF ORANGE COUNTY FOR THE YEARS 1860, 1866, AND 1906.

PERSONAL PROPERTY.	1860.		1866.		1906.	
	No.	Assessed Value.	No.	Assessed Value.	No.	Assessed Value.
Horses	2,991	$150,328 00	2,102	$119,040 00	3,881	$166,364 00
Cattle	6,599	90,631 00	4,981	80,003 00	8,263	102,482 00
Sheep	13,457	30,947 00	4,443	12,073 00	3,519	11,450 00
Hogs	10,704	19,838 00	7,187	24,128 00	6,102	14,224 00
Watches	386	11,876 00	344	12,313 00	762	6,107 00
Clocks	539	1,619 00	429	1,510 00	917	1,696 00
Pianos	74	10,400 00	75	9,655 00	361	15,010 00
Plate and silverware		8,111 00		6,001 00		2,300 00
Household and kitchen furniture		88,870 00		67,800 00		91,954 00
Bonds		355,191 00		36,549 00		222,974 00
Farming implements and other personal property		7,040 00		12,120 00		94,343 00
Total		$774,851 00		$381,192 00		$728,904 00

	No. Acres.	Assessed Value.	No. Acres.	Assessed Value.	No. Acres.	Assessed Value.
Real Estate	214,937	$2,279,222 00	214,158	$2,313,384 00	212,366	$1,209,567 00
Buildings		402,988 00		384,991 00		474,699 00
Town lots and buildings		84,075 00		93,246 00		239,984 00
Total		$2,767,285 00		$2,791,621 00		$1,924,250 00

CHAPTER XXI.

Miscellaneous.

The Marquis's Road is one of the historic highways of the County, extending, originally, from old Raccoon Ford to Brock's Bridge, from the Rapidan to the North Anna.

The general impression that La Fayette constructed this road is an error. Retreating rapidly before Cornwallis, from the neighborhood of Richmond, the latter boasting that "the boy can not escape me," he crossed the Rapidan, probably at Germanna, subsequently moving up to Raccoon Ford, where he awaited reinforcements under Wayne. On Wayne's arrival, he began his march towards Albemarle old Courthouse, (Scottsville,) where, and also at the Point of Fork (Columbia, in Fluvanna County,), supplies were stored which Tarleton was menacing. The following extract from Burk's History of Virginia, 1816, Vol. IV., 507, indicates the portion of the road opened by La Fayette.

From a respectable officer of militia, at that time, the subjoined description of La Fayette's route has, been obtained;

"I joined the Marquis's army the night they left Richmond, and encamped with the army at Winston's plantation, I believe in the County of Hanover. * * * The route from thence was to Culpeper

County, near the Rackoon Ford, where we halted until Wayne's brigade joined. The route from thence was in bye-roads in the direction of the Rivanna River, through Orange, and the upper end of Louisa and Fluvanna Counties. Near Boswell's Tavern the army halted one night, and the next day was marched along a new road to Mechunk Creek, which road goes by the name of 'the Marquis's road' to this day."

Citations from the order books in the chapter, "Orange in the Revolution," prove that Brock's Bridge was regarded as an important structure, and that a guard was constantly kept there long before this march occurred; which seems to be conclusive, that the Marquis did not construct the road in Orange.

This road passes La Fayette, a station on the Narrow Gauge Railroad, named in honor of the Marquis. Here he encamped for a night, his headquarters being under a large tree on one of the boughs of which he hung his sword. This tree was blown down during a storm some years since, and later converted into cross ties. The Rev. Dr. Howison of Fredericksburg, author of a history of Virginia, and also a history of the United States, purchased some of these ties and had walking sticks made out of them.

The items following, not susceptible of grouping under a general chapter, are inserted as interesting miscellanies.

At the rating of prices for ordinaries in 1742, "whiskey" is mentioned for the first time, though something denominated "rye brandy," which was probably the same thing, had been rated some years earlier.

In that year also, there was a difference of two pence

in the quart for "Virginia ale;" six pence "below the ridge," four pence "over the ridge." The probable explanation is that this commodity was manufactured in the Valley, and hence could be sold more cheaply there. Philip Long, who came from Alsace, was a notable citizen of that part of the county now called Page, and his lineal descendants are still prominent citizens of the latter county. Philip Long's name, often spelled Lung, appears frequently in the early records of Orange. His descendants say he was an accomplished brewer, and it is not unlikely that he was the first manufacturer of this Virginia ale.

The names of Augustine and of Lawrence Washington appear as parties plaintiff, during the forties. George Wythe, presumed to be the "Signer," and afterwards the famous "Chancellor," appeared as counsel for John Willis in 1747. Edmund Pendleton, also, appeared as counsel, but the name of his client is not given.

Chief Justice Marshall was counsel for Johnny Scott, and his receipt for his fee is still extant.

In 1751 Henry Downs, who had been a King's justice and a member of the House of Burgesses, is mentioned in a court order as a "Runaway." He was expelled from the House of Burgesses of Virginia for "stealing a white sheep," in Maryland, before he settled in this State.

It is stated in a note to the "Dinwiddie Papers," Vol. II., 167, that John Spotswood was County Lieutenant of Orange in 1755. This is an error, as John Baylor was then County Lieutenant, a fact which these same papers establish.

A county seal is first mentioned in 1774. The seal is an excellent cut of a lion, encircled by the name of the County. The cost of it was fifty shillings.

Smallpox created more consternation in the old days than now. In 1778, "on the petition of Joseph Spencer leave is granted him to inoculate for the smallpox at his house in this County;" and in April, 1797, "on the motion of John Stevens for leave to inoculate for the smallpox it is granted him, it appearing to the Court that he and his family are in immediate danger of taking the said disorder; such inoculation to take place on or before the 10th of May, next ensuing, and not less than half a mile from the road."

There was another alarm in 1848, when the Court directed Dr. David Pannill to take charge of the malady, erect a hospital or hospitals, employ servants, agents, etc., and clothed him with plenary power to do what he thought best, promising $500 to pay expenses.

In 1823 the Court contracted with Reuben Lindsay to make an accurate chart of the County at a cost of $1,500. This was probably for the well-known "Nine-Sheet" map of the State, far and away the best that has ever been made, the copper plates of which are yet in the State Library.

A committee of prominent citizens was appointed by the Court in 1833 to see the "free people of color," and ascertain what number of them would avail themselves of a recent Act of Assembly providing for their transportation to Liberia. Nothing appears to have come of it, though James Madison, Jr., was an ardent member of the American Colonization Society and remembered it in his will. The mill at Toddsberth once belonged to this society.

Madison died in 1836, and his widow qualified as executrix, giving bond for $100,000. Judge Philip P. Barbour's will was proved in 1841, and the administration bond was for $120,000.

In Dr. Taylor's "Virginia Baptist Ministers" it is stated that Mr. Craig was imprisoned in both Culpeper and Orange. The Orange records do not sustain this statement.

Although interest in improved stock, and especially in horses, was never so great in former times as now, yet the importation of thoroughbreds for breeding purposes began long ago, Governor Barbour having imported several notable horses from England early in the last century. Mr. R. B. Haxall, who resided at Rocklands, gave quite an impulse to the breeding of fine stock of every kind, and also to high-grade farming. He introduced what is commonly known as "Japan clover" in the County, and kept in stud for many years several of Major Doswell's highest bred horses, and others of equally famous pedigree.

Some years prior to the war a joint stock company built a training stable at Lee's Crossing, near Madison Run, known locally as the "Horse College," and placed an imported English trainer, named Carrier, in charge. Here was kept "Voltaire," probably the most famous "sire" ever known in Orange, and this history would be incomplete if Voltaire's name were omitted.

A general officer bought him during the war, and he

was killed in battle; but to be able to trace lineage back to him still establishes a horse genealogy throughout the County.

For many years, so many that the oldest inhabitant forty years since knew not how long, an old dismounted cannon lay on the old turnpike, a few hundred yards below the County seat. It was the custom of the boys, at Christmas and on the Fourth of July, to load it up and fire a round of salutes, and about 1860 it was overcharged and burst. Most probably it was left there during the Revolution, but this is only surmise. Another, just like it, was at the Orange Springs. This was not only burst by a discharge, but the man who touched it off was killed by the explosion—a valuable servant of Mr. Coleman who owned the Springs.

The name "Old Trap," the modern Locust Grove, appears as early as 1785. The old names for Poplar Run were "Baylor's Run" and "Beaver Dam Run," and the name for the bend in the Rapidan near where this run enters it was the "Punch Bowl," and it is so printed on the maps. Prior to 1800 there was an incorporation of a prospective village under the name of "Mechanic." It was somewhere between Barboursville and the Greene line, but it never became a village; a "boom" perhaps in the chrysalis state. Verdiersville, in the grim humor of the soldiers, was known as "My Dearsville," during the war.

In the one hundred and seventy three years that the County has existed, there have been practically but five King's and Commonwealth's Attorneys; Zachary Lewis, John Walker, Gilbert H. Hamilton, Lewis B.

Williams, and John G. Williams; an average term of nearly thirty-five years.

These are some of the old land grants in the County: In 1772, to Bartholomew Yates, Latane, Robinson, Clouder, Harry Beverley, William Stanard, and Edwin Thacker, 24,000 acres on south side of Rapidan, one quarter of a mile below mouth of Laurel Run. To Harry Beverley, 6,720 acres, north side head of Pamunkey. To James Taylor, 8,500 acres, both sides Little Mountains, south of Rapidan, adjoining John Baylor's land. To same, 5,000 acres. To William Beverley, 2,500 acres. In 1723, to Ambrose Madison and Thomas Chew, 4,675 acres. In 1726, to William Todd, two grants of 4,673 acres each, on both sides of Little Mountains, south of Rapidan; grant mentions Taliaferro's Run, and calls for a corner with Ambrose Madison. To Francis Conway, 576 acres. To John Taliaferro, the younger, 935 acres, South West Mountain. To Benjamin Porter a tract adjoining Colonel Spotswood, J. and Lawrence Taliaferro; and in 1727, to John Downer, a tract adjoining James Taylor.

In nearly all of the earlier grants, the Southwest Mountains are called the Little Mountains and Blue Run is invariably spelled "Blew."

Many more items, curious rather than historical, might be added, but these are deemed to be quite enough.

CHAPTER XXII

Biographical Sketches.

BARBOUR, B. JOHNSON. Youngest son of Governor Barbour, born 1821, died 1894; had great literary accomplishments and extraordinary gifts as a speaker and conversationalist; was long Rector of the University of Virginia, and Visitor to the Miller School, and, like his father, was greatly devoted to the cause of general education. He was elected to Congress immediately after the war, but was not permitted to take his seat under the proscriptive régime that then prevailed. He represented the County in the Legislature and was one of the earliest supervisors; was the orator on the occasion of the dedication of the Clay statue in the Capitol Square in Richmond; and such was his eloquence and scholarship that he was always in demand as an orator.

BARBOUR, JAMES. Born June 10, 1775; died June 7, 1842; served in the legislature from 1796 to 1812, and during his service in that body was the strenuous advocate of Madison's famous "Resolutions of 1798–99;" was elected Governor, January, 1812, and served as such with patriotic zeal, practically until the end of the War of 1812; was elected United States Senator in 1815, where he served until 1825, then becoming Secretary of War until 1828, when he was sent as Minister Plenipotentiary to England, whence he was recalled in 1829 on the election of Andrew Jackson to the Presidency; was chairman of the National Convention which nominated William Henry Harrison in 1839, and for years the president of the Orange Humane Society, in which position he fostered education in every possible way. Though others claim that distinction, there is little reason to doubt that he was the originator of the Literary Fund of Virginia which has been the mainstay of popular education from its creation until now, greatly supplemented, certainly, since the public free schools have become a State institution. His wish was that public service only should constitute his epitaph. He is said to have been a majestically handsome man, of great eloquence, and a wonder as a conversationalist. He lies buried at Barboursville in an unmarked grave. It would be a just tribute to his memory, and a tardy recognition of his great services to the cause of education in his County and State, for the school authorities to erect some memorial over it.

BARBOUR, PHILIP PENDLETON. Born May 25, 1783; son of Thomas and brother of the Governor. After he had been admitted to the Bar and had practiced law, he studied at William and Mary College; member of the Legislature 1812–14; of the United States House of Representatives 1814–21, and Speaker of the House; resigned in 1825, and was appointed United States District Judge; again Member of Congress from

1827 to 1830; was President of the Virginia Convention of 1829, succeeding James Monroe, and was a notable member of that eminent body of statesmen; appointed associate justice United States Supreme Court by Andrew Jackson in 1836; and was found dead in his bed in Washington, February 25, 1841. He is buried in the Congressional Cemetery.

BARBOUR, THOMAS. Born 1735, about one and one-fourth miles east of Barboursville village, and one-fourth mile south of the turnpike; died at Barboursville, 1825; appointed King's Justice in 1768, and was continuously in the commission until his death. More minutes of court are signed by him than by any other justice. He long represented the County in the House of Burgesses, was a member of the Conventions of 1774 and 1775, and County Lieutenant, with the rank of colonel, in the later years of the Revolutionary War. He was the father of Governor James and Judge P. P. Barbour.

BARTLEY, JAMES AVIS. Author of two volumes of poems which have now become quite rare; was educated at the University of Virginia shortly before the war, and died not long afterwards.

CHEW, COLBY and LARKIN. Sons of Col. Thomas Chew, sheriff of Orange in 1745, and Martha Taylor, great-aunt of President Madison and great-grand-aunt of President Taylor. Colby served in the expedition against the Shawnees in 1756, was ensign in Washington's regiment in 1757, was wounded near Fort Duquesne in 1758, and falling into the river, was drowned.

Larkin, his brother, had his arm shattered by a ball in battle in 1754, and was a lieutenant in the Second Virginia Regiment. (VI. Va. Hist. Mag. 345.)

CLEVELAND, BENJAMIN. Born and raised in Orange, some six or eight miles from the mouth of Blue Run. He married Mary Graves, also of Orange; was a gallant and efficient officer during the Revolution and one of the commanders at Kings Mountain. (VII. Va. Hist. Mag, 4, 128.)

Wheeler (History of North Carolina) says he was born in Prince William County, Virginia, but the fact of his birth in Orange seems incontestible. Cleveland's Run, about a mile northeast of Barboursville, was doubtless named for him or his family, as his parents and grandparents lived near it. They were Baptists, and doubtless members of old Blue Run church.

CRENSHAW, CAPTAIN WILLIAM G. Born July 7th, 1824, in Richmond, Virginia, and married, May 25th, 1847, Miss Fanny Elizabeth Graves of Orange County. He died May 24th, 1897, at Hawfield, about six months after his wife, and both are buried in Hollywood, at Richmond.

He was a man of remarkable ability. When the Civil War broke out, though not yet thirty-seven years of age, he was the senior member of Crenshaw & Co., whose business extended over a large part of the world, much of their foreign trade being done in vessels built and owned by himself and his brothers.

As soon as Virginia seceded he determined to discontinue business and go into the army, and raised and equipped at his own expense a battery of artillery, known as "Crenshaw's Battery," which became famous. After the ardous campaign of 1863, having participated in every battle from Mechanicsville to Sharpsburg, he was detailed by the Confederate Government to go to Europe as its commercial agent. This position he held to the end of the war, accomplishing large results in obtaining ordnance, clothing, provisions, and other supplies for the government; in building steamers to get these supplies into the blockaded ports; and also building several notable privateers for the Confederacy. He remained in England until the summer of 1868, and was thereafter for many years engaged in business in New York.

Throughout his life he was an ardent, enthusiastic and successful farmer and stock breeder, spending all the time he could spare at Hawfield, where he resided permanently the last ten years of his life.

FRANKLIN, JESSE. Born in Orange, March 4, 1760; died 184–; was adjutant to his uncle, Colonel Cleveland, at the battle of Kings Mountain; member of North Carolina Legislature, and Member of Congress; was United States Senator for two terms and president *pro tempore* of the Senate, 1805, and Governor of North Carolina in 1820. (VII. Va. Hist. Mag., 128.)

FRY, PHILIP S. Born —; died July 1859; was long the honored and beloved clerk of the county and circuit courts. He was deputy clerk in 1821, a justice in 1834, and was elected clerk in February, 1844, by the full bench of justices, receiving eighteen votes, to one for John M. Chapman.

GORDON, JAMES. Planter, of Germanna, known as "James of Orange," to distinguish him from his first cousin, the second James of Lancaster, was born in Richmond County in 1759. He was the eldest son of John Gordon, who emigrated to Virginia from County Down, Ireland, where his progenitors had been seated at "Sheepbridge," near Newry, since 1692. John Gordon married in Middlesex County, in 1756, Lucy Churchill, daughter of Col. Armistead Churchill and his wife, Hannah Harrison, of Wakefield. James Gordon represented Richmond County in the House of Delegates in 1781; and Orange, as the colleague of James Madison, in the Virginia Convention of 1788 which ratified the Federal Constitution. He died at Germanna, December 14, 1799, and was buried there in the Gordon family burying ground.

GORDON, WILLIAM FITZHUGH. Planter, lawyer, and statesman; was the second son of James Gordon, of Orange. He was born at Germanna, January 13th, 1787, and after reading law in Fredericksburg practised for several years at Orange. He was a member of the House of Delegates from Albemarle, serving for a long period as chairman of the judiciary committee, and was instrumental in the enactment of legislation establishing the University of Virginia. For several sessions he was a member of the United States House of Representatives, and was the originator of the Independent or Sub-Treasury system. He was a member of the famous Convention of 1829–30, and formulated the scheme of representation, which was finally accepted by the Convention, known as as the "Mixed Basis."

He was brigadier, and later, major-general of the State Militia. He married, first, December 12, 1809, Mary Robinson Rootes, "Federal Hill," Fredericksburg, who died without issue; second, January 21, 1813, Elizabeth Lindsay, daughter of Col. Reuben Lindsay, of Albemarle County, and of this marriage were born twelve children.

General Gordon was a democrat of the States' Rights school, and a fervid and eloquent speaker. He died at his residence, "Edgeworth," in Albemarle, five miles west of Gordonsville, August 28, 1858.

KEMPER, JAMES LAWSON. Born in Madison County in 1824; descended from one of the German colonists at Germanna of 1714; educated at Washington College, Virginia; commissioned Captain by President Polk in 1847, and joined General Taylor's army in Mexico, but too late for active service; served ten years in the House of Delegates and was Speaker of the House; Colonel of the Seventh Virginia Infantry in 1861; Brigadier-general in 1862; desperately wounded and left on the field in Pickett's charge at Gettysburg. Major-general, March, 1864, in command of reserve forces around Richmond; elected Governor of Virginia in 1873, defeating Judge Robert W. Hughes, and, after the end of his term, residing at "Walnut Hills," near Orange Courthouse, until his death in 189–, practicing law in Orange and adjacent counties. He was a gentleman of fine presence, something didactic in manner, and a speaker of excellent ability. He was the first Governor from among our own people after the war.

LELAND, JOHN. A Baptist preacher, born in Massachusetts in 1754. He came to Culpeper in 1775, and was made pastor of Mt. Poney church, where he soon had trouble, and came to Orange in 1776.

There is a local tradition of an all-day-long discussion between him and James Madison, when the latter was a candidate for the Convention of 1788, at a famous spring near Nason's. A fine oak tree, still standing near the spring, is known locally as "Madison's Oak."

As neither the "Life" of Leland, nor the sketch of him in Sprague's "American Pulpit," makes any mention of this discussion, the incident is believed to be wholly apocryphal; and had not Judge Dabney, who married a great-niece of Madison's, attempted to dignify the myth by publishing an account of it overloaded with errors in Harper's magazine, this sketch would have been wholly unnecessary.

MADISON, JAMES. Born March 16, 1752; died June 28, 1836; was the son of James Madison of Orange, and Nelly Conway, of King George, in which latter County he was born while his mother was on a visit to her parental home at Port Conway. The place of his birth has been marked in recent years by the Federal government. The encyclopædias and all of his biographers state that he was born in March, 1751, but inasmuch as there was no month of March in that year, the "New Style" of reckoning the calendar year from January 1, instead of from March 25, beginning with 1752, having cut out March from 1751, it is manifest that their date is incorrect. Even so painstaking a historian as Charles Campbell locates his birthplace as "near Port Royal, in Caroline County."

The biographies of Madison are so numerous that no sketch of him is a necessary part of this book, but extracts from a remarkable panegyric by the late eminent Virginian, Hugh Blair Grigsby, in his excessively rare "Discourse on the Virginia Convention of 1829–30," published by the Virginia Historical Society in 1853, is substituted.

> Perhaps the most important act in our history was the adoption of the Federal Constitution, an act the full purport of which was not known at the time of its adoption, if indeed it is fully known at present, and the history of that instrument and of the measures of those who carried it into execution, was wrapped up in the lives of the men who then sat in that hall. If to any one individual more than another the paternity of the Federal Constitution may be ascribed, James Madison was that man. It may be that the present form of that paper is from the pen of Gouverneur Morris, but Madison was the inspiring genius of the new system. He it was who, while a member of the old Congress, drew the celebrated appeal to the people at the close of the war to adopt some efficient mode of paying the debts of the Confederation; who procured in 1786 the passage of the resolution of this Commonwealth, inviting the meeting at Annapolis, which resulted in the assembling of the Convention at Philadelphia; who attended the sessions of that body, and as much as any one man, if not more, guided its deliberations. He, too, was the author of the letter accompanying the Constitution signed by Washington, and addressed to the President of Congress, He it was who, with Jay and Hamilton, sustained the Constitution by those essays, which under the name of the "Federalist," have attained the dignity of a text-book and a classic He it was who, more than any one man, braced the nerves of the Convention of 1788, while Henry, George Mason, Grayson and Monroe were breathing awful imprecations on the head of the new system; and who drafted the form of ratification of that instrument by the body, a form destined to be known better hereafter than it is at present.

[This was prophetic, as the people of Virginia learned to their sorrow in 1841.] He it was who repaired to New York and assisted in the deliberations of the first Congress. He it was whose influence was felt in the Federal councils, either by his personal presence as a member of the House of Representatives, Secretary of State, and President, or by his writings from 1786, when Virginia adopted his resolution inviting the meeting at Annapolis, to the moment of the assembling of the body of which he was then a member. The history of that one man was the history of his country. There, to the extreme left of the chair, as it then stood, dressed in black, with an olive-colored overcoat, now and then raising his hand to his powdered hair, and studiously attentive to every speaker, he was sitting before you.

When Mr. Madison took his seat in the Convention, he was in the seventy-ninth [78th] year of his age; yet, though so far advanced in life, and entitled alike by age and position to ease, he attended the meetings of the body during a session of three months and a half, without the loss, so far as I now remember, of more than a single day. That he was entitled to the chair, and that the universal expectation was that he should receive that honor, none knew better, or could have acknowledged more gracefully, than Mr. Monroe. He spoke but two or three times, when he ascertained that his voice was too low to be heard; possibly, too, he might have been averse from mingling too closely in the bitter strifes of a new generation. When he rose to speak, the members, old as well as young, left their seats, and, like children about to receive the words of wisdom from the lips of an aged father, gathered around him. That he still retained the vigor of his intellect, and that unapproachable grace in his written compositions, his two short speeches, written out by himself, and his letters to Mr. Cabell, Mr. Everett, and Mr. Ingersoll, on the tariff, bank and nullification controversies, show clearly enough.

As a speaker, Mr. Madison was more distinguished by intellectual than physical qualities. * * * Several of the finest passages in his speeches in the Virginia Federal Convention are lost to posterity from the weakness of his voice.

*   *   *   *   *   *

When it is remembered that the favorable vote of Virginia was alone wanting to save the Constitution, eight States having already ratified it, and that North Carolina and Rhode Island afterwards refused to adopt it, it is more than probable that its rejection by the largest State in the Union, as Virginia then was, would have settled its fate, and the Federal Constitution would have sunk to rise no more.

If the adoption of that system were wise and proper; if it has shed boundless blessings on our own people, and lifted its cheering light to the eyes of the oppressed of every clime; and if such a glorious result can be traced to the action of any one State and any one man, Virginia is the State, and JAMES MADISON is the man, to whom honor is due.

Whatever he did was thoroughly done. The memorial on religious freedom, prepared by him in 1780, in which he demonstrated, perhaps for the first time, the cardinal doctrines which ought to control governments in matters of religion, was mainly efficient in putting an end to that unnatural connection between church and state to which some of the ablest statesmen of the Revolution, guided by early prejudices, too closely adhered, and will henceforth appear, as well from the beauty of its style as from the weight of its philosophy, among the most conspicuous religious landmarks in the history of our race. He was the delight of the social circle, and seemed incapable of imputing a harsh motive to any human being.

His wife, whose elegance diffused a lustre over his public career, and who was the light of his rural home, accompanied him to Richmond, and, as you left their presence, it was impossible not to rejoice that Providence had allotted to such a couple an old age so lovely.

"If I were called upon," said Chief Justice Marshall, "to say who of all the men I have known had the greatest power to convince, I should, perhaps, say Mr. Madison, while Mr. Henry had, without doubt, the greatest power to persuade." (Henry's Life of Patrick Henry, Vol. II. 376.)

He was the author, in part, of Washington's "Farewell Address," and of the splendid inscription on Houdon's statue of Washington, which has no superior of its kind:

"The General Assembly of the Commonwealth of Virginia have caused this statue to be erected as a monument of affection and gratitude to George Washington, who, uniting to the endowments of the hero the virtues of the patriot, and exerting both in establishing the liberties of his country, has rendered his name dear to his fellow citizens, and given to the world an immortal example of true glory."

MILLS, ROGER Q. Born in the Pamunkey neighborhood, March 30, 1832, and went first to Kentucky, and then to Texas; served through the war; Member of Congress, 1872–92; chairman of House Committee of Ways and Means and author of the "Mills Tariff Bill," which became a political issue and was defeated; United States Senator, 1892–99.

MORTON, JACKSON. Brother of Jeremiah, was United States Senator from Florida, 1849–1855; member of the Confederate Provisional Congress.

MORTON, JEREMIAH. Born 179–; died 187–; elected to Thirty-first Congress as a democrat over John S. Pendleton, of Culpeper, and served from 1849 to 1851; represented the County in the Convention of 1861; was a secessionist. His home was "Morton Hall," near Raccoon Ford.

NEWMAN, JAMES, of "Hilton." Born 1806, died 1886; was a noted agriculturist and a gentleman of large information; was president of the State Agricultural Society, and did much to promote the improvement of stock in Orange, introducing and long maintaining the notable Cotswold breed of sheep. His most important work was a series of sketches, published in a local paper, relating to the early history and traditions of the County, at the request of Dr. George W. Bagby. Most diligent search has been made for these sketches, but no trace of them has been found.

SPOTSWOOD, or SPOTTISWOOD, ALEXANDER, called by Colonel Byrd the "Tubal Cain of Virginia," the real protagonist of Orange County, was born at Tangier, in 1676. He entered the army, was wounded at the famous battle of Blenheim, and rose to the rank of lieutenant-colonel. In 1710 he was appointed Lieutenant-Governor of Virginia under the nominal Governor, the Earl of Orkney, and showed himself a conspicuously energetic administrator, laboring for the good of the Colony in divers ways. He rebuilt the college of William and Mary, of which college he makes mention in his will, recorded in Orange, and took measures for the conversion and instruction of Indian children. He was the first to cross the Appalachian Mountains, the Blue Ridge, in 1716, and he dealt resolutely with the enemies of the Colony, capturing and putting to death the famous pirate, Edward Leach, known as "Blackbeard," and holding the Indians in check on the frontiers. He was superseded as Governor in 1722 but continued to live in Virginia, and founded Germanna, where he carried on extensive iron works and cultivated vines. In 1730 he was appointed deputy postmaster for the Colonies. Commissioned major-general in 1740, he was engaged in collecting forces for the expedition against Carthagena, dying at Annapolis in that year. Several of his lineal descendants still reside in Orange, and some of the products of his iron works are still preserved in the family, notably some fire backs with the family crest on them. There are portraits of the Governor, of Lady Spotswood, and of her brother, General Elliott, in the State Library, imputed to Reynolds and Sir Peter Lely, but this claim has not been substantiated. See "Dictionary of National Biography" (English) and the chapter *infra*, "Progress to the Mines."

SUMPTER, GEN. THOMAS. Born in Orange, 1734; died in South Carolina 1832; was probably at Braddock's Defeat, and was known, like Gen. Francis Marion, as the Swamp Fox of the Revolution; was Member of Congress and United States Senator from South Carolina; Minister of United States to Brazil. (VII. Va. Hist. Mag. 243.)

TALIAFERRO, JAMES PIPER. Son of Dr. Edmund P. Taliaferro, was born at Orange Courthouse, September 30, 1847; was educated at William Dinwiddie's classical school at Greenwood, in Albemarle, leaving school in 1864 to enter the Confederate army, where he served to the end of the war. Soon after the war he engaged in business at Jacksonville, Florida, and was elected to the United States Senate from that State in 1899, and re-elected in 1905, as a democrat.

TAYLOR, JOHN, "of Caroline." Nearly all the Encyclopædias allege that this eminent statesman was born in Orange. This statement is, after most careful inquiry, ascertained to be an error. The Taylor family of Orange was a distinguished one from the beginning, which probably gave rise to the statement. A letter from his grand daughter, Mrs. Hubard, confirmed by his great-grandson, Mr. Henry T. Wickham, seems to establish the fact that his birthplace was "Mill Farm" in Caroline; so Orange will have to resign this distinction.

TAYLOR, ZACHARY. Twelfth President of the United States; was born in Orange, November 24, 1784; son of Lieut.-Col. Richard Taylor, an officer of the Revolution and one of the first settlers of Louisville, Kentucky, where Zachary was taken in early childhood and grew up to his twenty-fourth year, working on a plantation, with only the simplest rudiments of an education. His elder brother, a lieutenant in the regular army, died in 1808, and he was appointed to the vacancy; promoted captain in 1810. In 1812, with fifty men, two-thirds of them ill with fever, he defended Fort Harrison, on the Wabash, against a large force of Indians, led by the famous Tecumseh. Promoted major for gallantry, he was employed during the war of 1812 in fighting the Indian allies of Great Britain. In 1832 he served as colonel in the Black Hawk War, and in 1836 he gained an important victory over the Seminole Indians at Okechobee, and was made a brigadier and commander of the United States forces in Florida. In 1846 he defeated General Arista at Palo Alto, with a force of 2,300 against 6,000, and, a few days after this battle, drove him across the Rio Grande at Resaca de la Palma; September 9, being now a major-general, with 6,625 men he attacked Monterey, defended by 10,000 regular troops, and after ten days' siege, and three of hard fighting, the city capitulated. General Scott, advancing on the city of Mexico, withdrew a portion of Taylor's troops, leaving him only 500 regulars and 5,000 voluntiers to meet an army of 21,000 commanded by President Santa Anna. Taking a strong position at Buena Vista he fought a desperate battle and won a signal victory. This victory, against enormous odds, created great enthusiasm and General Taylor, popularly called "Old Rough and Ready," was nominated for the presidency over Henry Clay, Daniel Webster and Gen. Winfield Scott, and was triumphantly elected over Lewis Cass, the Democratic nominee, and Martin Van Buren and Charles Francis Adams, Free Soil candidates.

Worn down by the unaccustomed turmoil of politics, the good-natured old soldier did not long enjoy his honors. He died of bilious colic within less than five months after his inauguration. (Chambers's Encyclopædia)

In 1848 the General Assembly of Virginia voted him a sword with the inscription: "Presented by Virginia, to her distinguished son, Major-Gen. Zachary Taylor, for his gallantry and conduct at Palo Alto, Resaca de la Palma, Monterey and Buena Vista." He was also presented, as the chief hero of the Mexican war, with the splendid silk sash on which the body of General Braddock was borne from the field of his defeat; which, stained with Braddock's blood, is still the property of his granddaughter, who was lately living in Winchester, Virginia.

WADDEL, JAMES. Born 1739, either in Ireland or else on the Atlantic while his parents were en route to this Country. It is not known that he ever resided in Orange, but his name is indelibly associated with that of the County by reason of William Wirt's celebrated apotheosis of him in the "British Spy", which follows. He built the church, known as "Belle Grove" of which there is a picture and description herein. His home was "Hopewell," the residence of the late Mr. Clay Baker, on the Charlottesville road, near the corner of Orange with Louisa and Albemarle. He was buried at Hopewell, and an imposing but unpretentious marble shaft marked his grave. The "Waddell Memorial" Church near Rapidan was named for him, and permission was got from his heirs to remove his remains thither. Mr. Baker superintended the exhumation. He told me that after having dug very deep in the grave, no sign, even of a coffin, could be found. After the closest scrutiny something that looked like the dust of decayed wood was discovered, and then a few nails, nearly consumed by rust, and a button. A spadeful of dust was taken out of the grave along with the nails and button, and reverently deposited in the churchyard. He had been buried about seventy-five years. Mr. Madison's remains, after twenty years' interment, showed little sign of dissolution. (See the paragraph about his tomb.)

The following extract from Mr. Wirt's writings has long been considered a masterpiece of rhetoric, and it ought to be read, marked, learned and inwardly digested by every citizen of Orange; and though it has been often published in sundry books, no history of the County ought to omit it.

It was one Sunday, as I travelled through the county of Orange, that my eye was caught by a cluster of horses tied near a ruinous old wooden house in the forest, not far from the roadside. Having frequently seen such objects before, in travelling through these States, I had no difficulty in understanding that this was a place of religious worship.

Devotion alone should have stopped me, to join in the duties of the congregation; but I must confess that curiosity to hear the preacher of such a wilderness was not the least of my motives. On entering, I was struck with his preternatural appearance. He was a tall and very spare, old man. His head, which was covered with a white cap, his shrivelled hands, and his voice, were all shaking under the influence of a palsy; and a few moments ascertained to me that he was perfectly blind.

The first emotions which touched my breast were those of mingled pity and veneration. But ah! sacred God! how soon were all my feelings changed! The lips of Plato were never more worthy of a prognostic swarm of bees than were the lips of this holy man! It was a day of the administration of the sacrament; and his subject, of course, was the passion of our Savior. I had heard the subject handled a thousand times. I had thought it exhausted long ago. Little did I suppose that in the wild woods of America I was to meet with a man whose eloquence would give to this topic a new and more sublime pathos than I had ever before witnessed.

As he descended from the pulpit to distribute the mystic symbols, there was a peculiar, a more than human solemnity in his air and manner, which made my blood run cold, and my whole frame shiver.

He then drew a picture of the sufferings of our Savior; his trial before Pilate; his ascent up Calvary; his crucifixion, and his death. I knew the whole history; but never, until then, had I heard the circumstances so selected, so arranged, so colored! It was all new, and I seemed to have heard it for the first time in my life. His enunciation was so deliberate that his voice trembled on every syllable, and every heart in the assembly trembled in unison. His peculiar phrases had that force of description, that the original scene appeared to be, at that moment, acting before our eyes. We saw the very faces of the Jews: the staring, frightful distortions of malice and rage. We saw the buffet; my soul kindled with a flame of indignation, and my hands were involuntarily and convulsively clenched. But when he came to touch on the patience, the forgiving meekness of our Savior; when he drew to the life, his blessed eyes streaming in tears to heaven; his voice breathing to God a soft and gentle prayer of pardon on his enemies, "Father, forgive them, for they know not what they do"—the voice of the preacher, which had all along faltered grew fainter and fainter, until his utterance being entirely obstructed by the force of his feelings, he raised his handkerchief to his eyes and burst into a loud and irrepressible flood of grief. The effect is inconceivable. The whole house resounded with the mingled groans, and sobs, and shrieks of the congregation.

It was some time before the tumult had subsided so far as to permit him to proceed. Indeed, judging by the usual, but fallacious standard of my own weakness, I began to be very uneasy for the situation of the preacher. For I could not conceive how he would be able to let his audience down from the height to which he had wound them, without impairing the solemnity and dignity of his subject, or perhaps shocking them by the abruptness of the fall. But no; the descent was as beautiful and sublime as the elevation had been rapid and enthusiastic.

The first sentence with which he broke the awful silence was a quotation from Rousseau, "Socrates died like a philosopher, but Jesus Christ like a God!"

I despair of giving you any idea of the effect produced by this short sentence, unless you could perfectly conceive the whole manner of the man, as well as the peculiar crisis in the discourse. Never before did I completely understand what Demosthenes meant by laying such stress on delivery. You are to bring before you the venerable figure of the preacher; his blindness constantly recalling to your recollection old Homer, Ossian, and Milton, and associating with his performance the melancholy grandeur of their geniuses. You are to imagine that you hear his slow, solemn, well-accented enunciation, and his voice of affecting, trembling melody; you are to remember the pitch of passion and enthusiasm to which the congregation were raised; and then the few minutes of portentous, deathlike silence which reigned throughout the house; the preacher removing his white handkerchief from his aged face, (even yet wet from the recent torrent of his tears), and slowly stretching forth the palsied hand which holds it, begins the sentence, "Socrates died like a philosopher;" then pausing, raising his other hand, pressing them both clasped together with warmth and energy to his breast, lifting his "sightless balls" to heaven, and pouring his whole soul into his tremulous voice "but Jesus Christ like a God!" If he had been indeed and in truth an angel of light, the effect could scarcely have been more divine.

WILLIAMS, LEWIS BURWELL. The youngest son of William Clayton and Alice Burwell Williams, was born in the city of Fredericksburg, Virginia, on January 27, 1802. His parents moved to the city of Richmond when he was six years old.

Mr. Williams attended school in Richmond and at the age of fourteen entered Princeton; he studied law and began the practice of his profession in Culpeper. In 1825 he removed to Orange, where he practiced his profession until his death in 1880. He represented his county in the Virginia Legislature in 1833. In 1831 he was appointed attorney for the Commonwealth, which office he filled by successive appointment and election until his death in 1880, a period of forty-nine years.

Opposed to secession, he was a candidate for the Convention of 1861, and was defeated by Jeremiah Morton, a pronounced secessionist.

After his State seceded he became an ardent supporter of the Southern cause, his four sons entering the army.

He was a devoted member of St. Thomas Episcopal Church. For many years he was its senior warden and frequently represented his church in the Diocesan councils.

WOOLFOLK, JOHN. Born —; died 1858; represented the county in the Reform Convention of 1850–51, and was greatly beloved by all his contemporaries, as the following resolutions, entered of record in the order book of January, 1858, on the motion of Lewis B. Williams, abundantly prove:

That in his death, the people of the County of Orange, have lost a friend, who in the varied relations of representative, lawyer, and citizen was able, honest and faithful, brave, generous and disinterested, with talents of the highest order, and an integrity of purpose and action, which was never subjected to suspicion, he has left behind him the memory which will be cherished by his countymen, of eminent ability, enlightened patriotism and incorruptible virtue.

CHAPTER XXIII.

Historic and Other Homes.*

BARBOURSVILLE. Near the village of the same name. The illustration is the least pleasing of all, failing as it does, to reproduce the fine proportions of the handsome old mansion. The water color from which it was taken was painted in the long ago, and before the fine box hedges, which have constituted a striking feature of the lawn for many years, had attained any size.

The house was built by Governor Barbour, about 1822. The exterior was not unlike Frascati; the interior was far and away the handsomest in the County and probably in Virginia. From a massive pediment portico the entrance was into a spacious hexagonal salon, having a dome ceiling and an elevation to the roof; adjoining this was the drawing-room, an octagon of like stately proportions and more ornately finished, which opened on another handsome portico. On the same floor was the state dining-room with nearly as lofty a pitch.

This house, which Mr. Jefferson helped to plan, and which was the abode of refined hospitality during the Governor's time and that of his son, Mr. Johnson Barbour, was burned down Christmas Day, 1884. The walls and the columns of the porticos are yet stand-

*The illustrations are, with very few exceptions, after photographs taken by Mr. Cook, of Richmond, in 1907.

ing, mantled now by a luxuriant growth of English ivy and other vines.

Remembering many happy days there, I pay the ruins the passing tribute of a tear.

BURLINGTON. Burlington, proper, is a handsome home built by James Barbour Newman, about a mile east of Barboursville. The illustration represents a house in the back yard, historic because John Randolph of Roanoke lived there while at school in Orange.

In colonial times the place was owned by the Burnleys, who are buried there, one of whom was a Burgess, and an officer in the Revolution.

CAMERON LODGE. Near Gordonsville; the seat of Col. Alexander Cameron, on the crest of the Southwest Mountains. Here is a tower where all the charms of an extended and beautiful landscape may be seen. To the right, the Blue Run and Rapidan valleys, with a background of the Blue Ridge; in front the undulations of the Southwest range; on the left, the town at the base of the mountain and far as the eye can reach the wooded plain extending to Richmond and beyond.

The illustration shows the house; it does not show the handsome approach to it, nor the ornamental hedges which line the way, nor the fields where Jerseys and Southdowns are cropping the green herbage.

CAMPBELLTON. Near Barboursville; was the home of Captain William Campbell, of the Revolution and subsequently a major in the United States army. Here Gen. Winfield Scott was a frequent visitor.

CHURCH OF THE BLIND PREACHER. This stood near Gordonsville, and was known as "Belle Grove" church. The illustration is from an old print in Howe's History of Virginia, published in 1845. Mr. Hunt, in his Life of Madison, narrates that the latter's mother was a frequent attendant there and a great admirer of Mr. Waddel. (See sketch of Waddel, and the chapter on Colonial churches.)

CLIFTON. Near Madison Run; said to be the oldest framed house erected in the County, though "Bloomsbury" contests that distinction, and it is probable that Governor Spotswood's residence at Germanna antedated both. There is nothing notable about the house but its age, and the fact that it was built of pit-sawn lumber, with hand-wrought nails, and that some of the window-panes, said to be the first in the County, almost prove their antiquity by their greenish tint and uneven surfaces. It was built about 1729 by John Scott, whose son was a member of the Committee of Safety, captain of a company of Minute Men in the Revolution and whose record is sufficiently disclosed in the general narrative.

The oldest tombstone standing in the County is in the graveyard here—Jane, wife of John Scott "born 1699, died 1731."

FRASCATI. Near Somerset; was built some time before 1830 for Judge Philip Pendleton Barbour, the workmen being of those who had been engaged in building the University. Until long since the war, there was a "serpentine" brick wall around the garden, identical with those now at the University and at Barboursville house. Since Judge Barbour's death there have been many owners. Col James Magruder owned it for some years prior to the war, and there the gallant Magruder boys, whose history is sketched in another chapter, were reared. There have been some alterations in the interior, and dormer windows have been set in the roof in recent years. The house, as the illustration shows, is very imposing in appearance. It is constructed of such excellent material and with such fine workmanship that it is said the floors will hold water like a bucket.

It is now owned by Mr. A. D. Irving, Jr., a near relative of Washington Irving one of the most famous of American authors whose writings are cherished in every land where the English language is known.

HAWFIELD. About midway between Orange and Raccoon Ford. It was bought in 1847 by Mr. Jonathan Graves for his only daughter, Fanny Elizabeth, the wife of William G. Crenshaw, and since that time has continued in the Crenshaw family. The original house, built before 1790, was enlarged in 1881 to its present handsome proportions by Captain William G. Crenshaw, with the least possible change of the old mansion. It adorns a beautiful estate of more than three thousand acres, which constitute an object lesson in intelligent farming. A portion of the tract once belonged to the Conway family, of Revolutionary memory.

LOCUST LAWN. On the Marquis's road in Pamunkey; was a tavern during the Revolution. Now owned by Mrs. Margaret Pannill, widow of Dr. David Pannill, and her sisters.

MADISON'S TOMB. This monolith was erected about 1856 by private subscriptions, mostly by admirers of Madison outside the County The date of birth is an error, as explained in the sketch of Madison, *infra*. The smaller tombstone in the illustration is that of Mrs. Madison, and curious to say, Maude Wilder Goodwin, in her "Life of Dolly Madison," complains of a wrong inscription on her tombstone also. She died July 12, not July 8, as the inscription reads, and she signed her name "Dolly," not "Dolley," to her will, which was dated on the 9th. She was buried first in Washington, D. C., in 1849, and her remains were not brought to Montpelier until about 1858. As her own nephew, not Madison's, erected the tombstone, the error must be imputed to him.

The inscription on Madison's tomb is:

MADISON
BORN MARCH 16, 1751.
DIED JUNE 28, 1836.

I have been told that when the stone was erected it was necessary to take up his remains in order to get a safe foundation. The coffin was opened, and, except that one cheek was a little sunken, his appearance was the same as in life; but disintegration began immediately, and the coffin had to be closed. He had been buried about twenty years.

MAYHURST. Near Orange Courthouse; the residence of Mr. William G. Crenshaw, Jr. This farm was embraced in the Baylor grant, and the mountain near by is still known as Baylor's Mountain. The first residence was that of Mr. Howard who married a Miss Taylor, of Orange. Col. John Willis bought the farm about 1859, and built the handsome residence shown in the illustration. Gen. A. P. Hill's headquarters were in the yard in the winter of 1863-64, and one of his daughters was christened in the house.

Mr. Crenshaw has furnished his countymen with an object lesson in road building by constructing a model macadamized road from Mayhurst to the county road.

MONTEBELLO. Near Gordonsville. Here was born Zachary Taylor, though a tablet has been erected to mark another spot as his birthplace, "Hare Forest," about midway between Orange and Rapidan and near the Southern Railway; a mere thicket now. It can not be gainsaid that there is some ground for the claim for the latter place, but the evidence, collected many years ago, seems conclusive as to Montebello. I was so informed nearly forty years since by Mr. Benjamin Johnson, whose ancestor owned the place and lived there when Taylor was born; by Mr. Johnson Barbour, whose parents, were kinspeople and contemporaries of the Taylors, and who had often so informed him; by Col. John Willis, who said he had often heard "Uncle Howard," another contemporary, who married a near kinswoman of the General, say so; and finally Major Erasmus Taylor, who died recently, said to me that there was no doubt as to the fact. The deed books do not show that Col. Richard Taylor, his father, ever lived at "Hare Forest," and his name does not appear in the census of 1782, though he may then have been with the army. The evidence, all of which is traditional, seems overwhelmingly in favor of Montebello. The house has been much modernized. Mr. Benjamin Johnson, the proprietor, gave me this tradition certainly as long ago as 1875. The Taylor family, he said, started to remove to the West in road wagons. The Johnsons were their kinspeople, and their house was the goal of the first day's journey. One of the company became very ill during the night and this illness occasioned a delay of six weeks. During that time Zachary Taylor was born. That is the "tale as told to me," nearly forty years ago.

MONTPELIER. About four miles from Orange Courthouse. The first dwelling house stood not far from the cemetery, in the direction of the present mansion. Nearly five thousand acres were patented by Ambrose Madison and Thomas Chew in 1723.

Col. John Willis, a great-nephew of James, Jr., was told by him' that the nucleus of the present structure was built when he was a mere lad, capable of carrying in his hands some of the lighter furniture from the old house to the new: which would fix the date at about 1760. It was a plain rectangular structure, with a hall running through the centre having two rooms on each side. Its identity has been so merged in the grander house that it can not now be differentiated from it. The chief enlargements were made in 1809, after designs by William Thornton, architect of the Capitol at Washington; and Latrobe lent his assistance in further improvements, which included the addition of the wings. "The result was simplicity, but symmetry of proportion and faultlessness of taste." The grounds are as handsome as the buildings, and the prospect very commanding—an unbroken stretch of ninety miles of the Blue Ridge, which constitutes an almost perfect crescent. Arlington is the only place in Virginia that can compare with it in the beauty of its immediate surroundings.

The present owner, William du Pont, Esq., has added another story to the wings, but the addition was so artistically made that it is impossible to tell where the old work ended and the new began.

The beautifully terraced garden laid out in the form of a horseshoe was Madison's own plan. Subsequent owners sadly neglected it, to say the least. This Mr. du Pont has not only restored, but has also converted into a flower garden exclusively, which for richness and variety of color and foliage is not surpassed, if equalled, by the horticultural gardens at Washington; and he has also decorated it with pleasing statuary. The ice house, which is surmounted by an ornamental colonnade, was dug in 1809, and is believed to have been the first attempt at keeping ice made in the Piedmont section.

MOUNT SHARON. Near Nason's; the residence of Mr. C. C. Taliaferro, to whom the plantation has descended in a direct line from a Crown grant. The illustration shows the stately and graceful proportions of the mansion. There is a greater variety of prospect from it than from any other point known to me in the County. There are perhaps more picturesque views of the Blue Ridge at other points, but for majestic and rugged outlines there are none to compare with the outlook from Mt. Sharon; and the varied landscape of Clarke's Mountain adds another charm to the prospect.

OAKHILL. Two miles northeast of Gordonsville, was the home of Francis Cowherd, of Point Pleasant fame, who was a captain in the Revolution. Present owners, his descendants of the same name.

PLEASANT VIEW. In the lower part of the County, not far from the Spotsylvania line. It was built for Mr. Jonathan Graves about 1830, and is now owned by Mr. W. G. Crenshaw, Jr., his grandson. It was long the residence of Capt. R. Perrin Graves.

ROCKLANDS. Near Gordonsville. The first residence on this plantation was built for Mr. Edmund Henshaw, near the middle of the last century. He soon sold to Mr. Richard Barton Haxall, who gave it the name "Rocklands," and greatly enlarged and improved both the house and farm. The present owner, Mr. Thomas Atkinson, had about completed many improvements of the mansion when it was burned down in 1905.

The present mansion is one of the handsomest houses in the County, and, as the illustration shows, is in the colonial style of architecture. The "outlook" from the front portico is pleasing, near and far; beautiful greensward, ornamental hedges, an artificial water view and undulating fields constitute the nearer landscape; to the left the highest reaches of the Southwest Mountains in full view, and in front the inspiring horizon of the Blue Ridge—a moral and a mental tonic to any lover of nature.

Well did Sir Walter say that if he could not see the Scotch heather once a year he would die. So feel those whose occasional view of the Blue Ridge has become almost a necessary part of their enjoyment of life.

Rose Hill. Near Rapidan; the home of Lawrence Taliaferro, first colonel of the "Culpeper" Minute Men, whose grave there is in a sad state of neglect and almost if not quite unknown. The fine mansion, built by Mr. Lewis Crenshaw and enlarged by Mr. Bresee, is not the simple story-and-a-half colonial structure with dormer windows and without a porch in which Col. Taliaferro lived; but the place is historic, as having been his home.

Soldier's Rest. Near Raccoon Ford; not Kelly's Ford (which is on the Rappahannock,) as stated in the genealogy of the Bruce family in the Virginia Historical Magazine, Vol. II. 328. It was built prior to the Revolution by Charles Bruce, a captain in that war, and was later the residence of his son-in-law, James Williams, captain in the Revolution and major-general in the war of 1812; and then of Dr. George Morton, who married General Williams's daughter.

The place is now owned by Judge James W. Morton, of Orange. The house, as reproduced herein from a cut in the above named magazine, was burned down in 1857.

SOMERSET. Near the railroad station named for it. Probably no house in the county occupies such a commanding site as this, blending in one prospect the water view of the Rapidan and Blue Run, the latter stream running quite through the plantation, and both ranges of mountains in all their convolutions.

The mansion was erected in 1803 for Mr. Thomas Macon, who married a sister of President Madison. Shortly after its completion there came an unprecedented windstorm which lifted the massive roof and slightly changed its position. The same storm struck "Tetley", near the mouth of Blue Run, and left not a fragment of a barn nearly completed, but swept every piece of timber across the river into Madison. Such is the tradition, as narrated to me by the "elders."

This plantation, one of the finest in the County, has long been owned by the Goss family, and the beauty of the surroundings of the mansion is wholly due to the taste and energy of Mrs. Ann Goss, the mother of the present owners.

WOODLEY. Near Madison Run; the colonial part built by Ambrose Madison, brother of James, Jr., who was a captain in the Revolution. The commodious. wings were added by his daughter, Mrs. Nelly Willis, and it is now a handsome home, owned by Mr. W. W.

Sanford, who has greatly improved this naturally fine estate.

WOOD PARK. Near Rapidan. The first building was erected by Mr. Baldwin Taliaferro, son of Col. Lawrence Taliaferro of "Rose Hill," of which estate this was a part.

This is a composite building of many architects, but to Col. George Willis, the grandfather of the present owner, Dr. Murat Willis, belongs the credit of its embellishment, the drawing-room especially being of very fine porportions, and notably handsome. It is a delightful and charming old country home in one of the most fertile and beautiful sections of the County.

OTHER HISTORIC HOUSES. Beginning at the upper end of the County, and not including houses specially mentioned, the following ought to be named; and doubtless others also, about which the writer is not informed. He does not, purposely, omit any that are entitled to mention, but names all that he has knowledge of, either personally or on the information of friends. He was promised information that has not been furnished, and the book must come to an end without further waiting:

The residence of the Barbours at Gordonsville was a famous hostelry and relay house in the stagecoach days, being on the main line to Philadelphia and New York, the former Federal capitals, where the statesmen of that day stopped, going and coming. Some apocryphal stories of John Randolph, Henry Clay and others are still told in connection with this house. From its porch LaFayette addressed an enthusiastic assemblage of citizens from Orange and the surrounding counties, who came to bid him welcome on his triumphal tour in 1826. It belonged to the Gordon family, and, indeed, with the two houses nearly opposite, constituted Gordonsville for many years.

Bloomingdale, near Somerset, was the home of Thomas Barbour, whose house stood several hundred yards northeast of the present mansion. "Tetley," nearby, was the home of a Capt. William Smith, but was so named by Mr. Charles J. Stovin, who owned it for many years. Bloomfield is the old Newman home, now owned by Judge Newman, and greatly improved. Hazelhurst is the handsome home of Mr. Frank Nalle, near Somerset. The old Winslow house, near Poplar Run, burned down six years ago, was a genuine type of the colonial period. Walnut Hills, near Madison Mills, was the Orange home of Governor Kemper. Greenfield, now owned by Mr. Richard Booten, was one of the old Taylor homes; the present house was built for Mr. Thomas Scott; some of the oldest tombstones in the county are there. Yatton, so named by Mr. Lewis B. Williams who lived and died there, was formerly "Midland," another of the Taylor homes, as is also Meadow Farm, which is still in the Taylor family. Selma was the home of the "beloved physician," Dr. Peyton Grymes. Retreat, formerly Willis Grove, now owned by the heirs of Dr. Charles Conway, was the home of "Gentleman Billy" Willis, and a merry place in days of yore. Chestnut Hill, now owned by Mr. W. G. Crenshaw Jr., was the home of Dr. Uriel Terrell, famous in old days as a favorite hostlery of Henry

Clay and other statesmen; the old Taliaferro home, near Rapidan, a Crown grant in 1726, now owned by Mr. John Taliaferro; Morton Hall, Lessland, former homes, of Hon. Jeremiah Morton; Vaucluse, of the ancient and aristocratic Grymes family; another Somerset, near Germanna—these are all old, and in a sense, historic homes.

CHAPTER XXIV.

Being a Personal Retrospect.

After more than five years of research and endeavor, this book is submitted to the indulgence of the public in the confidence of work conscientiously done; yet not without misgivings.

In writing history the personal note may never be sounded, and this chapter, not intended to be a part of the "history," is added, that some things not consonant with dignified narrative may be said.

Imprimis, it would be ungrateful not to acknowledge with genuine cordiality the encouragement received at the hands of gentlemen not native to the County and therefore not intimately interested in its history, yet without whose public spirit and liberality it is more than doubtful whether this book could ever have attained the dignity of type. He is an indifferent philosopher who is ashamed of being poor; he is none at all who does not recognize the limitations of that condition. So, let it be said at once and once for all, that its publication is due to the liberality of those who have contributed to the illustrations; which, in the writer's judgment, constitute a very valuable historical feature.

Some of these have been contributed by personal friends who have, perhaps, denied themselves in order to perpetuate cherished historical memories; others by gentlemen who know the writer casually, or not at all, and who have taken on trust his promise to write a history of the County.

He can not forbear to thank both friends and strangers, nor to hope that they will think he has at least tried to keep faith.

And now comes the inevitable and irrepressible *Ego*, being a summary of the reasons that induced me to attempt this book. I knew many of the old people of the County—Dr. Uriel Terrell, who died aged 94; Mr. James Barbour Newman, a kinsman, who died aged 97; Mr. Johnson Barbour, my kinsman and my Mæcenas, whose mind was stored and saturated by his father and mother with the history and traditions of Orange.

Only suppose that I had collected from them, and had preserved in this book, *all* they could and gladly would have told me! What a book it might then have been, which now it can never be!

History ought to be a picture of the time it attempts to describe, a picture held up in substance, as it were, before the eyes of the reader; as Hamlet says it should "hold the mirror up to nature, and show the very age and body of the time his form and pressure."

I came to the age of immature observation shortly after the Reform Constitution of 1850–51 was ratified.

I remember well the old County Courts before they became field-days for fakirs and horse-traders. Though now but little past three-score, I remember people who wore queues and short breeches—not many but a few. I remember when the usual apparel of country gentlemen consisted of blue broadcloth "swallow tail" coats with brass buttons, nankeen waistcoats and trousers; and becoming apparel it was. "Vests" and "pantaloons" are modern, and the cut of the trousers is wholly different from what it used to be. The Rev. Dr. Philip Slaughter told me that he wore the first pair of trousers without the old fashioned "flap" ever seen in Orange; and Mr. Johnson Barbour told a story of an old family servant who asked his mother, "please not to let the sempstress make any of them blackguard breeches for him."

I remember Henry A. Wise and the great Know Nothing Campaign of 1856.

On the court green at Orange, I have seen Mr. Johnson Barbour, Mr. James Barbour Newman, Mr. Woodson Campbell, Mr. Benjamin Johnson, Mr. John S. Cowherd, Mr. Robert Taylor, Dr. James L. Jones, Col. James Magruder, Mr. Barton Haxall, Mr. E. Goss, Mr. Charles Stovin, Dr. James Madison, Col. John Willis, Major John H. Lee, Messrs. James, Reuben, Thomas and John F. Newman, Col. Garrett Scott, and his brothers John and Charles, Mr. David Meade Bernard, Mr. Thomas Scott, Dr. Peyton Grymes, Mr. Lewis B. Williams, Mr. Richard Henry Willis, Col. George Willis, Mr. Philip B. Jones, Mr. Joseph Hiden, Mr. Ferdinand Jones, Hon. Jeremiah Morton, Mr. George Morton, of Pamunkey, Col. John Woolfolk, Mr. Travers Daniel, Mr. William C. Moore, Col. Elhanan Row, Mr. Lancelot Burrus, Dr. David Pannill, Mr. George Pannill, Mr. Philip S. Fry, Dr. Thomas Slaughter, Dr. Horace Taliaferro, Dr. Edmund Taliaferro, Captain Dick Chapman,

Mr. John F. Taliaferro, Capt. William G. Crenshaw, Col. B. F. Nalle, and many more of the like kind. They were mostly past the military age in 1861, but though not "the men behind the guns," they were behind the men who were behind them, from 1861 to 1865. Court days *were* court days in those times; a real educational influence.

I remember the John Brown raid in 1859, and the wild excitement it occasioned, and the apprehension of an insurrection, and the nightly patrols.

I saw Gen. Robert E. Lee, when he passed through Orange, April 22, 1861, and I ran off the next day and joined the Montpelier Guard, then at Harpers Ferry.

In a log schoolhouse, on the plantation now owned by Mr. Thomas Atkinson, I went to school with all the Magruder boys but the eldest, and I was in the same company with the Burrus boys, whose tragic history is narrated in the chapter on the war period.

I served throughout the world famous "Valley Campaign," and while a member of the V. M. I. Cadet Battalion, fired a farewell shot over the grave of Stonewall Jackson, the prelude to Appomattox.

The night before the battle of Winchester, September 19, 1864, one of the most fateful battles of the war to Orange soldiers, I slept in a tent with Wilson S. Newman, then commanding the Montpelier Guard, Lieut. Martin S. Stringfellow, and Phillip H. Scott, my brother. Our reveille the next morning was the bursting of shells in the camp. Newman was left for dead on the field. Stringfellow was twice wounded during the day, and

Scott, after the surging lines had twice passed over him, was taken off the field on the shoulders of John Noland, a comrade, the son of his father's tenant, as Early's army began its final retreat. He was carried to a hospital where Dr. Grymes barely had time to amputate his leg near the hip; leaving him on the operating table to avoid capture himself.

Nearly all day long, Christmas, 1864, then a member of the Black Horse Cavalry, I was on the enemy's flank while they were at Mr. Barton Haxall's stables, now Mr. Atkinson's, their object being the destruction of the railroad at Gordonsville. Our people at Gordonsville fired up an old disabled locomotive which they would take very quietly down the road to Trevillian, and then reversing it would rush back, the whistle screeching as if the world were about to come to its end. The raiders thought that infantry reinforcements were being rushed from Richmond, and after a slight skirmish with the home guards, stationed on the crest of the mountain near Col. Alexander Cameron's gate, retired across the Rapidan.

I got home from Appomattox April 12, 1865, and my brother, one legged and on crutches, met me at the door, and, for a few anguished moments, refused to believe that Lee had surrendered. I saw and endured Reconstruction, including the Black Crook Convention of 1867–68, negroes, aliens and all.

I remember this old Commonwealth in her tranquil happiness, before the war; in her majesty during the war; in her defeat and humiliation afterwards. Thank God! I see her in 1907, peaceful, prosperous, hopeful, recalling with proud emotions the memory of Pocahontas and John Smith at Jamestown, and celebrating with joyous acclaim the three-hundredth anniversary of her settlement.

APPENDICES.

APPENDICES

APPENDIX A.

(No Appendix is Indexed.)

Importations.

A list of persons who imported themselves, or were imported as servants by others, and who afterwards proved their importation in order to obtain their "head rights" to land in the colony. The date shows the year in which proof of importation was made and recorded. This list was kindly furnished by Mr. Philip H. Fry, for many years clerk of the County and Circuit Courts.

1736. ABEL, JOSEPH
1740. ANDERSON, JOHN
1740. ANDERSON, GEORGE
1741. APPLEBY, ROBERT
1753. ANDERSON, HANNAH
1735. AMBURGER, CONRADE
1735. BOURKS, MARTIN
1736. BUTLER, JOHN
1735. BICKERS, ROBERT
1740. BRACKENRIDGE, ALEX.
1740. BELL, JAMES
1740. BROWN, WM.
1739. BLAIR, ALEX.
1739. BUTLER, JOHN
1740. BLACK, THOS.
1740. BRAWFORD, SAML.
1740. BASKINS, W. M.
1740. BAMBRIDGE, ANN
1741. BRYNE, HENRY
1741. BRADSTREET, FRANCIS
1741. BANKS, WM.
1741. BROWN, THOS.

1746. BUNTINE, WM.
1747. BROWN, JOHN
1741. BRADY, WM.
1749. BIRD, SAML.
1755. BAILEY, ROBT.
1755. BEASLEY, BENNET
1756. BRAMHAM, FRANCIS
1756. BROWN, ANNE
1735. BURK, THOMAS
1735. BOURKS, JOHN
1735. BRYAN, DENNIS
1735. BILLINGSLEY, FRANCIS
1736. CAVENAUGH, PHILEMON
1740. CROCKET, ROBT.
1740. CAMPBELL, PATRICK
1740. CALDWELL, JAMES
1740. CARDHAUT, JOHN
1740. COLE, WM.
1740. CALDWELL, GEO.
1740. CRAWFORD, PATRICK
1739. CATHEY, JAMES
1739. CAMBLE, JOHN

1739. Cross, Richd.
1740. Carr, John
1740. Christopher, Nicholas
1740. Carr, Jacob
1741. Crawford, John
1745. Crawford, Wm.
1745. Chambers, Elizabeth
1750. Collins, Ann
1751. Carney, Timothy
1752. Carney, Easter
1751. Chaney, Joseph
1744. Coleman, John
1744. Coleman, Margaret
1750. Cook, Geo.
1749. Collins, James
1751. Cole, Edward
1747. Cook, James
1743. Cross, Ellioner
1743. Cooper, Wm.
1738. Cummins, Alex.
1755. Cocke, Chas.
1756. Cussins, Richd.
1746. Campbell, Dougald
1735. Cotton, Joseph
1735. Drake, Samuel
1735. Dealmore, John
1740. Daley, James
1740. Davidson, John
1740. Davis, James
1740. Danning, Elizabeth
1743. Dungan, Margaret
1752. Dooling, Thomas
1749. Durham, John
1751. Drake, Hannah
1755. Davis, John
1746. Duff, Arthur
1746. Duff, Mary
1746. Duling, John
1735. Dyer, James
1735. Dunn, Arthur
1740. Edmiston, David
1745. Edgear, Wm.

1750. Eve, Joseph
1741. Fink, Mark
1745. Frazier, Alex.
1746. Forester, John
1753. Finley, Patrick
1750. Fields, Mary
1740. Fox, James
1749. Ferrell, Honner
1740. Frazer, Robt.
1755. Flanders, Wm.
1746. Frazer, John
1735. Floyd, John
1735. Finlason, John
1735. Floyd, Charles
1736. Grant, John
1740. Gilasby, James
1740. Gelasby, Jesse
1740. Gay, Saml.
1739. Givins, Saml.
1739. Grady, Mary
1740. Gilasby, Margaret
1740. Gilasby, Matthew
1745. Gaines, James
1746. Gibson, Abel
1746. Gibbins, Wm.
1752. Grant, Alex.
1750. Gully, Thos.
1742. Gibson, Margaret
1743. Green, Edward
1747. Gahagan, Thomas
1757. Golder, John
1746. Grace, Ann
1735. Green, Robt.
1735. Gray, Wm.
1740. Hays, John
1740. Hays, Patrick
1740. Hook, Robt.
1740. Harrell, John
1740. Hall, Edward
1740. Hutcheson, Wm.
1740. Henderson, Thomas
1740. Hutcheson, Geo.

APPENDIX—IMPORTATIONS. 227

1740. HOPKINS, ELIZABETH
1741. HANEY, JOHN
1741. HART, HENRY
1741. HARRIS, JOSEPH
1746. HOWSIN, THOMAS
1749. HUSSEE, EASTER
1750. HERRENDON, JOHN
1743. HOPKINS, JAMES
1755. HENDERSON, ALEX.
1756. HANEY, DARBY
1735. HOME, GEORGE
1735. HUMPHREYS, GEORGE
1750. IRWIN, ANTHONY
1738. JONES, THOMAS
1740. JOHNSTON, WM.
1740. JOHNSTON, WM.
1746. JENNINGS, EDWARD
1751. JOHNSON, PETER
1750. JOHNSON, PETER
1750. JERMAN, THOMAS
1741. JOHNSON, ARCHIBALD
1746. JONES, THOS.
1735. JOHNSON, WM.
1735. LAMBOTTE, EDWARD
1740. KING, ROBT.
1740. KING, WM.
1740. KINDLE, THOMAS
1741. KINES, JOHN
1746. KELLY, WM.
1752. KELLY, MICHAEL
1737. KENDALL, HENRY
1755. KENDALL, HENRY
1735. KELLY, WM.
1735. KERCHLER, MATHIAS
1740. LOGAN, DAVID
1740. LONG, WM.
1739. LEDGERWOOD, WM.
1739. LEPPER, JAMES
1739. LAMPART, EDWD.
1740. LEONARD, PATRICK
1746. LYNCH, JOHN
1750. LYON, MICHAEL

1749. LAMB, RICHD.
1746. LERNAY, THOMAS
1735. LATHAM, JOHN
1740. MCONNAL, ANDREW
1740. MCDOWELL, ROBT.
1740. MCCOWIN, FRANCIS
1740. MCCLURE, JAMES
1740. MAXWELL, JOHN
1739. MCCADDAN, PATRICK
1739. MCKAY, AGNES
1739. MCKAY, WM.
1739. MCKAY, JAMES
1739. MORPHET, JOHN
1739. MCDOWELL, ROBT.
1739. MITCHELL, DAVID
1739. MCDOWELL, JOHN
1739. MCMURRIN, MARGARET
1739. MCDOWELL, EPHRAHIM
1739. MCALEGANT, JAMES
1739. MCCANLESS, WM.
1739. MCCANLESS, ELIZABETH
1739. MULHALAN, JOHN
1739. MCLEAN, WM.
1739. MCLEAN, MARGARET
1739. MCDANIEL, WM.
1741. MCPHERSON, ROBT.
1741. MCPHERSON, MARGARET
1741. MCPHERSON, ALIX.
1741. MCPHERSON, SUSANNA
1741. MILLS, JAMES
1745. MCNIEL, PATRICK
1745. MCKENSEY, JOHN
1746. MCCULLOCK, ANN
1748. MORRIS, WM.
1752. MCFIELD, JOHN
1748. MASON, MARGARET
1750. MULHOLLAND, OWEN
1744. MORGAN, JOHN
1744. MORGAN, MARY
1735. MCCAN, JOHN
1735. MCMURRIN, DAVID
1750. MCGINNIS, JAMES

1749. Monroe, Wm.	1738. Ramsey, Robt.
1749. Morris, Jane	1741. Rosse, Alex.
1751. Mannen, Andrew	1755. Rakestraw
1755. Morgan, Thomas	1755. Rouse, Francis
1755. Mitchell, John	1756. Rigby, John
1756. McDonald, John	1756. Ryan, John
1735. McCulley, James	1735. Rouse, Edward
1735. McCoy, John	1735. Robinson, Charles
1735. McKenny, John	1747. Ross, David
1735. Mitchell, Wm.	1735. Read, John
1735. Nicholls, Wm.	1735. Roberson, James
1741. Newport, John	1740. Stevenson, Thos.
1740. Ofrail, Morris	1740. Scott, Samuel
1752. Ogg, John and wife	1740. Scott, Robert
1750. Onaton, Mary	1740. Steavenson, John
1735. Parsons, Richard	1740. Smith, John
1736. Parks, John	1740. Skillim, Wm.
1740. Patterson, Robert	1739. Steavenson, David
1740. Poage, Robert	1739. Smith, Wm.
1740. Pickens, John	1739. Smith, Elizabeth
1746. Page, John	1739. Stanton, Elizabeth
1746. Piner, Thomas	1740. Smith, Wm.
1746. Price, Edward	1753. Sheets, John
1746. Parsons, George	1750. Sims, Joanna
1752. Parsons, Mary	1750. Smith, Owen
1752. Poor, Michael	1744. Scales, Richard
1754. Phillips, Joseph	1749. Sims, Wm.
1755. Peacock, Thos.	1749. Scott, James
1741. Parks, Thomas	1742. Sevier, Valentine
1741. Phillips, Edmund	1743. Sears, Joseph
1735. Pitcher, Thomas	1738. Stewart, George
1735. Phillips, Joseph	1750. Sleet, James
1736. Ryly, Mical	1750. Smith, Thomas
1741. Ralson, Robert	1755. Smith, Elizabeth
1740. Ray, Joseph	1756. Stokes, Elizabeth
1740. Reads, Joseph	1741. Sutherland, Wm.
1736. Rood, James	1735. Small, Oliver
1740. Reed, Agnes	1735. Stackall, John
1740. Robinson, James	1735. Stanton, Matthew
1746. Raney, John	1740. Trimble, John
1751. Riche, Patrick	1740. Thompson, Wm.
1737. Ryan, Solomon	1740. Thomason, Moses

APPENDIX—IMPORTATIONS.

1740. THOMASON, ALEX.
1739. TURK, ROBT.
1752. TERRET, NATHANIEL
1751. TIBBIT, MATTHEW
1743. THOMPSON, ROBT.
1743. THURSTON, SARAH
1749. TERRILL, HONNER
1738. THOMSON, JOHN
1755. THOMPSON, ALEXANDER
1735. THOMAS, JOSHUA
1747. UPTON, HENRY
1747. UPTON, MARY
1735. VAUGHT, JOHN PAUL
1735. VAUGHT, MARY CATHERINE, wife,
1735. VAUGHT, JOHN ANDREW, JOHN CASPER, sons
1735. VAUGHT, CATHERINE, MARGARET and MARY CATHERINE, daughters
1735. VINYARD, JOHN
1735. WARTHAN, JAMES
1735. WALKER, JOHN

1735. WEAVER, PETER
1740. WILSON, DAVID
1739. WILSON, RICHARD
1740. WALSH, PATRICK
1740. WILLIAMS, THOMAS
1740. WILSON, JOHN
1740. WALKER, JOHN
1745. WALSH, JOSEPH
1746. WOOD, THOS.
1746. WALLACE, HUMPHREY
1750. WILLSON, MARY
1738. WHITE, JOHN
1751. WHITMAN, WM.
1744. WHEELER, JOHN
1756. WALKER, THOMAS
1735. WOOD, JAMES
1735. WELCH, JOHN
1735. WARFIN, RICHARD
1735. WALKER, JOHN
1735. WILHITE, MICHAEL
1735. WILHITE, JOHN
1740. YOUNG, ROBT.

These importations were almost without exception from "Great Britain," though in many cases Ireland is given specifically as the place whence imported.

The following list is wholly of "German Protestants," the importations having been all proved, and the parties naturalized, January 28, 1743.

BLANKENBACKER, ZACHARIAH
BOMGARDNER, FREDERICK
CHRISTLE, DUVALD
FLESHMAN, PETER
GARR, ANDREW, JOHN ADAM, and LAWRENCE.

GRAYS, LAWRENCE
THOMAS, JOHN
UHLD, CHRISTOPHER
VALLICK, MARTIN
ZIMMERMAN (alias Carpenter), JOHN

And on February 24, 1743:

BROYLE, COURTNEY
MANSPILE, JACOB
MILLER, JACOB

WILHITE, JOHN
WILHITE, TOBIAS

APPENDIX B.

Census, 1782.

The Number of People Taken in Orange County by Catlett Conway, Gent., October, 1782.

	White	Black		White	Black
WILLIAM HUNTER...	7	39	JOHN COOKE........	5	2
MARY MOTHERSHEAD.	9	9	DANIEL JAMES......	8	2
CHARLES BRUCE.....	11	30	HENRY COOKE......	9	
WILLIAM MORTON...	3	30	RICHARD LONG......	3	
JESSE F. CLARK.....	8		JOHN LONG.........	3	
WILLIAM STROTHER.	3	4	ROBERT BRADLEY...	7	
WILLIAM THORNTON.	7		ZACHY. COGHILL.....	9	
RICHARD REYNOLDS..	7	6	WILLIAM LANCASTER	7	4
THOMAS MORRISON...	6	4	JOHN MILLER.......	7	4
JAMES BARKER......	5		JAMES TINDER......	10	
JOHN HANSFORD.....	10		ANN SCOTT.........	4	
JOSEPH HILMAN.....	8		REUBEN SCOTT......	3	
WILLIAM PANNELL..	11	19	THOMAS SUMMERS...	6	
JOHN CHAMBERS.....	11	2	THOMAS WELCH.....	6	6
JONATHAN GIBSON...	5	8	JAMES WETHERSPOON	6	
JOHN BRAMHAM.....	5		ADAM GOODLET......	21	6
BENJAMIN MARTIN...	11	2	JOHN FAULCONER ...	6	6
JOHN KING.........	2	1	JOHN DAWSON......	10	
RICHARD GRAVES....	10	11	JOHN CHISHAM......	8	1
GEO. STUBBLEFIELD.	5	3	LEWIS PERRY.......	4	3
JAMES ROBB........	13	17	RICHARD ABELL.....	8	1
CATLETT CONWAY ...	7	27	CALEB ABELL.......	4	1
FRANCIS HUGHS.....	8	2			
URIEL MALLORY.....	9	17	Total........	335	267

The Number of People Taken in Orange County by Johnny Scott, Gent., October, 1782.

	White	Black		White	Black
WILLIAM ACRE......	9	1	ELIJAH CRAIG.......	9	20
JOHN ACRE.........	6	2	JONATHAN COWHERD.	8	14
FRANCIS BUSH......	6	2	JOSEPH DAVIS.......	9	7
JOHN BOSWELLS.....	13	16	ROBT. DEARING, JR..	5	2
JOHN BELL.........	8	20	JONATHAN DAVIS....	10	5
WILLIAM BUCKNER..	11	11	JOHN DEARING......	4	1

APPENDIX—CENSUS, 1782.   231

	White	Black		White	Black
Edward Dearing...	4	11	Ann Martin........	8	3
James Davis........	4	1	George Smith......	7	8
John Daniel.......	3	8	Joseph Smith.......	12	27
Elizabeth Eastin../.	6	10	John Sutton, Jr....	3	2
Nancy Eve.........	6	1	Johnny Scott......	5	20
David Gellaspy....	11	9	Joseph Silvester...	3	1
Richard Gaines....	2	5	Zachary Taylor....	5	15
David Hill.........	12		Alexander Taylor.	7	
Moses Harrod......	8		Harry Winslow....	5	5
John T. Hamilton..	7	24	William Webb.....	10	18
Thomas Jones......	12	9	John Willis	4	24
Robert Martin.....	10	9	Jonathan White...	4	
Ann Martin........	1	7	John Young........	6	17
Prettyman Merry..	7	7	John Hawkins......	8	2
Alexander Marr...	8	5	William Young....	5	12
Roger Mallory....	10	2			
John Morris.......	6		Total........	307	363

The Number of People Taken in Orange County by Benj. Grymes, Gent., October, 1782.

	White	Black		White	Black
Benjamin Grymes...	5	40	Thomas Morris.....	5	
Robert Gaines.....	9	2	Richard C. Webb...	6	3
John Spotswood....	8	39	John C. Webb......	9	
Robert C. Jacobs...	2	13	Obediah Overton...	6	
Churchill Jones...	2	23	George Overton...	7	
William Hume.....	6	4	Major Oakes.......	12	
John Woolfolk....	4		Thomas Lucas......	8	
George Wills......	4		Timothy Connor....	9	1
Joseph Rossen.....	2		John Rhodes.......	4	
Elisha Hawkens...	2		John Jennings.....	10	
Henry Martin.....	7	8	John Jones.........	1	
George Chapman...	3	1	Benjamin Bradley..	4	1
Stephen Smith.....	8	4	Joseph Richards...	5	
Nathl. Sanders....	13	2	John Robinson.....	9	1
Joseph Parish.....	9		Benjamin Head.....	3	1
George Bledsoe....	2		Daniel Singleton..	1	5
William Sullivan..	7		John Bledsoe......	2	9
James Smith........	5	1	Wm. Humphreys.:...	4	
Reuben Morris.....	1		Jesse Smith........	8	

HISTORY OF ORANGE COUNTY

	White	Black		White	Black
JAMES GORDON	1	15	AMBROSE RICHARDS	4	
WILLIAM HAWKINS	7	3	THOMAS JONES	5	
JOHN LANCASTER	7		HENRY PERRY	2	
PEIRCE PERRY	8		MOSES BLEDSOE	4	
REUBEN HAWKINS	5		EDMUND ROW	8	4
JOHN WOOD	4		THOMAS ROW	6	
JAMES WOOD	3		GEORGE WHARTON	9	
JOHN PROCTER	3	3	THOMAS FAULCONER	11	1
MOURNING PIGG	7				
ELIJAH JONES	7		Total	313	184
PHILEMON RICHARDS	5				

The Number of People Taken in Orange County by Jeremiah White, Gent., October, 1782.

	White	Black		White	Black
LEWIS BIDDLE	3	6	RICHARD RAINES	2	
EDM'D SHACKLEFORD	7	4	EDWARD LANE	6	4
EDWARD ANSILL	6	3	JOHN WHITE, JR	12	4
JAMES RIDDLE	9	10	HENRY DAVIS	7	
SAMUEL HAM	6		LITTLEBERRY LANE	8	1
THOMAS LAMB	7		JOHN SHEFLETT	3	
JAMES HAINEY	1		H. SHACKLEFORD	6	
WILLIAM COLLIER	3		THOMAS SNOW	13	
MARTIN COLLIER	5		JOHN BRYSON	7	
WILLIAM ROGERS	8		WILLIAM EASTER	9	2
ALEXANDER OGG	9	2	THOMAS HARVEY	4	
SAMUEL ESTIS	6	2	EPHRAIM SIMMONS	7	
JOHN GOODALL	9	11	MARGARET DOUGLAS	2	
WILLIAM COX	9	4	FRANCIS HERRING	4	
JOHN LAMB	11		ELIZA. BRUCE	4	2
JOHN HODGHELL	12		AGNESS SLATER	6	
RICHARD LAMB	11		JAMES HEAD	5	8
WILLIAM LAMB	7		JOSEPH HARVEY	4	
JOHN OGG	4	4	THOMAS BROOK	3	
JAMES EARLEY	10	33	JEREMIAH WHITE	12	16
DAVID WILLIAMS	6		WILLIAM BELL	2	17
JOHN HANEY	3		EPHRAIM SIMMONS	4	5
SAMUEL HAM. JR	5				
MARTIN PETTUS	3		Total	299	138
WILLIAM SMITH	10				

Appendix—Census, 1782.

The Number of People Taken in Orange County by Thomas Barbour, Gent., October, 1782.

	White	Black		White	Black
Thomas Barbour...	10	30	Thomas Herring...	4	
John Brookes's....		24	Benjamin Johnson	5	18
May Burton, Jr....	5	7	Martin Johnson...	3	7
John Burton.......	8	4	William Jones.....	7	
Ambrose Burton...	9	1	John Lucas........	10	
James Burton......	4	1	William Lucas.....	8	17
David Bruce.......	9		Nathan Mallory...	9	3
Thomas Ballard, Jr	7		Tabitha Oliver....	6	5
Robert Beadles...	4	3	Robert Pearson....	8	2
Philip Ballard....	10	3	John Payne........	10	3
Philip Ballard, Jr.	5		Joseph Patterson..	6	
Philip Ballard, the younger........	1		Richard Payne.....	6	5
Elijah Ballard....	6		John Rucker.......	10	6
James Beazley, Jr..	3	1	Peter Rucker......	4	4
William Ballard...	8		Ephraim Rucker, Jr	4	
May Burton.......	4	7	John Rogers.......	7	
Mordecai Bruce....	3		Thomas Smith......	4	3
William Collins....	5	1	Robert Sanford...	11	14
John Carters, Jr...	16	30	John Snell, Jr.....	11	10
James Connoley....	6	6	Joshua Staff......	1	7
Joseph Chapman....	7	3	Joshua Staff, Jr...	9	3
John Carrell......	5	6	Thomas Staff......	5	
Belfield Cave.....	4	5	Achilles Staff.....	1	
James Coffer......	12		Joel Hodghell.....	4	
Charles Creel.....	5	1	Richard Sebree....	2	1
Thomas Daughoney	11	13	Richard Sebree, Jr	7	
James Daughoney ..	5		William Sebree....	6	1
Jacob Ehart.......	4		Joshua Underwood	8	
Enoch Gulley......	5		James Wayt........	13	2
Lewis Garr........	3	7	John Wilhoit......	8	
Benjamin Head.....	8	11	Wm. Lucas, Jr.....	5	
Benjamin Haney...	5		Total........	401	285

The Number of People Take in Orange County by Thos. Bell, Gent., October, 1782.

	White	Black		White	Black
Richard Allen.....	6	8	Joseph Boston.....	10	5
Joseph Atkins......	5	12	Robert Cockburn..	6	

	White	Black		White	Black
Rosanna Campbell.	9	2	Abner Porter......	7	12
James Davis........	3	1	Sanford Ransdell,	4	3
John Finnell......	7	5	John Samuel.......	7	7
Simon Finnell.....	9	1	James Sleet ,......	8	6
George Grace	4	1	Samuel Thompson..	5	2
James Hawkins	2	4	Francis Taliaferro	6	33
William Ingram....	2		Thomas Bell.......	10	30
John Jackson's		18	Lawr. Taliaferro..	10	61
John Lee..........	9		Francis Dade......	2	12
William Lee.......	8				
Edward Marsh.....	2	3	Total........	141	226

The Number of People Taken in Orange County by William Moore, Gent., October, 1782.

	White	Black		White	Black
Edward Atkins.....	4		Vivian Daniel......	6	3
James Atkins.......	6		John Embre........	4	6
Benjamin Atkins ..	4		Isaac Freeman.....	7	
John Atkins.......	4		Isaac Graves	7	10
John Alcock.......	6	10	Uriah Gaston......	7	
James Atkins, Jr...	8		James Gaines.......	7	2
John Atkins.......	4		William Groom.....	10	
William Atkins....	5		John Goodrich.....	8	
Lewis Brockman...	11	5	Lindsay Harris....	5	
Ann Boling........	3		John Henderson...	4	17
John Boling.......	12		Thomas Harris	6	6
Richard Bullock ..	10		Thomas Lendrum...	5	
Thomas Bell.......	8	2	Caleb Lindsay.....	1	3
Thomas Burrus....	5	12	Reuben Lendrum ..	7	
Saml. Brockman, Jr	4	6	William Moore.....	15	53
William Brockman	3	2	Michael Manspoel..	8	4
Saml. Brockman....	3	13	Andrew Manning ..	2	13
John Brockman....	8	4	George Morton....	8	13
Mary Burrus......	9	1	John Oakes........	7	
John Bledsoe......	4		William Payne.....	8	2
Henry Chiles......	7	2	William Pollock...	9	16
Jeremiah Chandler	10		Indy Payne........	1	2
Jacob Crosthwait..	12	4	John Page.........	5	
James Cooper......	12		Thomas Payne......	10	5
Joseph Duncan.....	6	7	Aaron Quisenberry	4	14

APPENDIX—CENSUS, 1782. 235

	White	Black
A. Quisenberry, Jr.	8	5
Wm. Quisenberry	4	10
Moses Quisenberry	9	1
John Quisenberry	7	1
Jas. Quisenbeery	5	1
William Richards	9	1
Ann Smith	3	
James Smith	9	6
Steph. I. K. Smith	2	1
Zachy. Shackleford	10	2
Henry Tandy	12	17
Edward Thomas	9	3
William Thomas	4	4
John Wright	7	3
Jacob Williams	11	1
Total	438	293

The Number of People Taken in Orange County by Rowland Thomas, Gent., October, 1782.

	White	Black
Rowland Thomas	10	13
Rowland Thomas, Jr	3	3
Robt. Stubblefield	7	9
Thomas Sharpe	10	4
Robert Daniel	4	5
John Brown	4	
John Loyd	9	
Noah Knowles	8	
George Moore	6	
William Peacher	10	2
John Collins	11	
David Allen	3	1
Joseph Reynolds	4	5
Peter Mountague	7	
Benjamin Stevens	4	1
Stephen Smith	3	3
Nichs. Fisher	4	
Uriah Proctor	5	
Robert Lancaster	3	
John Proctor	8	
Richard Lahcaster	5	
Eliza Daniel	3	13
James Coleman	9	14
David Barrett	4	
Elijah Morton	5	12
Elisha Arnold	4	
William Herndon	1	
Henry Clayton	7	1
John Wright	8	2
James Grady	4	1
Stephen Hiatt	4	4
Rush Hudson	8	2
John Dear	5	1
William Reynolds	8	7
Catherine Dear	5	
Robert Chandler	5	1
William Bradley	9	
Richard Bradley	3	
Charles Dear	2	
Joseph Chandler	7	11
Sarah Heath	6	
Thomas Dear	6	1
William Wright	7	2
James Herndon	8	3
Total	256	121

The Number of People Taken in Orange County by James Madison, Gent., October, 1782.

	White	Black
John Baylor		84
Mary Bell	10	32
Henry Barnett	7	
Robert Bickers	8	

HISTORY OF ORANGE COUNTY

	White	Black		White	Black
WILLIAM BICKERS...	6		JOHN PETTY........	5	
YOWELL BOSTON....	6		BENJAMIN PORTER...	5	11
JAMES BLAIR.......	3		PHILIP ROMAN......	6	
WILLIAM BROWN....	8		THOMAS STEVENSON..	9	3
WILLIAM BEALE.....	1	19	SAMUEL SUTTON.....	6	
GARLAND BURNLEY..	7	12	WILLIAM SUTTON....	7	
THOMAS COLEMAN...	7	6	PEIRCE SANFORD....	8	
WILLIAM BROWN, JR	7		JOHN STOCKDELL....	4	16
JAMES COLEMAN.....	4		ANDREW SHEPHERD .	8	13
JOSEPH CLARK......	6		VINCENT SELF......	5	2
MARTHA CHEW......	4	9	JEREMIAH SMITH....	6	
RICHARD CARLTON...	5		HAY TALIAFERRO....	1	21
WILLIAM EDWARDS..	8		JAMES TAYLOR......	2	40
WILLIAM FINNELL ..	11		JAMES TAYLOR, JR ..	6	22
ZACHARY GASTON ...	8		ERASMUS TAYLOR ...	12	34
JOHN GRAVES	2		FRANCIS TAYLOR....	1	1
ANDREW GLASSEL...	1	5	GEORGE TAYLOR		21
ZACHY. HERNDON ...	7	18	CHARLES TAYLOR....	4	14
WILLIAM HANCOCK..	7		CHAPMAN TAYLOR...	2	5
NICHOLAS JONES.....	5	2	ROBERT TERRELL ...	4	21
JOHN LEATHERS.....	14		SARAH THOMAS......	2	12
SPENCER MOZINGO. .	6		JAMES VAUGHN	5	
WILLIAM LEAK......	5	2	BENJAMIN WINSLOW	8	6
JAMES MADISON.....	6	88	LEWIS WILLIS.......	4	6
AMBROSE MADISON...	3	30	SAMUEL WATSON....	5	
THOMAS MALLORY...	12	1	MICHAEL RICE......	9	3
JAMES NEWMAN.....	7	19	THOMAS BICKERS....	3	
WILLIAM NEWMAN .	8	1			
JOHN NOELL........	4		Total........	346	581
GEORGE NEWMAN....	6	3			

The Number of People Taken in Orange County by Zach'y. Burnley, Gent., October, 1782.

	White	Black		White	Black
BENJAMIN POWELL...	7	5	CHARLES TAYLOR....	8	
WILLIAM SULLIVAN ..	4	10	DAVID ROACH.......	4	
ROBERT MILLER.....	11	2	ELIZA. FURNIS......	3	
THOMAS FORTSON....	8	6	CHARLES WALKER...	9	6
SIMON KEE.........	9		JAMES TAYLOR (son of Charles)	5	
SOLOMON JARRELL...	5				

Appendix—Census, 1782.

	White	Black		White	Black
William Collins	6	13	James Taylor	5	
Mary Powell	7	1	William Taylor	1	
Eliza. Shiflett	5		Francis Powell	8	4
Abner Cross	8		James Duncan	8	
James Bush	4		Eliza. Furnis	7	
James Jarrell	11		Joseph Eddins	3	18
Edward Bryant	5		John Rucker	2	
John Kendall	7		Wm. Stanard's		52
Daniel Crow	7		Mace Pickett	3	3
John White	9	17	Jesse Plunkett	6	6
John Beadles	3	2	James Simpson	8	5
Jacob Coffer	5	4	Wm. Scott	3	7
Thomas Powell	9		John Page	10	3
Reuben Underwood	9		Macajah Neal	2	
George Thornton	6	19	Zach. Burnley	9	60
Thomas Walker	1	6			
Marg't Underwood	8		Total	258	249

The Number of People Taken in Orange County by And'w. Shepherd, Gent., October, 1782.

	White	Black		White	Black
Joseph Banner	3		William Herring	4	
Henry Bourn	11		George Jones	10	1
William Bourn	6		Hugh Jones	3	
James Beckham	10		James Jameson	6	2
Spencer Bramham	10		Margaret Jameson	1	4
Benjamin Bohan	5		William Jameson	3	2
Benj. Bohan, Jr.	3		John Kendall	8	
John Bohan	4		Thomas Lantor	5	
John Booth	7		Francis Moore	3	14
Thomas Bryant	6	1	Francis Moore, Jr.	12	10
William Castie	4	6	Reuben Moore	7	10
Patrick Cockran	4	5	Nath. Mothershead	2	3
John Clark	8	7	Jeremiah Minor	9	2
Alexander Dale	6		William Minor	4	
Thomas Davis	3	6	Richard Morton	7	
Anthony Foster	5	2	Lucy Moore's estate		5
Thomas Foster, Jr.	5	2	Alex. Newman	8	3
Catherine George	11	8	Abner Newman	3	1
Lawrence Gillett	4	1	Charles Porter	14	20

	White	Black		White	Black
John Price	6	5	Daniel Thornton	11	
Richard Price	4	3	John Terrell	9	
Jesse Ransdell	5		William Tweesdell	4	
John Ransdell	8		Joseph Thomas	9	7
William Ransdell	11		Alexander Waugh	2	16
Joseph Spencer	11	10	George Waugh	2	7
William Thornton	7				
John Thornton	3		Total	326	168
James Thornton	10				

Grand Total.................... { 3410 Whites.
2848 Blacks.

APPENDIX C.

Will of President Madison.

I, James Madison, of Orange County do make this my last will and testament, hereby revoking all wills by me heretofore made.

I devise to my dear wife during her life the tract of land whereon I live, as now held by me, except as herein otherwise devised; and if she shall pay the sum of nine thousand dollars within three years after my death, to be distributed as hereinafter directed, then I devise the same land to her in fee simple. If my wife shall not pay the said sum of money within the period before mentioned, then and in that case it is my will, and I hereby direct that at her death the said land shall be sold for cash, or on a credit as may be deemed most for the interest of those entitled to the proceeds thereof. If my wife shall pay the said sum of money within the time before specified as aforesaid, so as to become entitled to the fee simple in the said land, then I bequeath the said sum of money to be equally divided among all my nephews and nieces which shall at that time be living, and in case of any of them being dead, leaving issue at that time living, then such issue shall take the place of its or their deceased parent.

It is my further will, that in case my wife shall not pay the said sum of money within the time before named, and it shall therefore be necessary to sell the said land at her death as before directed, then after deducting the twentieth part of the purchase money of the said land, which deducted part I hereby empower my wife to dispose of by her will, I bequeath the residue of the purchase money and in case of her dying without having disposed of such deducted part by her will, I bequeath the whole of the purchase money of the said

land to my nephews and nieces or the issues of such of
them as may be dead, in the manner before directed in
regard to the money to be paid by her in case she shall
pay the same. I devise my grist mill with the land
attached thereto, to my wife during her life, and I
hereby direct the same to be sold at her death, and the
purchase money to be divided as before directed in
regard to the proceeds of the tract whereon I live.

I devise to my niece, Nelly C. Willis and her heirs
the lot of land lying in Orange County, purchased of
Boswell Thornton, on which is a limestone quarry, and
also my interest in a tract of land lying in Louisa County
reputed to contain two hundred acres, and not far
from the said limestone quarry. I devise my house
and lot, or lots, in the City of Washington, to my beloved
wife and her heirs. I give and bequeath my owner-
ship in the negroes and people of color held by me to
my dear wife, but it is my desire that none of them
should be sold without his or her consent, or in case of
their misbehavior, except that infant children may be
sold with their parents who consent for them to be
sold with him or her, and who consent to be sold.

I give all my personal estate of every description,
ornamental, as well as useful, except as hereinafter
otherwise given, to my dear wife, and I also give to her
all my manuscript papers, having entire confidence in
her discreet and proper use of them, but subject to the
qualification in succeeding clause. Considering the
peculiarity and magnitude of the occasion which produced the convention at Philadelphia in 1787, the
characters who composed it, the Constitution which
resulted from their deliberation, its effects during a
trial of so many years on the prosperity of the people
living under it, and the interest it has inspired among
the friends of free government, it is not an unreasonable
inference that a careful and extended report of the
proceedings and discussions of that body, which were

with closed doors, by a member who was constant in his attendance, will be particularly gratifying to the people of the United States and to all who take an interest in the progress of political science and the cause of true liberty, it is my desire that the report as made by me should be published under her authority and direction, as the publication may yield a considerable amount beyond the necessary expenses thereof; I give the net proceeds thereof to my wife, charged with the following legacies to be paid out of that fund only—first I give to Ralph Randolph Gurley, secretary of the American Colonization Society and to his executors and administrators the sum of two thousand dollars, in trust nevertheless, that he shall appropriate the same to the use and purposes of the said Society, whether the same be incorporated by law or not.

I give fifteen hundred dollars to the University of Virginia, one thousand dollars to the College at Nassau Hall at Princeton, New Jersey, and one thousand dollars to the College at Uniontown, Pennsylvania, and it is my will that if the said fund should not be sufficient to pay the whole of the three last legacies, that they abate in proportion. I further direct that there be paid out of the same fund to the guardian of the three sons of my deceased nephew, Robt. L. Madison, the sum of three thousand dollars to be applied to their education in such proportions as their guardian may think right. I also give out of the same fund to my nephew Ambrose Madison two thousand dollars to be applied by him to the education of his sons in such proportions as he may think right, and I also give out of the same fund the sum of five hundred dollars to each of the daughters of my deceased niece, Nelly Baldwin, and if the said fund shall not be sufficient to pay the whole of the legacies for the education of my great nephews as aforesaid and the said legacies to my great nieces, then they are to abate in proportion.

I give to the University of Virginia all that portion of my library of which it has not copies of the same editions, and which may be thought by the Board of Visitors not unworthy of a place in its library, reserving to my wife the right first to select such particular books and pamphlets as she shall choose, not exceeding three hundred volumes.

In consideration of the particular and valuable aids received from my brother-in-law, John C. Payne, and the affection which I bear him, I devise to him and his heirs two hundred and forty acres of land on which he lives, including the improvements on same, on which he has bestowed considerable expense, to be laid off adjoining the lands of Reuben and James Newman in a convenient form for a farm so as to include woodland, and by the said Mr. Newmans.

I bequeath to my stepson John Payne Todd the case of medals presented me by my friend George W. Erving, and the walking staff made from a timber of the frigate Constitution and presented me by Commodore Elliot, her present commander. I desire the gold mounted walking staff, bequeathed to me by my late friend Thomas Jefferson, be delivered to Thomas J. Randolph, as well in testimony of the esteem I have for him as of the knowledge I have of the place he held in the affecttions of his grand-father.

To remove every doubt of what is meant by the terms tract of land whereon I live I here declare it to comprehend all land owned by me and not herein otherwise devised away.

I appoint my dear wife to be sole executrix of this my will and desire that she may not be required to give security for the execution thereof and that my estate be not appraised.

In testimony hereof I have this fifteenth day of April, one thousand eight hundred and thirty five, signed,

sealed, published and declared this to be my last will
and testament.

                       JAMES MADISON. [Seal.]

We have signed in presence of the testator, and of each other.

ROBERT TAYLOR,
REUBEN NEWMAN, SR.
REUBEN NEWMAN, JR.
SIMS BROCKMAN.

I, James Madison, do annex this codicil to my last will as above and to be taken as part thereof. It is my will that the nine thousand dollars to be paid by my wife and distributed among my nephews and nieces may be paid into the Bank of Virginia, or into the Circuit Superior Court of Chancery for Orange, within three years after my death. I direct that the proceeds from the sale of my grist mill and the land annexed sold at the death of my wife, shall be paid to Ralph Randolph Gurley, secretary of the American Colonization Society, and to his executors and administrators in trust and for the purposes of the said society, whether the same be incorporated by law or not.

This codicil is written wholly by, and signed by my own hand this nineteenth day of April 1835.

                                      JAMES MADISON.

APPENDIX D.

"War of 1812."

So little is known of the part Orange played in the War of 1812, that it can all be easily embraced in an appendix. It certainly was not conspicuous; yet the names of such of her sons as volunteered in the war which the New England States denounced as "Madison's War," ought to be handed down to posterity.

It was a curious coincidence that one son of the County, Madison, was the chief executive of the nation, and another, James Barbour, the chief executive of the State, during this war. William Madison, brother of the president, attained the rank of major-general at that period, but it is not believed that he ever had a command in action.

From an official publication by the State in 1852, "Muster Rolls of the Virginia Militia in the war of 1812," the following roster is copied, being that of "Capt William Smith's Company of the Second Regiment, Virginia Militia, in the County of Orange, called into actual service, under the general orders of the 28th of June, 1813, from the 5th of July till the 10th of August:" one month and twelve days in all.

CAPT. WILLIAM SMITH

Lieutenants.	*Sergeants.*
HAY TALIAFERRO	JOHN T. MANN
GEORGE W. SPOTSWOOD	HENRY CONWAY
Cornet.	JAMES YAGER
PATRICK PITTY	CHAS. S. STONE

APPENDIX—WAR OF 1812. 245

Corporals.
WM. S. JINKINS
THOS. TOMBS
HENRY CLARK
GEO. H. INSKEEP

Privates.
DANL. ANDERSON
ROLAND BRADLEY
PETER BOGARDER
JOHN BRADLEY
JAMES BROWN
THOS. BROWN
WM. CLARKE
JONATHAN CATHIN
JOHN CLARKE
EDWARD COLLING
JACOB DAVIS
HORATIO DADE
JOHN DICKSON
WM. FOARD
FRANCIS FORD
WM. FANBOONER

Privates.
THOS. GETTING
MONROE HANCOCK
JOHN C. HARRIS
LINSFIELD JONES
WM. JONES
JOHN LEWIS
JOHN J. LEWIS
CONWAY MOWER (or Mawr),
MOSES MCKENNY
BRAXTON OSBORN (or Oborn)
ABNER PITTS
ISAAC RIGHT
THOS. STUBBLEFIELD
LAWRENCE SANDFORD
WM. TALKEN
LAWRENCE TALIAFERRO
HAY TALIAFERRO
WM. TAYLOR
JAMES WALLER
JAMES WEBB
JOHN H. WEEKS

The name Colling ought probably to be Collins, and Right, Wright; the spelling of the roll is followed.

William F. Taylor was commissioned an ensign of infantry in 1813. (Calendar, State Papers.)

There was also a company of "mounted riflemen" from the County, commanded by Capt. William Stevens. This company of the Third Virginia Regiment was stationed at Hampton, for two months, in 1814, but diligent search has failed to discover a roll. Among the Orange "Petitions" in the State Library is one from Charles M. Webb, of this company, which sets out the facts here stated. Webb's horse impaled itself and died from his wounds, and his petition for pay for it was rejected.

Application was made to the War Department, through the courtesy of Senator Thomas S. Martin, for a roster of this company, but without success, there being a "lack of clerical force;" yet others than the official force are not permitted to examine the files, which is as it should be.

APPENDIX E.

War of the Revolution.

In this appendix, names are sometimes duplicated, no doubt, yet it is impossible now to tell whether persons of the same name were always the same person. Authorities are generally given that statements may be verified.

It is not assumed that this record is exhaustive, but it is believed to be much the fullest that has yet appeared. Unfortunately the official records of the Revolution, which are fairly complete in the State Land Office and Library, seldom disclose the county from which the soldiers came, and hence are not useful, except for comparison, in compiling a roster of this kind.

Permission was asked to examine the files of the departments at Washington. It was refused on the ground that the rolls have become so fragile that handling them is very injurious; yet the Government does not publish them, and the archives of the State and County are the only resource of the investigator.

The following persons are named in the order books, at the indicated dates, as being active participants in the Revolution. The orders are greatly condensed.

1778. JERE CHANDLER
———STAVES, (Two sons of widow Staves, names not given.)
JOSEPH EDMONSON
FRANCIS MCCLARNEY
1779. SOLOMON GARRETT
———HENSLEY (son of Jane).
1784. JOHN TRACEY. Died in service.
1785. JAMES CHISHAM (Chisholm). Died in service in '78
WM. ROSSON. Died in service.

1785 JOHN BARNETT
JOSIAH LANDRUM
JAMES LINTOR
ROBERT WATTS. Died in service.
AMBROSE WHITE. Died in Va. Regt. of Guards.
1786. JOHN BUSH. 7th Va; died in Continental service.
CATLETT JONES. Not wounded in public service; discontinued from pension list, as able to earn his living
JOHN GROOM. Lost leg; entitled to pension.
ANDREW LEACH. Pensioner; dead.
WILLIAM PALMER. Pensioner; lost leg.
1787. FINLASON SLEET. Allowed £50 for acting as adjutant for six years from 1777.
JAMES GAINES. Allowed £30 as clerk of court-martial five years.
1789. JOHN MILLER. Died of wounds received in United States service. Judith, his wife, pensioned.
1792. WM. BOLLING. Enlisted in 2d Va. Feby. 1777; died Aug., '78, in service.
PEACHY BLEDSOE. Sergt. in 2d regiment, (proved foregoing item.)
1811. JAMES BURTON'S oath as to his service.
WILLIAM CAMPBELL'S oath; both Captains.
1813. JESSE THORNTON. In Capt. Spencer's Co. 7th Va. in '76, as fife major; served to end of war.
1817. HERMAN VAWTER. Sergt. in 17th Va.
1818. JOHN ATKINS. Aged 69; in Capt. Geo. Stubblefield's Co., 5th Va., in '76,; discharged in '78.
THOMAS MARSH. Aged 72; in Capt. Thos. Gaskin's Co., served 3 years; discharged in N. C.; in battles of Trenton, Brandywine, Germantown; re-enlisted in cavalry and served till end of war.
JOSEPH THOMAS. Aged 61; enlisted in '76 in 2d Va. Cont. Regt., Capt. Francis Taylor's Co., served till '78; discharged at Valley Forge, Pa.; in battles of Brandywine and Germantown.
JOHN BOURN. Aged 66; enlisted '76, 2d Va. Contl., Capt. Taylor's Co.; served till '81; captured at Charleston, S. C.
JULIAN, or JULIUS, KING. Aged 62; enlisted in '77, 3d Regt. Light Dragoons, Col. Geo. Baylor; served 3 years; battle of Germantown.

APPENDIX—WAR OF THE REVOLUTION. 249

1818 WM. KNIGHTON. Aged 62; enlisted '78 in Capt. Grant's Co., 16th Va. Contl.; also in 3d Va.; served 3 years; battle of Monmouth, and seige of Charleston, where he was made prisoner.
JOHN SNOW. Aged 59; enlisted '76, Francis Taylor's Co.; served 2 years; discharged at Valley Forge; battles, Brandywine and Germantown.
CHARLES MURPHY. Aged 72; enlisted in '77 in Capt. John Gillason's Co. 10th Va.; served 3 years; afterwards in 6th Regt. till discharged at Cumberland old C. H. in '82; battles of Brandywine, Germantown, Monmouth.
GEO. MANSFIELD. Aged 59; enlisted '81 in Capt. James Gunn's Co. 1st Regt. Light Dragoons; served till '83; battles of Guilford C. H. and Camden.
JOHN D. FITZPATRICK. Deed conveying bounty land in Illinois Territory.
PETER MONTAGUE. Aged 85; enlisted in '77 in Capt. Alex. Parker's Co. 2d Va. Regt.; served 3 years; battle of Savannah.
1832. JAMES CHILES. Aged 70; proved 2 years service in Revolution, on the oath of .
STARKE WRIGHT, of Louisa; in same company with him.

Also the following, during this year, proved two years service:

ZACHARIAH TAYLOR,	aged	72
JEREMIAH WHITE,		77
JAMES HANEY,		73
RICHARD GOODALL,		74
ABSALOM ROACH,		72
JOHN DAVIS,		76
JAMES JONES,		73
PHILEMON RICHARDS,		78
JAMES DANIEL,		74
GEO. NEWMAN,		85
JOHN SMITH,		
ROBT. MANSFIELD,		70
WM. DAVIS,		74
RICHARD WHITE,		76
WM. JARRELL,		79

JOHN WILLIAMS, aged 78
KENNETH SOUTHERLAND, 70
WILLIAM WAYT, 71
WILLIAM FISHER, 75
1833. GEO. SHERMAN, 71
DR. CHARLES TAYLOR, Army Surgeon.
1834. GEO. MORRIS
PETER APPERSON
WILLIAM RANDALL, aged 74
CHURCHILL GORDON, midshipman.
1836. WM. PARROTT
1847. MORDECAI BARBOUR, pensioner.
ROBERT CLARK

The following names are collected from the Orange "Petitions," on file in the State Library.

THOS. BUSH, ensign, Capt. Dudley's Company, 2d Va.
THORNBERRY BOLING, same Company.
PEACHY BLEDSOE, sergt., Capt. Nathaniel Welch's Co., same Regt.
CATLETT JAMES, pensioner.
JAROT MORTON, regular, Francis Taylor's Company.
WM. BOLING, minute man.
JESSE BOLING, minute man.
REUBEN FINNELL, minute man and regular.
JOHN FINNELL, minute man and regular.
GEO. DOUGLAS
WM. BOHON
JOHN BOHON
BENJAMIN BOHON
WM. TWISDELL

The following list, compiled from records of the War Department, is copied from the VII Virginia Histtorical Magazine, page 24, etc., some corrections having been made as to residence. Where rank is not given private soldier is understood.

CAPT. GARLAND BURNLEY
CAPT. MAY BURTON
CAPT. BELLEFIELD

CAPT. JAMES BURTON
CAPT. CHARLES BRUCE
JOHN BEADLES

APPENDIX—WAR OF THE REVOLUTION. 251

CAPT. COURSEY	KENNETH SOUTHERLAND
CAPT. WM. CAMPBELL	CAPT. JOHN SULT
CAPT. FRANCIS COWHERD	CAPT. SPENCER
COKER	CAPT. JOSEPH SPENCER
BELLEFIELD CAVE	COL. STUBBLEFIELD
LIEUT. BELLEFIELD CAVE	LIEUT. BENJ. SMITH
JAMES CHILES	COL. TAYLOR
CRAVENS	COL. JAMES TAYLOR
JOHN DAVIS	LIEUT-COL. FRANCIS TAYLOR.
CAPT. REUBEN DANIEL	COL. TAYLOR, 3d Va.
WM. FISHER	LIEUT. WM. TAYLOR
LT. JOHN GOODELL [Goodall].	CAPT. FRANCIS TAYLOR
RICHD GOODELL [Goodall].	ENSIGN JOHN TAYLOR
CAPT. REUBEN HAWKINS	ZACHY. TAYLOR
LIEUT. ZACH. HERNDON	FRANCIS TACKETT
CAPT. BENJAMIN JOHNSON	COL. TEMPLE
JAMES JONES	CAPT. RICHD. WELL
CAPT. AMBROSE MADISON	LIEUT. GEO. WAR
CAPT. FRANCIS MOORE	LIEUT. (Corporal) RICHARD
GEO. NEWMAN	WHITE
CAPT. NELSON	CAPT. JOHN WAUGH
WM. ROACH	CAPT. GEORGE WAUGH
ABSALOM ROACH	JERE WHITE
PHILEMON RICHARDS	LIEUT. RICHD. WHITE
CAPT. JOHN SCOTT	LIEUT. WM. WHITE
JOHN SNOW	SERGT. JOHN WILLIAMS

"A Muster Roll of Capt. Ambrose Madison's Company of foot in the Regiment of Volunteers Guards at the Barracks in Albemarle County, whereof Col. Francis Taylor is Commander, to June 1, 1779." Original in possession of Mr. John Willis, of Gordonsville, his great grandson.

CAPT. AMBROSE MADISON	*Corporals*
LIEUT. JAMES BURTON	AMBROSE WHITE
ENSIGN JOHN GOODALL	RICHD. QUINN
Sergeants	NORMAN KIDD
JOHN SNOW	*Privates*
JOHN WAYT	JEDITHON CANTERBERRY
JAMES GOODALL	AMBROSE LUCAS

Privates
JAMES FARGUSON
JOHN BARNETT
JOHN DAVIS
LEWIS DAVIS
ZACHA. LEWIS
WM. HAYNE
JONATHAN ROACH
WM. GOODALL
DAVID ROACH
JOHN LANE
DAVID VAWTER
JAMES HANEY
ABSALOM ROACH

Privates
CALEB JENNINS
WM. HARRIS
JOHN YOUNG
WM. BALLARD
JAS. MCGINNESS
BEAN LANNAM, not joined.
ALEX WHITE, deserted 12th April.
STARK RIGHT
REUBEN ROACH, died 15th April.
ALEX MACKENNY

"Sworn to before me this 22d day of July 1779 by James Burton, Lieutenant.

THEO^K. BLAND, *Colonel-Commanding,*

Post Charlottesville".

A Roll of Capt. Francis Taylor's Company enlisted between Jany. 29 and March 17, 1776, from a MS. account book and papers in Va. State Library.

Enlisted by F. TAYLOR.

EDWARD BROADUS
JAMES QUINN
JEREMIAH COX
TURNER THOMASON
JOHN ALMAND
ELISHA ESTES
JOSEPH HARVEY
THOMAS BALLARD
JAMES BROADUS
WILLIAM DAVIS
BELL SIMMONS
THOMAS SHELTON
WILLIAM MEDLEY
ROBERT DAWSON

THOMAS MORRIS
JAMES BEASLEY
ACHILLES FOSTER
GEORGE BROOKS
STEPHEN HAM
HENRY RUSSELL
BENJAMIN DAWSON
RICHARD CHANDLER
W. BOWLING
THORNBERRY BOWLING
WILLIAM WARD
LEWIS PINES
JAMES LONG

APPENDIX—WAR OF THE REVOLUTION.   253

Enlisted by WILLIAM TAYLOR.

JOHN GILLOCK
ROBERT CHANDLER
WILLIAM SAWYER
LEONARD SALE
EDWARD ATKINS (in service).
HOWARD BLEDSOE
JOHN FINNELL
ALEXANDER THOMAS
LEWIS COOK
SAMUEL CLAYTON
PRAT HUGHES
JAMES COURTNEY

WILLIAM HARVEY
BENJAMIN CAVENAUGH
WILLIAM MARTIN
THOMAS BREEDLOVE
THOMAS SHIP
LEWIS WILLIS
EVAN BRAMHAM
JAMES JACKSON
JACOB BURRUS
JOHN SNOW
THOMAS FLEEMAN

Enlisted by BENJAMIN PORTER,
resigned Aug. 28, 1776.

JAMES WELSH
THOMAS PORTER
PERRY PATTERSON
FRANCIS MCLARNEY
WILLIAM FINNELL
JOSEPH PRICE
HENRY BARNETT
JOHN BOWEN

REUBEN HAWKINS
ELISHA HAWKINS
GERARD MORTON
JOHN HAMMOND
WILLIAM MORRIS
JOSEPH THOMAS
JAMES BARNETT
JOHN CHOWNING

Enlisted by FRANCIS COWHERD.

WILLIAM TOWNSHEND
JAMES BROWN
SAML. WARREN
JAMES BROOKS
MICHAEL GAVIN

SHADRACH HILL
BENJA. RUCKER
JONATHAN DAVIS
JAMES DEERING

The names, James Gibbons and James Barton, and Elijah Deer, John Boyd, taken in place of Thomas Porter, who deserted.

Wm. Taylor and Benjamin Porter were lieutenants; and Francis Cowherd, ensign; James Burton, a cadet.

Pay roll of Captain Francis Taylor's Company of the 2d Virginia Battalion, from the 28 January to the 28 February, 1777. (Vol. VI, Va. Hist. Magazine page 127.)

<table>
<tr><td>Francis Taylor, captain,</td><td>40 Dollars.</td></tr>
<tr><td>William Taylor, first lieutenant,</td><td>27</td></tr>
<tr><td>Francis Cowherd, second lientenant,</td><td>27</td></tr>
<tr><td>James Burton, ensign,</td><td>20</td></tr>
<tr><td>Samuel Clayton, sergeant,</td><td>8</td></tr>
<tr><td>James Broadus, sergeant,</td><td>8</td></tr>
<tr><td>James Welch, sergeant,</td><td>8</td></tr>
<tr><td>Jeremiah Cox, drummer,</td><td>7½</td></tr>
<tr><td>James Quin, corporal,</td><td>7½</td></tr>
<tr><td>Evan Bramham, corporal,</td><td>6½</td></tr>
<tr><td>Thomas Shelton, corporal,</td><td>7½</td></tr>
<tr><td>John Brown, corporal,</td><td>7½</td></tr>
</table>

Privates at 6⅔ Dollars.

Archilles Foster
Henry Russell
George Brooks
Ransdell Abbot
William Medley
William Ward
Thomas McClanahan
Robert White
Andrew Harrison
Stephen Ham
Elijah Deer
Leonard Sale
John Almand
Gerard Morton
Elisha Hawkins
Robert Chandler
James Brown
John Chowning
John Gillock
Samuel Warren
William Morris
Joseph Thomas
James Long
Henry Barnett

Turner Thomason
Joseph Henry
Shadrach Hill
Benjamin Dawson
Thomas Morris
John Finnel
Thornberry Bowling
James Deering
Thomas Breedlove
Jacob Burrus
Elisha Estes
William Martin
John Snow
Thomas Fleeman
Lewis Pines
Joel Foster
James Jackson
Thomas Ballard
James Beazley
William Turner
Edward Broadus
Perry Patterson
William Davis
James Gibbons

HUMPHEY SHAY, 28 Dec., 1777, 13½ Dollars. Of the 1st Virg. Battalion Ordered to join my Comp. by Gen. L (———?).
JOHN JOHNSON, 28 Jan. 1776, 6⅔ Dollars. Of Col. Rall's Maryland Battalion Ord. to join my Compy. at Baltimore, Md.
The above is a just Pay Roll.

(Signed) FRANCIS TAYLOR.

WILLIAM MORTON, ancestor of the Mortons of Orange, was a Revolutionary officer, and was killed on Clarke's Mountain while attempting to arrest a deserter named Nixon who fled to West Virginia and changed his name to Mixon.

PHILIP MALLORY, 2d Lt. in 1777; 1st Lt. 1778; Capt. 1779; taken prisoner at Charleston 1780; served to close of war. (Heitman.)

DAVID PANNILL, captain of artillery. Received large bounty land grants after the war. He was the uncle of the David Pannill who was the maternal grandfather of Gen. J. E. B. Stuart. (Va. Land Office.)

WM. TERRELL, 2d Lt. 5th Va. Dec. 1776; resigned 1778.— (Heitman.)

WM. STEVENS, 1st Lt.; Prisoner at Charleston. (Heitman.)

There was a distribution of salt by the general Committee of Safety in March 1776, when Orange was credited with 600 militia, and received 300 bushels of salt. (Calendar Va. State Papers. VIII. 140.)

Captains Spencer and Taylor, with their subaltern officers, April 1, 1776, allowed till the 20th instant to complete their companies. The companies were reviewed May 8, and the officers commissioned.

Abram Maury, adjt. Continental Line. (*Ibid*. VI. 393.)

In 1781, Thomas Barbour (County Lieutenant, *Ibid*. IV. 639) reports the people badly armed because the men ordered into service were required to carry their arms but not allowed to bring them back. All clothing required had been collected and delivered, and the County had furnished its full quota of men, thirty-seven, upon the last call. Two had absconded and one became insane. (*Ibid*. II. 607.)

In Mr. Wm. Kyle Anderson's book on the Robertson and Taylor families, is this remarkable account of the Orange Taylors in the Revolution.

George Taylor, member of the Committee of Safety*, was the father of twelve sons, one of whom died before the Revolution, and one was only thirteen years of age when the war ended. The other ten all volunteered and served in the Revolution as follows:

JAMES, sergeant-major
JONATHAN, lieutenant
EDMUND, captain
FRANCIS, colonel
RICHARD, captain in navy

JOHN, lieutenant in navy
WILLIAM, major
CHARLES, surgeon
REUBEN, captain
BENJAMIN, midshipman

The same book is authority also for these Taylors:

JAMES, colonel; RICHARD, lieutenant-colonel, father of General Zachary Taylor; JOHN, captain.

Revolutionary Pensioners from Orange.

(*From Report of Secretary of War, 1835.*)

Under Acts 1785, 1816.

THOMAS PHILLIPS, invalid   ALEXANDER TURNER, invalid

Under Act of 1818.

ELIJAH ALVIS
JOHN ATKINS
JOHN BOURN
FRANCIS HUGHS
JULIAN (or Julius) KING

WILLIAM KNIGHTER[Knighton.]
CHARLES MURPHY
GEO. MANSFIELD
PETER MONTAGUE

All privates in the Virginia Line.

---

*George Taylor was not a member of the committee.

Appendix—War of Revolution

Under Act of 1832.

Nicholas Bickers
James Chiles
Wm. Crittenden, wagon master
John Davis, private
Isaac Davis, senr. lieutenant, captain
James Daniel
Wm. Fisher
Richard Goodell [Goodall]
Richard Hill
James Haney
Wm. Jarrell
Robt. Mansfield
James Nelson
Geo. Newman
Jonathan Pratt
Absalom Roach
John Smith
Geo. Sheaman
Bland Shiflet
Zachariah Taylor
Jere. White
Thomas Walker
John Williams, sergeant
Richard White, (corporal, ensign, lieutenant)
Wm. Wayt

All privates, except as otherwise indicated.
Greene yet a part of Orange.

Officers Pensioned, Act of May, 1828.

James Burton, captain. Died 1829, widow, Elizabeth.
Francis Cowherd, captain. Died 1833, widow, Lucy.
Wm. White, captain. Died 1828,

Revolutionary Pensioners Residing in Orange, Census 1840.

John Almond
Lucy Cowherd
Susan Campbell
Wm. Crittenden
James Chiles
Wm. Fisher
Geo. Morris
Jonathan Pratt
Philemon Richards
Danl. Young
George Waugh, lieutenant and captain, who married Elizabeth Boston, and died in 1814—Widows' File number 9873—was also a pensioner.

APPENDIX F.

Commissions, 1734-1783.

1735
GOODRICH LIGHTFOOT
MORGAN MORGAN
ROBERT CAVE, lieut. of horse
1738
JOHN LEWIS
1740
Captains:
  JOHN RUCKER
  EDMUND SPENCER
  GOODRICH LIGHTFOOT
  BRYAN SISSON
Lieutenants:
  CHRISTOPHER ZIMMERMAN
  GEO. MORTON
  FRANCIS MICHAEL, cornet
  ROBERT SLAUGHTER, major
1741
HENRY DOWNS, captain
WM. BELL. cornet, of horse
WM. Beverley, county lieutenant, Orange and Augusta Counties
THOS. CHEW, colonel
RORT, SLAUGHTER lieutenant-colonel
JOHN FINLASON, major
WM. RUSSELL, captain
RICHD. WINSLOW, captain
GEO. DOGGETT, lieutenant

Ensigns:
  FRANCIS MICHAEL
  PHILIP BUSH
1742
JAMES PATTON, colonel, Augusta County
Captains:
  JOHN BUCHANNON
  JOHN SMITH
  SAML. GAY
  JAMES CATHEY
  JOHN CHRISTIAN
  EDWARD SPENCER
  HENRY FIELD
  ROBT. GREEN
  HUGH THOMPSON
  PETER SHOLL
  JOHN WILSON
  JOHN MCDOWELL
  ROBERT EASTHAM
  JAMES GILL
  GEO. TAYLOR
  ANDREW CAMPBELL
  THOS. RUTHERFORD
  JOHN HIBS
  JOHN PICKENS
  ISAAC PENNINGTON
  JOHN DENTON

APPENDIX—MILITARY COMMISSIONS 259

Captains:
THOS. LOW
LEWIS NEIL
GEO. ANDERSON
RICHARD MORGAN
ROBERT BRACKENRIDGE
JEREMIAH SMITH
THOMAS ASHBY
RICHARD WOODS
JOSEPH COALTON
JOHN BROWN
DANL. MCKEERE
JOHN MATTHEWS
SAML. BALL
DANL. HARRISON
ROBT. CRAVAN
ALEX. DUNLOP
WM. EVANS
Lieutenants:
JOHN MOFFETT
WM EVANS
GEO. MORTON
PHILIP CLAYTON
THOMAS JONES
C. ZIMMERMAN
CHAS. DEWITT
BENJ. ROBERTS
ROBERT SCOTT
THOS. JONES
JOHN QUINN
GEO. HOBSON
JACOB HITE
JOHN HARRISON
SAML. MORRISS
JOSEPH CARTER
EDWARD WATTS
THOS. SWEARINGEN
ROBERT JONES
WM. PEYTON

Lieutenants:
WM. CROCKETT
DAVID VAUNCE
Ensigns:
GEO. SCOTT
SAML. FARGUSON
WM. DUNCAN
WM. ANDERSON
FRANCIS MOORE
JOHN ROBERTS
RICHARD YARBOROUGH
PETER RUSSELL
JOHN FUNK
JAMES WOOD, colonel of horse and foot
JOHN LEWIS, colonel of foot
MORGAN MORGAN, major
JOHN BUCKANNON, lieutenant-colonel of foot
1743
Captains:
ROBERT SCOTT
WM. LINOVELL
BENJ. ALSOR
Lieutenants:
JOHN DOBBIN
THOMAS WEST
Ensign:
JOHN WATTS
Cornets:
THOS. LINOVELL
THOS. HARRISON
1744
Captains:
JOHN KARR
WM. SMITH
BENJ. BORDEN
Lieutenant:
GEO. SCOTT

The claims of Capt. John Smith and his company, Capt. John Christian and his company, of Capt John Wilson, of Capt. John Guy and his company, of Capt. Bohannon, of Lieut. Just Stephonicus Smith, and of Lieut. John Douglas ordered to be certified to the General Assembly.

Captains:
WM. THOMPSON
ANTHONY GARNETT
ANDREW BYRD, lieutenant
1745
WM. JAMESON, captain
JOHN WETHERELL, ensign
1749
GEO. TAYLOR, lieutenant colonel

1755
JEREMIAH MORTON, captain
JAS. WALKER, lieutenant
1757
FRANCIS MOORE, major
RICHARD BARBOUR, captain
Lieutenants:
RUST HUDSON
JOHNNY SCOTT

1758. The Court purchased thirty-seven muskets, for the use of the militia unable to provide themselves with guns, for £31. 15s.

1761
Captains:
REUBEN DANIEL
THOS. JAMESON
JOHNNY SCOTT
1762
JAS. WALKER, captain
JAS. SUGGETT, lieutenant
1763
Militia marched to Augusta.
1764
WM. TALIAFERRO, colonel
1767
JAMES MADISON, county lieutenant
Captains:
WM. MOORE
JAMES TAYLOR
ZACHARY TAYLOR, lieutenant
1768
Captains:
LAWRENCE TALIAFERRO
WM. MOORE

Lieutenants:
HAY TALIAFERRO
THOMAS MERRY
1770
JOHN BELL, captain
1772
CHARLES BRUCE, captain
1773
THOS. JAMESON, ensign
1774
Captains:
ZACHY TAYLOR
VIVIAN DANIEL
JONATHAN TAYLOR, lieutenant
1777
Recommended to the Governor, for appointments:
NATHANIEL MILLS, as captain vice V. Daniel, resigned.
SAML. BROCKMAN, lieutenant
TOLIVER CRAIG vice Uriel Mallory, resigned.

APPENDIX—MILITARY COMMISSIONS 261

RICHARD CRITTENDEN WEBB,
  as lieutenant.
JOSEPH PARRISH, ensign
Lieutenants:
  R. C. WEBB
  MANOAH SINGLETON
  WM. SMITH
  ROBT. MILLER
  ROBT. DANIEL
  BENONI HANSFORD
  JAMES HAWKINS
  ROBT. JOHNSON
  WM. BUCKNER
  GEO. STUBBLEFIELD
  RICHARD GRAVES
  JAMES HAWKINS
  GEO. WAUGH
  CALEB LINDSAY
  ZACHARY SHACKLEFORD
ROBERT THOMAS, captain
Ensigns:
  ROBERT THOMAS
  JAMES HEAD
  AMBROSE BURTON
  JOHN PROCTOR
  THOMAS CHAMBERS
  WM. WRIGHT
       1778
ZACHY BURNLEY, County Lieutenant, vice James Madison, resigned.
LAWRENCE TALIFERRO, lieutenant-colonel, vice Burnley, promoted.
THOS. BARBOUR, major, vice Wm. Moore, resigned.
BENJ. HEAD, captain, vice Jere White, resigned.
WM. BUCKNER, captain, vice Geo. Smith, resigned.

ZACHY HERNDON, captain, vice Johnny Scott, resigned.
RICHARD GRAVES, captain, vice Chas. Bruce, resigned.
Lieutenants:
  ROBT. MILLER
  MAY BURTON
  WM. YOUNG
  JOHN PROCTER
  BENONI HANSFORD
    promoted one grade.
Ensigns:
  RICHD. WHITE
  ROBT. MARTIN
       1779
JAMES HAWKINS, captain
Lieutenants:
  ABNER PORTER
  CHAS. PORTER, JR.
  RICHD. PRICE
  GEO. WAUGH
  REUBEN MOORE
  BELLEFIELD CAVE
Ensigns:
  CALEB SISSON
  JOHN SCOTT
  RICHARD MOORE PRICE
ROBT. MILLER, captain, vice Benj. Head, resigned.
MAY BURTON and RICHD. WHITE, promoted.
R. C. WEBB, captain, vice Toliver Craig, resigned.
Lieutenants:
  JAS. PARRISH
  RICHD. CAVE
  CHAS. PORTER
Ensigns:
  JAMES SAUNDERS
  MOSES WILLIS

1780
EDMUND SHACKLEFORD, captain, vice Coursey, resigned.
Lieutenants:
LEWIS RIDLEY
RICHD. PAYNE
JOHN RUCKER, ensign
GEO. WAUGH, captain, vice Francis Moore, Jr.
ROBT. DANIEL, captain, vice Conway, resigned.
MAY BURTON, captain
Lieutenants:
WM. WRIGHT
ROWLAND THOMAS, JR.
MOSES WILLIS
TIMOTHY CONNER
JAMES SAUNDERS
THOMAS CHAMBERS
JOHN PANNILL
WM. BURTON
THOS. FORTSON
JOHN BEADLES
PRETTYMAN MERRY
JOHN SCOTT, JR.
LEWIS WILLIS
Ensigns:
ALEX. NEWMAN
LEWIS COLEMAN

Ensigns:
JOHN HERNDON
JOHN ROBINSON
THOS. WHITE
1781
Lieutenants:
WM. THOMAS
JAMES BURTON
ZACHY SHACKLEFORD
Ensigns:
JAMES STEVENSON
WM. BURTON
JAMES MADISON, JR., county lieutenant vice Burnley, resigned.
THOS. BARBOUR, colonel, vice Madison, promoted.
BENJAMIN JOHNSON, lieutenant-colonel
AMBROSE MADISON, major
BELLEFIELD CAVE, captain
Ensigns:
JAS. EASLEY
JOHN DAWSON
JAS. DEERING
CHAS. THOMAS
JAS. SLEET
1783
GARLAND BURNLEY, captain, vice Zachy Herndon

This appears to have been the last appointment made during the period of the Revolutionary War.

The "Calendar of State Papers," shows, however, that Thomas Barbour was County Lieutenant in the later years of the war, and it would seem that James Madison, Jr., never acted as such.

APPENDIX G.

Roster of the Montpelier Guards During John Brown Raid, 1859.

This company was organized and uniformed about two years before the raid occured. It did not participate in the capture of Brown, but was ordered to Charles Town, where he was imprisoned, there being much talk of "rescue" at the time, and remained there until Brown and his accessories were hanged.

This company was Brown's military escort to the scaffold. The roster was furnished by Mr. W. H. Ricketts, treasurer of Orange.

LEWIS B. WILLIAMS, JR., capt.
GEO. CULLEN, first lieutenant
JAMES A. NEWMAN, second lieutenant
DR. THOMAS C. REVELY, surgeon
ISAAC T. GRAHAM, first sergeant
WM. H. RICKETTS, color-bearer
DON PEDRO GILABERT (Peter Gilbert), drummer

Privates:
  THOS. R. BLEDSOE
  T. C. BOULWARE
  IRA BROCKMAN
  L. T. BROCKMAN
  WM. BROCKMAN
  R. W. EDDINS
  PHILIP B. HIDEN
  R. H. HOUSEWORTH
  FRANK HUME
  JOSEPH L. JACKSON
  FLEMING KENDALL

Privates:
  ROBERT KENDALL
  JOHN LARMOND
  CHAS. C. MOORE
  JOHN MOORE
  ROBT. P. MOORE
  W. L. MORRIS
  J. Q. NEWMAN
  L. T. ODEN
  FLEMING PARKER
  THOS J. PEYTON
  M. D. PROCTOR
  ROBT. H. ROGERS
  A. F. STOFER
  W. R. TALIAFERRO
  JOHN G. TERRELL
  TOWLES TERRELL
  A. B. THOMAS
  THOS. R. TOWLES
  J. T. WILLEROY
  JOHN WOOLFOLK
  SNOWDEN YATES

APPENDIX H.

Roster of Confederate Soldiers, 1861 to 1865.

The Montpelier Guard, Co. A., 13th Va. Infantry.

(*Roster furnished by W. H. Ricketts.*)

Captains:
  LEWIS B. WILLIAMS †
  B. F. NALLE
  CHAMPE G. COOKE †
  GEORGE CULLEN

Lieutenants:
  ISAAC T. GRAHAM
  CHARLES C. MOORE
  WILSON S. NEWMAN †
  THOMAS T. WILROY †
  M. S. STRINGFELLOW
  H. C. COLEMAN
  J. S. JACKSON, orderly sergeant at Appomattox
  GEORGE C. WALTERS, second sergeant
  F. N. GOODWIN, third sergeant
  W. H. RICKETTS color sergeant

Privates:
  AMOS, GEO. A.
  AUSTIN, S. T.
  ATKINS, HUGH
  BELL, C. S.
  BELL, JOHN W.
  BICKERS, T. O.
  BROCKMAN, L. T. sergeant †
  BROCKMAN, WM.
  BROCKMAN, JOE

Privates:
  BROCKMAN, ASA
  BROCKMAN, IRA S. †
  BROCKMAN, A. T.
  BROCKMAN, W. A.
  BROWN, WM.
  BROWN, HENRY
  BERNARD, RICHARD S. †
  BLEDSOE, THOS. †
  BURRUS, G. M. †
  BURRUS, ROBERT †
  BURRUS, JOSEPH †
  BURRUS, W. T.
  BURRUS, LANCELOT
  BULLOCK, OSWALD
  BOULWARE, C. C.
  BOSTON, JOHN T.
  BRESAU, PETER
  CAVE, R. C.
  CAVE, R. L.
  CAVE, WALLACE L.
  COLEMAN, R. L.
  COLEMAN, L. L.
  COLEMAN, BURWELL
  CHAPMAN, WM.
  DONALD, NIMROD
  DOWNER, R. C.
  DOWNER, R. G.

† Killed.

Appendix—Confederate Soldiers 265

Privates:
DIGGS, HENRY A.
DIGGS, WM.
DIGGS, COLE †
DOWNIN, VIRGIL
ECKLOFF, R. G.
EDDINS, H. C.
ESTES, THOMAS
ESTES, JOHN
FAULKNER, CARTER B.
FLETCHER, T. N.
FORTNEY, W. H.
FRY, LUTHER C.
FRY, E. M. †
GOODWIN, L. T. †
GARRISON, GEORGE
GRAVES, ISAAC
GILBERT, PETER, drummer
HALSEY, P. W.
HENDERSON, JAMES M.
HAYS, THOS. (cook)
HERNDON, THEOPHILUS
HERNDON, REUBEN D.
HUNTER, WM. M.
HORTON, J. S.
HUME, F. D.
HOWARD, GEO. W. †
HIDEN, P. B.
HOUSEWORTH, R. H.
HOUSEWORTH, V. A.
HOLLAND, T.
HALSEY, ———
HOLLADAY, WALLER L.
JACOBS, A. E.
JONES, BENJ.
JONES, W. A.
KENDALL, F. M.
KENDALL, R. S.
LANCASTER, J. E.
LIPSCOMB, M. B.
LIPSCOMB, DAN

Privates:
LAYTON, J. T., †
MALLORY, D. C.,
MAUPIN, L.
MASON, ROBERT
MEADE, J. M.
MEADE, NAT.
MCCLARY, CHARLES
MOORE, R. P.
MOORE, J. M.
MOORE, JOHN, †
MORRIS, WM.
MILLER, CHRISTIAN
NEWMAN, GEO. A.
NEWMAN, JOHN
NEWMAN, JOHN HERBERT †
NEWMAN, R. M.
ODEN, L. T.
ONEAL, JAMES
POWELL, ROBERT †
POWELL, HUGH †
PEAKE, WM. B. †
PANNILL, P. P.
PANNILL, B. B.
PAYNE, B. B.
PAYNE, JOHN
PAYNE, JAS. W.
PEYTON, GEO. Q.
PRATT, JOHN
PROCTOR, MORGAN D.
PORTER, H. C.
RICHARDS, F.
RICHARDS, R.
ROACH, HENRY D.
ROBINSON, THOS. J.
ROBERSON, MARCELLUS
ROGERS, R. H. †
ROGERS, ROBT.
SCOTT, PHILIP H.
SCOTT, W. W.
SIZER, JAS. J. †

† Killed.

Privates:
SLAUGHTER, T. T. †
SLAUGHTER, JAS.
SMITH, WM. J.
STAPLES, EDWARD S. †
TALIAFERRO, PEACHY
TALIAFERRO, W. R.
TERRELL, TOWLES
THOMAS, A. B. †
TERRELL, O. T.
THOMPSON, A. H.

Privates:
TOWLES, T. R.
WAYLAND, MARTIN V.
WILLIAMS, CHAS. C.
WALTERS, ALFRED
WILLIAMS, JOHN G.
WILLIS, JOHN
WILLIS, H. LEE
WILLIS, R. G.
WOOLFOLK, JAS. H.
WRIGHT, WM. T. †

Captain Williams was promoted to the rank of colonel, and was killed in Pickett's charge at Gettysburg.

R. M. Newman, orderly sergeant of the company, January 1, 1864, subsequently an officer on the staff of Gen. George H. Steuart of Maryland, furnishes a roster of that date from his contemporaneous diary, from which a few names, not in the other list, have been incorporated.

On January 1, 1864, according to this diary, there were fifty-two enlisted men in the company subject to duty; to give some idea of the losses in the Wilderness Campaign there were present for duty June 8, fourteen men, on July 7, eighteen. The subsequent battle of Winchester, September 29, was one of the most destructive in which the company was engaged.

"The Gordonsville Greys," Co. C., 13th Va. Infantry.

(Roster by Capt. P. P. Barbour.)

Captain:
SCOTT, WM. C.
Lieutenants:
GOODMAN, G. A.
COWHERD, E. F.
RICHARDS, C. H.

Sergeants:
WEISIGER, WM. H.
BARBOUR, P. P.
BLACKBURN, A. J.
QUARLES, WM. R. †

---
†Killed.

APPENDIX—CONFEDERATE SOLDIERS 267

Corporals:
BAKER, BENJ. F.
BAUGHAN, RICHD. A.
JONES, WM. R.
MOYERS, GEO. W.
Privates:
AMOS, GARRETT
ATKINS, S. G.
ANDERSON, JNO. W. †
BATTAILE, J. R.
BEALE, C. W.
BEALE, N. G.
BEALE, JAS. N. †
BAKER, C. †
BAKER, J. O.
BIBB, JOHN †
BIBB, JAMES
BAUGHAN, J. N.
BEAR, BERNARD
BRAGG, JOHN
BRAGG, J. R.
BROWN, S. C.
BROCK, R. S.
BRUCE, W. D.
BRUCE, JERE
CARTER, CHAS. H.
COWHERD, CHAS. S.
COWHERD, YELVERTON †
COWHERD, M. D.
COWHERD, C. C.
COOKE, G. W.
COLVIN, ROBT.
COLVIN, GREEN
COLVIN JOHN
DAVENPORT, J. T.
DAVIS, THOS. A.
DAVIS, W. D.
DANIEL, J. BOLLING
DUNN, W. M.
DUVAL, GEO. W.
DUVAL, JNO. P.

Privates:
ESKEW, WM. J.
FAULCONER, G. W.
FEGAN, JOHN †
GOODMAN, MONOAH
GOODMAN, H. G.
GARRISON, JAMES †
GRUBBS, JOHN †
GIBSON, J. FRANK
GENTRY, J. R.
HEATWOLE, BENJ. †
HEATWOLE, JOHN
HALE, D. W.
HALE, JOHN †
HARLOW, BEN.
HARRIS, R. H.
HARRIS, WM.
HARPER, JAS.
LANCASTER, THOS.
LANCASTER, JOHN
LEAKE, AUSTIN M.
LOCKER, JOHN
LOCKER, WM.
MAGRUDER, DAVID W.
MAGRUDER, GEO. W. †
MANSFIELD, W. B. †
MEADE, RICHD.
MEADE, GEO.
MOORE, RICHARD †
MORRIS, REUBEN J.
MORRIS, LEMUEL
MAHANES, JAS. H.
MASON, JOHN
MALLORY, O. P.
NEWMAN, J. S.
NEWMAN, J. H. †
NEWMAN, R. M.
NOLAN, THOS. †
NOLAN, JOHN
OGG, JAS.
OGG, RICHD.

† Killed.

268   HISTORY OF ORANGE COUNTY

Privates:
OMOHUNDRO, MELTON †
PANNILL, JOHN †
PARRISH †
POWELL,
PARROTT, JOHN
PARROTT, THOS.
QUARLES, JAS. C.
QUARLES, CHAS.
RICHARDS, RICHD.
ROBINSON, LEWIS †

Privates:
ROBINSON ———
SMITH, W. T.
SMITH, HENRY
SULLIVAN, WM.
SPICER, ADDISON
SHEPHERD JAMES
TYLER, JOHN
TRAINUM, ELIAS
WHITLOCK, GEO. W.
WHITLOCK, THOMAS

The successive captains in this company were G. A. Goodman, P. P. Barbour, and Benj. F. Baker. John Grubbs became a lieutenant. Captain Scott resigned, and later joined Crenshaw's Battery, and became quartermaster of the artillery batallion, with the rank of major. G. A. Goodman became colonel of the Thirteenth Virginia Infantry. Dr. W. S. Grymes went out with this company as surgeon and became chief surgeon of the division. Dr. Colby Cowherd was assistant surgeon of the regiment, and was afterwards attached to the Twelfth Georgia Infantry. Lieut. E. F. Cowherd was adjutant while A. P. Hill commanded the regiment.

"*The Barboursville Guard,*" *Co. F, 13th Va. Infantry.*

(*From an original muster roll in the office of the Secretary of Virginia Military Records—from October 31, 1861 to December 31, 1861.*)

This company was organized about 1859, with the following officers. Capt. W. S. Parran, Lieutenants, 1st, Andrew Jackson Eheart; 2nd Andrew Jackson White; 3rd, Joseph T. Wood. At the reorganization in 1862, A. J. Eheart was elected captain; C. L. Graves

† Killed.

APPENDIX—CONFEDERATE SOLDIERS 269

first, Conway Newman, second, and R. C. Macon third lieutenant.

Captain Parran became an army surgeon and was killed at Sharpsburg, while helping to man a fieldpiece of the Washington Artillery.

Captain Eheart was killed in battle at Spotsylvania Courthouse, May 12, 1864. C. L. Graves was promoted captain in 1864 and retired disabled. Conway Newman became captain in 1865.

Following is the official roster October 31, 1861:

Captain:
PARRAN, W. S.
First Lieutenant:
EHEART, A. J.
Second Lieutenant:
WOOD, JAS. T.
Sergeants:
GRAVES, C. L.
FITZHUGH, O. S.
MUNDY, ALBERT
HERNDON, ROBT. N.
Corporals:
SHOTWELL, JERRY
MARSHALL, THOS. A.
PAYNE, RICHD. N.
WAYLAND, ABRAM C.
Privates:
BLEDSOE, A. B.
BROOKING, E. W.
BROCKMAN, JOHN
CASON, JOEL
CARPENTER, B. F.
CLARKE, W. S.
CHEWNING, JAS. L.
COBBS, T. S.
DAVIS, ASHMAN T.
CALVIN, JOSEPH A.
DICKENSON, ELIJAH
DOLIN, THOS.
EUBANK, T. P.

Privates:
FAULCONER, JOHN C.
HARVEY, JOHN L.
HARVEY, THOMAS
HERNDON, B. F.
JOHNS, JOHN S.
JOHNS, HENRY C.
KEETON, J. J.
KENNEDY, H. S.
LAMB, EZEKIEL
LUCAS, JOHN H.
MACON, R. C.
NEWMAN, CONWAY
PETTIT, IRA W.
PETTIT, T. J.
PITMAN, R. C.
ROACH, JOHN W.
ROURKE, O.
SHOTWELL, CASWELL
SIMPSON, JAS. M.
STOGDELL, J. E.
THOMAS, FOUNTAIN
WAYLAND, B. B.
WILHOIT, JOHN N.
WOOD, BELLFIELD W.
WOOD, E. R.
WRIGHT, WM. B.
JAS. W. THOMAS had been discharged in May.

The following names, in addition, are on a list furnished by W. H. Ricketts:

Privates:
BLEDSOE, E. T.
BLEDSOE, C. B.
BECK, F. B.
BROOKING, V. C.
BROCKMAN, BELLFIELD
BROOKMAN, JOHN
BROOKMAN, HENRY
BRADFORD, J. E.
CAMPBELL, H.
COLLINS, LEWIS
DICKERSON, BURNETT
DICKERSON, EDWARD
DAVIS, J. F.
DAVIS, G. W.
DOUGLAS, J. M.
DUNN, ALONZO
EARLY, G. W.
ESTES, W.
FAULCONER, W. F.
FAULCONER, NICHOLAS
FAULCONER, WM.
FULLER, GEO.
FERNEYHOUGH, JOHN
GAY, JOHN
GARNER, (or Garnes) ROBT.
GILBERT, HENRY

Privates:
HERNDON, HENRY
HERNDON, J. F.
HEAD, N. V.
HEATWOLE, BENJ.
JOHNS, ROBT.
LEE, JAMES
MILLER, DANL.
OSBORNE, DANL.
PARROTT, B. B.
PAYNE, R. N.
RICHARDS, R.
SIMMS, F.
SOUTHARD, BEN.
THOMAS, F.
THOMAS, HENRY
THOMPSON, WM.
THOMPSON, R. M.
THOMPSON, HENRY
WHITELAW, J. D.
WILLIAMS, J. M. P.
WHITE, J. H.
WHITE, T. P.
WOOD, W. B.
WOOD, DICK
WOOD, B. W.

On an official pay roll, lent the Secretary of Virginia Military Records by R. Henry Chilton, Ottoman Post Office, Virginia, from February 18, to April, 1862, nearly all the foregoing names are to be found and these additional:

BROOKMAN, P.
CAMPBELL, T. C.
CAMPBELL, J.

CAMPBELL, F. M.
CASH, J. P.
CASH, J. G.

APPENDIX—CONFEDERATE SOLDIERS 271

COLEMAN, G.
DECKER ———
DAVIS, T. J.
DRUMMOND, J. H.
FAULCONER, FRED.
GANNAWAY, J. M.
HENDERSON, J. V.
MAUTIPLY, J. G.
PAGE, R. J.
RAYNER, THOS.

RICKARDS, L. A.
SOTHARDS, B.
THOMPSON, J. W.
THOMPSON, H. H.
VIA, J. W.
WAYLAND, A. C.
WARE, T. W.
WOODSON, M. B.
WATTS, S. C.

Roster of Company C. 7th Va. Infantry.

(*Furnished by Lieut. N. T. Bartley.*)

This company was first commanded by Capt. John C. Porter of Culpeper, and all the other officers, James W. Green, John R. Strother and Daniel Brown were also from that County. Subsequently J. W. Almond of Orange became captain, and N. T. Bartley and Jeremiah Pannill, lieutenants.

Following is the roster of the soldiers from Orange:

APPERSON, WM.
APPERSON, C.
BLEDSOE, GEORGE
BLEDSOE, J. A.
CONWAY, ALBERT
COOK, W. J.
CHILDRESS, WM.
COLEMAN, THOS. P.
COLEMAN, JOHN
COLEMAN, J. A.
DAVIS, WM.
DAVIS, THOMAS
DEMPSEY, ROBERT
DEMPSEY, WM.
DEMPSEY, COLEMAN
DEMPSEY, LEVI
ENGLAND, ROBERT

ELIASON, GEO. P.
HUME, B. W.
HUME, BENJAMIN
HUME, FRANCIS
HALL, HENRY
HALL, JOHN
HAWKINS, BENJAMIN
HART, FREDERICK
HEFFLIN, GEORGE
JONES, J. H.
JOHNSON, JAS. S.
MINNICK, DANIEL
MORTON, JEREMIAH
MORTON, DR. C. B.
MORRIS, J. F.
MORRIS, GEORGE
MORRIS, THOMAS

Porter, Chas. W.
Rhoades, R. B.
Richards, Jas. P.
Richards, Jas. C.
Ruffner, P. H.
Smith, A. W.
Smith, R. A.
Smith, W. B.
Smith, William
Smith, Nathaniel
Sisson, N. H.
Tinsley, J. W.
Tinder, J. T.

Vass, James
Webb, Ed. C.
Webb, Ed. W.
Webb, R. C.
Webb, J. W.
Woolfrey, Jeremiah
Woolfrey, Benjamin
Woolfrey, Burruss
Willis, Isaac
Willis, Gordon
Willis, Lewis
Wiltshire, Alfred

In Company "E," of the same regiment were these Orange soldiers:

Jacobs, John
Watson, B. F.
Smith, J. K. P.

Peyton's Battery, later Fry's, in Cutshaw's Battalion.
(*List from W. H. Ricketts.*)

Captain:
  Peyton, Thos. J.
First Lieutenant:
  Fry, C. W.
Second Lieutenant:
  Moore, John
Third Lieutenant:
  Cannon, Robert
Sergeants:
  Cave, Wallace
  Frazer, John
  Rawley, W. H. H.
  Slaughter, Mercer
Corporals:
  Higgins, Geo. W.
  Newman, Jas. F.
  Darnell, J. F. †
  Payne, B. C.

Privates:
  Adams, J. †
  Aylor, B.
  Atkins, Hugh
  Amos Wm.
  Bell, John
  Bell, Orville
  Bell, Granville
  Bridwell, O. H.
  Brown, Wesley
  Ballard, Winfield
  Ballard, C.
  Bailey, ———
  Brock, A.
  Brock, J.
  Coats, E. †
  Coats, Jas.
  Campbell, J. S.

† Killed.

APPENDIX—CONFEDERATE SOLDIERS 273

Privates:
DAVIS, CHAS. †
ESTES, FRANK
ESTES, WM.
EVERETT, WM.
FAUDREE, J. M.
GILLESPIE, J. N. †
GRAHAM, THOS.
GARRETT, A.
GARRETT, JOE
GILBERT, P.
HERNDON, THOS.
HAWLEY, J. A.
HUGHES, TONEY
HUGHES, JOHN
HARRISON, WM. H.
HANSFORD, JOHN
HANSBROUGH, BYRD
HERRING, E. †
HERRING, F. T.
HEATWOLE, JOS.
JONES, WM. †
JERDONE, WM.
LEATHERS, ANDREW †
MARTIN, WM.
MASTIN, WM.
MASTIN, TIM
MASON, J. F.
MUNDAY, B.
MORRIS, CHAS.

Privates:
MORRIS, FENTON
MCCLARY, J. F.
MITCHEL, W. E.
NIGHTING, RUFUS
NIGHTEN, ———†
NEWMAN, T. T. †
ONEIL, JAS.
PEYTON, M. D.
RIFE, NOT.
ROGERS, J. N.
RICHARDS, ROBT.
RACER, JAS. †
REYNOLDS, G. W.
REYNOLDS, W H.
SCHOOLER, GARRETT †
SANDERS, JOHN
SANDERS, JAS.
SHIFLET, J. F.
SHEPHERD, HENRY
SMITH, JOHN
THACKER, WM.
THACKER, JOSEPH
WHITLOCK, G. W. †
WINSLOW, THOS.
WALKINS, R. S.
WAUGH, R. S.
WATTLES, ANDREW
WILLIAMS, JOSEPH

C. W. Fry became captain, Mercer Slaughter, lieutenant and W. B. Willis quartermaster sergeant.

The Orange Rangers, Co. I, 6th Va. Cavalry

This company was mustered into service at Rhoadesville, May 4, 1861, and "travelled thence to Culpeper Courthouse, where it arrived June 11, 1861." From

---
† Killed.

an original official muster roll, owned by Mr. Alexander T. Browning:

Captain:
BROWNING, G. J.
First Lieutenant:
WALKER, WM. H.
Second Lieutenant:
ROBERTS, JOHN A.
Third Lieutenant:
SALE, JOHN S.
Sergeants:
WOOLFOLK, JOHN W.
MORTON, WM. J.
TERRILL, ROBT, M.
ANDREWS, WM. S.
Corporals:
ROACH, JAMES
MALLORY, JOHN
STONE, WM. J.
COOPER, JOHN J.
Bugler:
CHILDRESS, HENRY P.
Privates:
ALMOND, L. V.
ALMOND, THOS.
BOURNE, W. T.
BURRUS, W. T.
BROWN, JAMES W.
BAKER, JOS. H.
BICKERS, JNO. W.
COLLINS, WM. S.
CARSON, THOS. S.
COOPER, ALEX. H.
COOPER, ALFRED
CLARK, S. T.
CANADY, J. T.
CRAWLEY, ADAM G.
CRAVEN, CHAS. M.
CORBELL, S. V.
DURRER, JOHN C.
GARTH, L. T.
GILBERT, J. E.

Privates:
HALSEY, JOSEPH J.
HART, MALCOLM
HANSFORD, W. A.
HARTLEY, THOS. J.
HOPKINS, Z.
HUGHES, JEFFERSON
JONES, LUTHER M.
JONES, M. A.
KUBE, LEWIS
LANCASTER, RICHD.
LEE, LAFAYETTE
MALLORY, W. M.
MALLORY, ROBT.
MARTIN, T. J.
MARTIN, ROBT.
MCCLAINE, ROBT.
MASON, HORATIO P.
MILLS, ALEX. H.
MCCULLOUGH, ROBT. S.
PARTLOW, J. M.
PROCTOR, MARCELLUS
PROCTOR, WALTER R.
PROCTOR, OSWALD C.
QUARLES, HENRY
ROW, ELHANAN W.
REYNOLDS, J. W.
REYNOLDS, JOS. B.
RICHARDS, GEO. W.
RHOADS, ACHILLES
SISSON, ABNER J.
STUBBS, JESSE
THOMPSON, CHAS. H.
THOMPSON, JAS. B.
TINDER, E. H.
WAUGH, CHAS. S.
WHITE, JAMES H.
WIGGLESWORTH, C.
WOOD, W. S.
YOUNG, J. R.

† Killed.

Appendix—Confederate Soldiers

From Judge D. A. Grimsley, who was major of the regiment, it is learned that subsequent captains were John Row, William J. Morton and John W. Woolfolk; lieutenants C. B. Brown and J. T. Mann, both killed at Brandy Station, June 9, 1863, William Willis, J. H. White, James Roach and Samuel Andrews.

Mr. J. M. Gardner gives the names of James Roach and Abner Sisson as lieutenants and the name of lieutenant Andrews as William H. instead of Samuel.

J. J. Halsey became quartermaster of the regiment with rank of captain and E. W. Row was appointed an assistant surgeon.

The surgeons from the county were—

Doctors:
GRYMES, W. S.
PARRAN, W. S. †
NEWMAN, GEO. S.
MORTON, C. B.
SLAUGHTER, A. E.
COWHERD, COLBY

Doctors:
ROW, E. W.
TALIAFERRO, H. D.
TERRELL, R. M.
MAGRUDER, H. P. †
JONES, LUTHER

Major William C. Scott, who was at one time orderly sergeant of Crenshaws' Battery, credits the following names of that company to Orange:

COLEMAN, J. C.
COLEMAN L. L. (temporary)
GRAVES, B. V.
GRAVES, THOS. E.
HERNDON, J. C.
HACKLEY, A. S.
HERNDON, R. S.
JOHNSON, T. T.
LUMSDEN, G. G.
LUMSDEN, C. L.

LANCASTER, D. M.
LOVING, TALIAFERRO P.
MALLORY, R. H.
MALLORY, THOS. J.
PROCTOR, A.
PROFFITT, W. W.
PAYNE, JOHN A.
QUISENBERRY, J. N.
WOOD, THOMAS

† Killed.

It is known that a number of Orange soldiers served in the Wise Artillery, but it has been impossible to get a list of them.

These names are added from personal memory:

In Albemarle Light Horse, Second Cavalry.

MAGRUDER, JAS. W., Lieut. †
NEWMAN, THOS. HENRY †
WILLIS, JOHN
NEWMAN, N. W.
MORTON, JAS. W.

In "Black Horse" Troop, Fourth Cavalry.

TALIAFERRO, C. C.
TALIAFERRO, ROBT.
WILLIS, H. LEE
SCOTT, W. W.

In Madison Company, Fourth Cavalry.

GRAVES, J. W. C.
HOUSEWORTH, R. H.

The following held Commissions:

TAYLOR, ERASMUS
NEWMAN, CHAS. SHERIDAN
GRAVES, R. P.
HERRING, WM.
TALIAFERRO, JOHN
JONES, PHILIP B.
WILLIAMS, WM. G.

The following were Chaplains:

DAVIS, RICHD. T.   HIDEN, JAMES C.   WILLIS, EDWARD

E. GOSS. was in Lee's Guard, THOS. A. B. SCOTT, was in Grandy's Battery, and BYRD CHARLES WILLIS, was in ninth Virginia Cavalry.

The following were in service, but regiments unknown:

GRAVES, WM. C.
TALIAFERRO, FRANK, a noted scout. †
WILLIS, THOS. BARBOUR
COWHERD, FRANK
JONES, A. SEDDON
BELL, REUBEN
LINNEY, C. B.
LINNEY, H. B.
COLE, WM. †
NEWMAN, J. B. Jr.

† Killed.

It is well known to the writer that this roster is far from complete; yet it is far and away the completest grouping of Orange soldiers yet compiled, and he has had endless trouble in compiling it. Unless the chapter of the "Daughters" at Orange take up the matter at once, and give it continuous and earnest attention, an exhaustive roster can never be compiled. It is vain to hope that either the State or federal government will ever compile one that will even approximate completeness.

APPENDIX I.

Members of The Various Conventions.

1775, March 20. Thomas Barbour, James Taylor.
1775, July 17. Thomas Barbour.
1775, December 1. Thomas Barbour, James Taylor.
1776, May 6. James Madison Jr., William Moore.
1788. To consider the Federal Constitution, James Madison Jr., James Gordon.
1829–30. To revise State Constitution, James Madison Jr., Philip Pendleton Barbour.
1850–51. "The Reform Convention," John Woolfolk.
1861. The Secession Convention, Jeremiah Morton.
1867–8. The Reconstruction, or Underwood Convention, Frederick W. Poor.
1901–2. To Revise and amend the constitution, A. C. Walter.

APPENDIX J.

Members of The Colonial House of Burgesses.

From Orange County from 1736 to the formation of the Commonwealth, June 29, 1776.—From Stanard's "Colonial Register."

1736-8, Robert Green, William Beverley.

1740, (Robert Green had become sheriff.) William Beverley.

1742, Henry Downs (expelled during session for misconduct prior to his candidacy), Robert Slaughter (unseated on contest and new election ordered for both seats). This assembly first met May 6, 1742, and by prorogation in 1744, twice in 1746, and was dissolved April 8, 1747. Orange appears to have been unrepresented during all these years by reason of the unseating of her members.

1747, George Taylor.

1748-9, George Taylor, John Spotswood,

1753-58, George Taylor, Benjamin Cave.

1758-60, Benjamin Cave, William Taliaferro.

1761. Benjamin Cave, James Taylor.

1761-65, James Taylor, James Walker.

1765-68, James Walker, Zachariah Burnley

1769-71, James Walker, Thomas Barbour.

1772-3, Thomas Barbour, Zachariah Burnley.

1774, Thomas Barbour, ——— ———

1775, Thomas Barbour, James Taylor.

INDEX.

A

Adams, Richard, 71.
Albemarle, 31.
Allen, Benjamin, 31.
American Archives, 64.
Anderson, George, 30.
Anderson William Kyle, 84.
Appalachian Mountains, 100, 104.
Army of Northern Virginia, 40.
Ashby's "bent" (gap), 30.
Assessments for taxation, comparative, 167.
Atkinson, Thos., 169.
Auberge, Conrad, 82.
Augusta, 29, 30(3), 31.

B

Bagby, G. W., 193.
Baker, Clay, 197.
Ball, 34; Sam'l, 26(2), 27(2).
Ballard, Garland, 40; Philip, 76.
Ballenger, Andrew, 82.
Baltimore furnishes seeds in 1865, 161.
Banks, 168.
Bank of Orange, 38.
Baptists, Separate, 47.
Barbour, 33, 44, 77; B. J., 129, 150, 151; Sketch, 181; James, 26, 27, 28, 127, 139(2), 142, 178; Sketch, 181–2; P. P., 139, 178; Sketch, 182–3; Richard, 44; Thomas, 63, 65, 70, 71; Sketch, 183; Thos, Jr., 124.

Barboursville, 47, 49; Sketch, 202–203.
Barnett, John, 29.
Barnett's, Ford, 29.
Bartley, J. A., Sketch, 183.
Battles in County, 155–6.
Baylor, 77; John, Co. Lieutenant, 176, 180.
Beale, Traverner, 36.
Beard, 31.
Becket, John, 44.
Bell, 44; Charles, 124; Mary, 75; Thos., 44, 65, 71, 124; Wm., 44, 65, 69, 71(2); Z. 134.
Benefit of Clergy, 8, 136.
Bennett, Bartlett, 71.
Beverley, 77, 98, 99, 111, 112; H, 180(2); Robt., 104; Wm., 35, 180.
Beverley Manor, 30 (2), 31.
Blackbeard, 193.
Blakey, James G., 40.
Black Hills, composition, 117.
"Black and Tan Convention," 163
Black Walnut Run, 28, 33, 35.
Blankenbaker, Balthaser, 82;Matthias, 82.
Bledsoe, Aaron, 48; Abraham, 30; Isaac, 30.
Blind Run, 108.
Bloomsbury, 87.
Blue Ridge, 30(2), 31.
Blue Run, 47(3), 48; 180.
Board of Supervisors, 40.
Bohannon, William, 30, 56.
Bomer, John, 30.
Borden, B., 26, 29, 134.

Bouquet, Colonel, 58.
Bradford, Col., 143.
Bransford, John, 30.
Brent, Geo. P., 40.
Brick Church, 42.
British Spy, 47.
Brock, William, 60, 61.
Brock's Bridge, 73, 130.
Broil, Jacob, 82; John, 82(2).
Brooke, 98, 100.
Brooking, 42.
Brown, John, Raid, 146.
Browning, Francis, 30(2).
Bruce, Captain, 71
Brumback, Melchior, 80.
Brunswick County, 31.
Bryan, Morgan, 49.
Bryant, William, 30.
Buchanan, John, 31.
Buckner, 72.
Bullard, Richard, 61.
Bullock, James, 59.
BURGESSES, LIST OF, Appendix J. 278.
Burlington, 127; Sketch, 203.
Burnley, John, 124; Zachary, 47, 50, 65, 71, 72; Capt. 76.
BURRUS BOYS, tragic story of, 157–8.
Burton, 44, 72; James, 139; Capt. May, 42.
Bush, Philip, 30.
Byrd, Colonel, 27, 58, 59, 87.

C

Calwell, Robert, 31.
Cameron Lodge, 203.
Campbell, 44, 98, 101; Gilbert, 31.
Campbellton, 203.

Cannon, old, near Orange and at Orange Springs, 179.
Cannon River, 25.
Cape Capon, 31.
Carpenter, William, 30, 82.
Carter, Charles, 35; John, 82.
Catawba Creek, 31.
Cave, 44, 77; Benj., 26, 28, 36; Richard, 71; Robert, 30; William, 60, 61.
Cave's Ford, 42.
Cedar Island Ford, 35.
CENSUS 1782; Appendix B.
Chandler, Jere, 71.
Chapman, Richard M., 40(2); Reynolds, 40; Capt. 76.
Charles River, 17.
Cherry Tree Bottom, 31.
Chesapeake and Ohio Railway, 31.
Chew, 44, 77; Colby, 183; Larkin, 184; Thomas, 26(2), 27, 28, 33(2), 35, 37, 38, 180.
Chew's Mill, 29.
CHURCHES, COLONIAL, 42–5; Middle or Brick, 42; plate, 43; desecration, 43; Pine Stake, 44; Families connected with, 44; Glebe Farm, 44; Modern St. Thomas, Zion, 49; Other Old, 46, 51; Blue Run, 47; The Blind Preacher's, 47; Old Zion, Pamunkey, 48; of Blind Preacher, 204; Number by Denominations, 172.
Church Wardens, 123.
Clark, Geo. Rogers, 14; Wm. 75.
Clerk's Office, 39, 40.
CLEVELAND, BENJ., sketch, 184.
CLIFTON, sketch, 204.

Clore, Michael, 82.
Clouder, 98, 112, 180; Run, 112.
Cobbler, Frederick, 82.
Coleman, James, 74; John, 72; Thos. 139.
COMMISSIONS, MILITARY, 1734-83. Appendix F., 258-62.
COMMITTEE OF SAFETY, 65-70; Wingate's disloyalty, 66-8; Address to Patrick Henry, 69.
Commonwealth's Attorneys, 179.
Confederate Chaplains, 275.
Confederate pensioners, pensions, 172.
CONFEDERATE SOLDIERS, ROSTER, 264-76; Montpelier Guard, 264-6; Gordonsville Grays, 266-8; Barboursville Guard 268-70; Company "C," 7th Va. Infantry, 271; of Orange Soldiers in Company "E;" ditto, 272; Peyton's Battery, later Fry's, 272-3; of Orange Rangers, 273-4; In Crenshaw's Battery, 275; in various commands, 275-6.
Confederate Surgeons, 275.
Conner, John, 30.
Conney, Captain, 71.
Convention, 1861; candidates for, 149.
CONVENTIONS, MEMBERS OF, Appendix I, 277.
Convention Troops, 72.
Conway, 44; Captain. 71: Catlett, 71, 139; F. 180.
Conway River, 24.
Cook, Michael, 82.
Cooke, John Esten, 101.
Coons, Joseph, 80.

County levy, 129; rate, 171.
County records, 5.
County Seat, statistics, 169.
County Standard, 30.
COURTHOUSES, 33-41; Col. Spotswood's offer, 34.
Cowherd, Francis, 38, 61, 139; James, 28, 59.
Craig, Captain, 71; E, 47, 48, 51, 71, 178.
CRENSHAW, W. G., sketch, 184-5; Battery, Orange Soldiers in, 275; Record of rainfall, 119.
CRIMES AND PUNISHMENTS, 133; Peter's decapitation; Eve burnt at stake, 135; Deserter sold, 134; Cropping ears, 136; Non-attendance at church, 177.
Crosthwait, 37, 59; Isaac, 59, 61; Jacob, 61; Timothy, 36, 37; William, 30.
Culpepper, 32, 37.
Culpeper Minute Men, 37. 57.
Curtis, Chas., 26, 37.

D

Dances, neighborhood, 125-6.
Daniel, 44; Reuben, 71; Vivian, 65, 69; Travers, 218.
Daughters of Confederacy, 158.
Davis, Samuel, 59.
Davis, Isaac, 139; Jonathan, 50.
Davison, Thos., 124.
Dinkle, Samuel, 40.
DISSENTERS, 46-9.
Douglas, Margaret, 71.
Downer, J., 180.

Downs, Henry, 30, 36; "Runaway," expelled from House of Burgesses, 176.
Dunmore, 63(2), 69.
du Pont, Wm., 168, 209

E

Earnest, Rev. Joseph 72.
Eastham, Robt., 26.
Edmondson, Joseph, 71.
Education, 126; of girls, 127.
Elevation, mean, 120.
Elk Run, 29.
England, Mr., 97.
Essex County, 79.
Euphrates, 110.
Eve, 35; Burnt at stake, 135.
Expedition Run, 100.
EXPLANATIONS, 7.

F

Falling Spring, 31.
Fairfax, Lord, 24, 93; Grant, 24.
Farmer, A., 68; A. W., 67.
Fennell, Jonathan, 30.
Fenney, 30.
Field, 34; A, 26, 27; Col., 61; M. G., 168.
Finks, Mark, 30.
Finlason, John, 26 (2), 27 (2), 34, 134.
Fishback, John, 80; Herman, 80.
FISCAL and STATISTICAL, 166–173.
Fisher, Patrick, 60, 61.
Fitzgerald, Thomas, 59.
Fleshman, Z., 82.
Fontaine, John, 81, 98(2), 99.
FONTAINE'S JOURNAL, tramontane expedition, 104–13.

Forbes, General, 58.
Fort Duquesne, 58.
Franklin, Edward, 30; Jesse, sketch, 185.
Frascati, sketch, 204–5.
Fredrick Co., 29, 30(2), 31(2).
Fredericksburg, 85.
Freedsmen's Bureau, 160.
Free people of color, their transportation, 177.
FRENCH and INDIAN WARS, 58–62; Anecdotes, 61.
Fry, P. S., 40; Sketch, 185.
FRY'S BATTERY, ROSTER, 272–3.
Furnace, John, 61.
Furnes, John, 59.

G

Gaines, James, 60–1.
Gaming, 124–5.
Garth, John, 29.
Gent, gentleman, 7.
GERMANNA, 28, 34, 42, 47, 78, 79, 80, 81(2), 82, 83, 84, 85, 86, 92, 94, 100, 112; AND FIRST SETTLERS, 77–86; First and second German Colonies, 80–84; English settlement, 84; Decadence, 85.
German Protestants, 77, 81.
German Road, 29.
Germantown, 81, 104.
Gibbs, Francis, 60, 61.
Gibson, John, 139; Jonathan, 27.
Gilbert, Peter, 125.
Glebe Farm, 44.
"Good Roads," bond issue for, 171.
Gooch, William, 29.

Index

Gordon, James, sketch, 186; R. L., 163; Wm. F., sketch, 186-7.
Gordonsville, 48, 49; "Boom," 169; Elevation, 115; Gazette, 129; "Greys" roster, 266-68.
Governor's Ford, 35.
Graffenreid, Baron de, 81.
Graves, 72.
Greame, Mr. 91.
Great Bridge, 64.
Green, Robert, 26, 27, 134.
Greene County, 32(2).
Grigsby, Hugh Blair, 188.
Grymes, Benjamin, 71; Peyton, 40; Wm. S. Camp Confederate Veterans, 158.

H

Haeger, Henry Rev., 81.
Hackley, Francis, 59.
Haley, Edward, 29.
Halsey, R. O., bank president, 168
Hamilton, G. H., 179.
Hamilton, Reuben, 124.
Hamilton, Wm., 124.
Harmon, Adam, 31.
Hartswell, Rev., Richard 45.
Hase, Moses, 73.
Hawfield, 44; Sketch, 205.
Hawkins, 72; William, 73.
Haxall, R. B., 178.
Head, Anthony, 30.
Head, Benjamin, 72.
Head, George, 30.
Hebron church, 47, 83.
Hedgeman's river, 25.
Henderson, William, 28.

Henry, P., 14, 68, 69, 70, 191.
Henshaw, Eliz. 3.
Hensley, Jane, 72.
Herndon, 72; Z., 74, 124.
Hervey, Henry, 60.
Hiden, 40; Dr. J. C. 129; Jos. 40.
Hill, A. P. 58; Headquarters, 155.
Hinke, William J., 83.
HISTORIC HOMES, sketches, 202-215; names, 213-15.
Hite, Joist, 26, 29, 30, 31.
Hitt, Peter, 80.
Hobson, G., 26.
Hoffman, John Henry, 80.
Hogg, Captain, 58.
Hog stealing, 133.
Holladay, H. T., 151.
Holt, Michael, 82.
Holtzclaw, Jacob, 80.
Hopewell, 197.
"Horse College," 178.
Houdon, inscription on his statue of Washington, 191-2.
Howard, John, 29, 30.
Howe, H., 22.
Hughes, Geo., 124.
Hume, 36.
Hunt clubs, "Tomahawk," "Blue Run," 168.

I

IMPORTATIONS, list of persons, Appendix A, 225.
INDIANS, ANTIQUITIES, 52-7; Mound, 52-7; Court orders, 56; Tomahawk, 57; Camp of Minute Men, 57.
Indians, 55.

J

Jones, Ferdinand, 163; on Committee to raise war subscription, and look after families of soldiers, 151–3; Rev. Hugh, 84; C., 74.
Joice, Tully, 45.
Johnson, Benjamin, 74.
Jerdone, 84.
Jefferson, Thomas, record of rainfall, 120, 202.
Jamestown, founded, 14.
James, River, 31(2), 109.
Jackson, "Stonewall," headquarters, 155.

K

Kaffer, Michael, 82.
Kelly, William, 30.
Kemper, C. E., 80; J. L., 83; Sketch, 187; John, 80; Andrew, 82.
King's Road, 31.
KNIGHTS OF THE HORSESHOE, 198–113; The party, 98; The journey, 99; Discrepancies, 99; The horseshoes, 100; Sic Juvat, 101; The poem, 103; Fontaine's Journal, 104–13; Distance travelled, 113.

L

La Fayette, Marquis de, 74; Station where Marquis camped, 175.

Lamb, James, 60; John, 59, 61; Richard, 59, 61; Wm., 60.
Land grants, old, grantees of, 180.
Lane, Littleberry, 61.
Latane, 180.
Leach, Edward, 193.
Lederer, John, 102.
Lee, Thomas, Hon., 37; J. H., 40. 149; Robt. E., 49, 150; Headquarters, 155.
Leland, Parson, 44, 188.
Lewis, John, 30; M., 127; Zachary 28, 179.
Liberty Mills, skirmish at, 156.
Licking Run, 81.
Lightfoot, Colonel, 30, 33, 77; Goodrich, 26, 134; John, 26.
Limestone, "String," 115; Quarries, analyses, 116.
Lindsay, 72; R., County Chart, 177.
Literary Fund, 139.
Locust Lawn, 206.
Long, Allen, 125; Philip, 176.
Lottery, to pave roads at C. H., 40.
Louisa R. R., 131.
Low, Littleberry, 60.
Lucas, John, 59.
Lutherans, 82; Church in Madison, 47.
Lyne, H. O., 168.

M

Magisterial districts, why so laid off, 164; whom named for, 164.
Magnetic declination, 120.
Marble, Todd's quarry, 116.
Marquis's Road, 174.

Massacre, the great, 16.
McClarney, 71.
McClayland, Daniel, 59, 136.
Madison, 37, 44, 77; Ambrose, 180(2); Mrs. Ambrose, 27; James, 44(2), 45, 50, 65, 71, 72(2), 73; James, Jr., 63, 65, 69, 71(2), 72, 124, 177, 178; Sketch, 188–92; his will 239–43; Wm., Jr., 124.
Marshall, Rev., Mungo, 43.
MAGRUDER BOYS, tragic story of, 156–7.
Mallory, Uriel, 71.
Manahoac Indians, 52.
Marshall, 43; John, 176, 191.
Martin, John Joseph, 80; Rev. Thos., 44.
Mahone, Wm., 49; Engineer Plankroad, 145.
Mason, 98, 112.
Maury, L. H., 127; Walker, 127.
Mayhurst, 207.
Meade, Bishop, 42.
"Mechanic," incorporated, 179.
Meherrin Indians, 105.
Mercer, 29; John, 28, 29.
Merry, Prettyman, 73.
Meyer, George, 82.
Middle Church, 42.
Military district, removal of officials, iron clad oath, 161–2.
Miller, 72.
Mills, Captain, 71; Roger Q., 192.
Mine River, 106.
Mine Run, 99.
Minerals, plumbago, 117; Iron, gold, 118.
Minor, Dabney, 38.
Minute Men, 64; Camp, 57.

MISCELLANEOUS, 174.
Missions, 45.
Mitchell, Henry, 66.
Monacan, Indians, 52.
Monroe, Wm., 138; Will of 138; grave of, 143; ORANGE HUMANE SOCIETY, 139.
Montague, 72; Peter, 71.
Montebello, 207.
Montpelier, sketch, 208.
MONTPELIER GUARDS, ROSTERS, John Brown Raid, 263; Confederate War, 264–6.
Moore, 77; Francis, 36, 44, 65(3), 69, 70, 71(2); J. B., 40; R. T., 38; Thos. 60, 66; Wm., 44, 63, 65, 71.
Morgan, M., 26, 29.
Morton, Elijah, 50; Geo. 73; Jackson, 192; James W., 164; Jeremiah, 192; Wm., 50, 74.
Mouldin, Richard, 26.
Mount George, 111.
Mountain Road, 29.
Mountain Run, 99, 106(2).
Mountains, "South West," 114; Water shed, 114; Elevation of, 115.
Mount Sharon, 209–10.
Mount Spotswood, 111.
Musters, militia, 125.

N

Negro Run, 133.
Newman, Abner, 124; James, sketch, 192; James Barbour, record of rainfall, 118.
New River, 31.

Newspapers, 128–9, "Expositor," "Express," "Native Virginian," "Observer," "Piedmont Virginian," "Southern Chronicle", at Orange; "Gazette" at Gordonsville.
Nichols, Albert, 40.
Northern Pass, 101.
North Mountains, 30.
North River, 31.
Northwest Territory, 14.

O

Oak Hill, 61, 210.
"Old Trap," 179.
Opechancanough, 16.
ORANGE, GENESIS OF, 17–25; Counties formed from it, 18; Name, 22; Established, 23; Boundaries explained, 24; ORGANIZATION, 26–32.
Orange Horseman's Association, 169.
ORANGE HUMANE SOCIETY, incorporated, 139; Trustees of, 139; General history, of, 139–143.
Orange C. H., incorporations and trustees, 40, 41.
ORANGE RANGERS, ROSTER, 273–4.
Ordinaries, regulation of, 122.
Overton, Captain, 59.

P

Page, Mann A., 40(2).
Pamunkey, 42, 47; Neighborhood, 170.
Pannill, Dr. D., 177; Wm, 65.

Patton, James, 31.
Paulitz, Philip, 82.
Payler, Christopher, 82.
Pearcey, Charles, 60.
Pendleton, Edmund, 176; John, 142.
Peter, slave, beheaded, 134.
PEYTON'S BATTERY, ROSTER, 272–3
Phillips, David, 30; Leonard, 30.
PHYSICAL FEATURES, 114–120; Elevations, 115.
Pillory, 34, 38.
Pine Stake Church, 29, 44.
Plank road, 131.
Pleasant View, sketch, 210.
Point Pleasant, 60.
Pollard, James, 26, 27, 34.
Pollock, John, 124.
Poplar Run, 179.
Population, white, free negroes, slaves, 1860, 172; whites, negroes, 1900, 172.
Porter, 77; Benjamin, 29, 30, 180; Charles, 74, 75, 136.
Porteus, James, 30.
Potatoe Run, 29.
Pounds, 7.
Powell, Ambrose, 58, 60, 61; Benj. 59; Simon, 60, 61; Thos., 59;
Price, John, 71.
Prison, 34, 38.
Prison bounds, 8.
"PROGRESS TO THE MINES," 87–97; The journey, 87; Arrival, 88; The visit, 88–94; Departure, 94; Inspection of mines, 95; Return, via Fredericksburg, 96–7.
Public Schools, statistics, 171.

Q

Quarles, William, 38.

R

Raccoon Ford, 33, 34.
Railroads, Louisa, Narrow gauge, Orange and Alexandria, Southern, 131; C. & O., 132; Mileage of each, 132.
Rainfall, 118, 119.
Randolph, John, 127, 203
Rape, 137.
Rapidan, 28, 29(2), 32, 33, 34, 99, 111; Neighborhood, 170.
Rappahannock, 32, 37; River, 87.
Ratings, prices of commodities, 122.
Rawlings, Richard, 40.
RECONSTRUCTION, 160-65.
Rector, Jacob, 80.
"Reform Convention," 145.
Revenues, state, county, district, 171.
REVOLUTION, (See appendix, not indexed), 63-70; Culpeper Minute Men, 64, 75; Committees of Safety 64; Great Bridge, battle of, 64; Sundry orders and allowances, 70-75; La Fayette's headquarters, 74.
REVOLUTION, WAR OF, Appendix E, 247-57.
Rice, Michael, 60, 61.
Richeson, William, 30.
Riddle, James, 60, 61; John, 134.
Roan Oak, 31.
Roanoke Island, 13.

Roberts, James, 60.
Robinson, 29, 98, 112, 180; Geo., 31; Thomas A., 40.
Robertson, 33(2), 98; William, 28, 33.
ROCKLANDS, sketch, 210.
Rogers, William, 59, 61; Wm. B, 116, 118; W. S., 168.
Rose Hill, 211.
ROSTERS, Montpelier Guard, John Brown Raid, Appendix G, 263; Confederate, 264-6.
Ruckers, 44.
Ruckersville, 42.
Russel, 94; Peter, 36; Wm., 60; 134.

S

St. George Parish, 21, 78, 79.
St. Mark Parish, 22, 42, 45(2), 79.
St. Thomas Church, 43.
St. Thomas Parish, 42, 45, 49.
Sanders, Nathaniel, 51, 71.
Sanford, Wallace. W., 212.
Sanford, Pierce, 38.
Sapony, Indians, 56.
Schools, 128.
Scott, 44, 77; E. W., 171; Garrett, 3, 162, 163; Johnny, 65, 71, (3), 74; W. W., 129.
Seal, County, 177.
SEVENTH VIRGINIA INFANTRY, list of Orange Soldiers in, 271-2.
Shackleford, Henry, 60, 61.
Sheible, George, 82.
Shepherd, 44; Andrew, 71, 75; James, 40.
Sherrando, 30, 31.
Shilling, 7.

Sims, William, 60.
Singleton, Edmund, 72.
Slaughter, Francis, 26, 27, 34, 134; Rev. Philip, 98; Robt., 26(2), 27, 30, 34, 134; R. C., 168.
Smallpox, permit to inoculate for, 177.
Smith, 33, 77; Capt., 71, 98; Austin 98, 104, 106; Augustine, 26, 27(4), 28; John, 26, 134; Michael, 82; Wm., 29, 60, 61.
Snow, John, 28, 29.
Snyder, Hendrick, 82; Henry, 82.
Social, customs, habits, dress, 122.
Soldier's Rest, 211.
Somerset, 42, 49; Sketch, 212; Neighborhood, 170.
Somerville's Ford, 36.
Southall, Stephen, 73.
Southern Chronicle, 129.
South River, 25.
South West Mountains, 180.
Spencer, Joseph, 50, 76, 177.
Spillman, John, 80.
Spotswood, 98; Col. Alex., 28, 34(3), 35, 42, 56, 77, 80, 81, 82, 83, 98, 150; Sketch, 193-4; Mrs., 88; John, 88.
Spotsylvania, formed, boundaries, 19, 23, 85, 100.
Spout Run, 31.
Springs, mineral, 117; Freestone, 118.
Stallings, G., 76.
Stanard, W., 180; W. G., 6.
"Starving Time," 15.
Staunton River, 25, 29.
Staves, Sarah, 71.
Stephen, Adam, Colonel, 60.
Stephensburg, 60.

Stevens, General, 74; John, 177.
Streams, principal, 114.
Stilfy, Lewis, 134.
Stocks, 34, 38.
Stodgill, James, 30.
Strother, Lawrence, 56.
Stuart, General, 49.
Stubblefield, 72.
Style, old and new, 7.
Sumpter, Gen., sketch, 194.
Swift, Run, 99; Gap, 99.

T

Taliaferro, 33, 38, 44, 76, 77; Jno., 15, 26, 27(3), 180(2); J. P., Sketch, 194; Lawrence, 64, 180; Wm., 361; W. R., 164; Tolever, 76.
Taliaferro, Road, 29.
TAXABLE VALUES, comparative table, 1860, 1866, 1906, 173.
Taylor, 33, 77, 98; Erasmus, 36, 47; Francis, 65, 66, 68, 76; Roster of Company in Revo., Appendix, 252; Geo., 36, 37; Hancock, 62; James, 29, 63, 65, 70, 84, 180(2); John, 38, 194; Robt., 38(2), 76, 139; Wm. B., 40; Z., 26; ZACHARY, sketch, 195-6.
Terrell, Edmund, 124; Wm, 124.
Temperature, mean, 120.
Test, the, 8.
Thacker, E., 180.
Thompson, Alexander, 31; David, 59, 61.
Thornton, Daniel, 74; F., 15.
Thornton River, old name for South River, 25.

Tinkling Springs, 31.
Thomas, 77; Joseph, 37; Robt., 73; Rowland, 44, 65, 71; Wm., 74; Thomases, 44.
Tithable, 7.
Tobacco, 129.
Todd, 98; Wm., 180.
Toddsberth, 48, 49.
Todd's Branch, 29.
Todd's Marble Quarry, 116.
Todd's Path, 29.
Tomahawk Branch, 57; Camp of Minute Men, 57.
Tombstone, oldest, 204; Madison's 206; Dolly Madison's, 206.
Turner, Robert, 28, 82.
Turnpike, Swift Run, 130; Rockingham, 146; Blue Ridge, 145.
Tuscarora Branch, 31.

U

Union League, 160.
Utz, George, 82.

V

Vaughan, William, 61.
Vawter, William, 59.
Verdier, Paul, 124.
Verdiersville, 44; "My Dearsville," 179.
Virginia, Company of London, 13; of Plymouth, 14; Charters, 14; Original limits, 14; SEATING OF, 13 et seq.
"Virginians of the Valley" poem, 103.
"Voltaire," a noted horse, 178–9.
Vote in 1860, 148.

W

Waddel, James, 44, 47, 127; Sketch, 197–200; Memorial Church, 197.
Wails, Major, 76.
Walker, Charles, 59; James, 65; John, 70, 179; Thos., 59.
Waller, Colonel, 90.
Wambersie, Mr., 44.
WAR PERIOD, 148–159; Cockades, 148; Appropriations by County Court, 151 et seq.
WAR of 1812, Appendix D, 244–46.
Warner, John, 60.
Washington, 58, 97; Inscription on statue, 192; Augustine, 176; Lawrence, 176.
Watkins, Evan, 31.
Watson, William, 60.
Watts, Charles, 60, 61; David, 61.
Waugh, Alexander, 29; Chas. S., 135; Waughs, 72, 77.
Weaver, Tilman, 80.
Webb, 47, 72; Wm., 73.
Westover Manuscripts, 87.
White, Jeremiah, 71; Willis, 124; Whites, 44.
White Oak River, 108.
William and Mary College, 28,193.
Williams, 40; Francis, 30; Jacob, 59; John, 59, J. G., 164, 168, 180; Lewis B., 40, 164, 180; sketch, 200; William, 49; W. G. 164.
Willis, Harry, 95; Henry, 26(3); Col. George, 27, 170; John, 36; Larkin, ten sons in Confederate Army, 158; Willis, 77; Col. 96; Willises, 44, 159.

Wingate, John, 66, 67.
Winslow, F., 139.
Wirt, William, 47, 197.
Wolford, General, 76.
Wolves' heads, bounty on, 130.
Wood, James.
Wood Park, 213.
Woodberry Forest, 27.
Woodford's Mt., 104, 112.
Woodley, sketch, 212-13.
Wood's Gap, 102.
Woods, George,
Wood's River, 31.

Woolfolk, 6; W., 6; John, sketch, 200-1; John L., Thomas, 139.
Wythe, Geo., 176.

Y

Yates, B., 180.
Yeager, Nicholas, 82.
York, 74.
York River, 17; head spring, 114.

Z

Zimmerman, Christopher, 29, 82.
Zion Meeting House, 48.

www.ingramcontent.com/pod-product-compliance
Lightning Source LLC
Chambersburg PA
CBHW071804300426
44116CB00009B/1194